THE
EYES
BEHIND THE
VIOLIN

Published in the United States by
Red Leaf Music and Publishing, Florida
Email: redleafmusicandpub@yahoo.com

ISBN 979-8-9889053-0-1 (Paperback)
ISBN 979-8-9889053-1-8 (Hardback)
ISBN 979-8-9889053-2-5 (ebook)
Library of Congress Control Number:
2023944578

Cover Design and Interior Formatting by: Nuno Moreira, NMDESIGN
Editor: Blair Parke

THE
EYES
BEHIND THE
VIOLIN

A Memoir: Finding My True Identity

KYENI MATEE

Acknowledgements

Writing this book has been a huge undertaking for me, and I definitely couldn't have done it alone. I, first and foremost, want to thank my heavenly Father for His love and support. To my husband Chuma Matee, thank you for loving me and allowing me to set some things aside to write. To my mother, Claudia Hendricks, of whom I love very much, thank you for being brave enough to endure the endless questions that I had and for going back through this journey with me. To my dad, James T. Bryant, who has crossed over to the other side, thank you for loving me and giving me your ear to free myself from that which was hidden. To my big brother Tommy, thank you for the endless conversations we had about our lives and childhoods, and thank you for looking out for me when I needed you the most.

To my sister, my confidante, and my best friend, Alberta, it is because of your support and counsel that I have gotten where I am today. I would be a totally different person without you. To my inner circle, Jacqueline and Paul Barattiero, Susan Ratz-Thomas, and Marsha and John Jones, my life has been full and rich because of your friendship and support. To my beta readers (Jacqueline Barattiero, Cindy Goodrich, Camille Clark Phillips, and Tim Hefner), thank you for taking the time to read this book and provide me with feedback. To my amazing editor, Blair Parke, thank you for your guidance and thank you for providing your talents and making sure that my voice was heard loud and clear in this book.

To Obeeyay and Yahosh Bonner, thank you for the song "What a Dream," because it truly blessed me at a time that I needed it. To Clotile

Bonner Farkas, thank you for guiding me vocally and sharing your talent with me. To the countless other family members, friends, and colleagues that have supported me over the years, you are all a part of me and have been a part of my growth and development. I love you all.

Introduction

Writing this book has been a desire of mine for the past twenty years. I attempted to write it twice over the years but never got past the first couple of paragraphs. At the time, I just chocked it up to being too busy, but now I know the reason for the delay was much deeper than that. Now that I have written this book, I realize I was not emotionally or spiritually ready to uncover the hurts and pain from my past and actually deal with them. It took a very pivotal moment in my life to force me to look at the trials, hurts, and painful memories of the past that I had hidden away, making peace with them in order to start healing from them.

This memoir is a story of forgiveness, redemption, healing, and self-identity. This journey I've been on has provided me with the opportunity to look at my past and learn that trials, as painful as they may be, are, and can be, opportunities for growth if we allow them to be. The trials throughout my life opened my eyes to a lot of learning and understanding about myself, and my personal strength and fortitude. One of the big things that I learned through writing this memoir is that we are not alone in our trials because the Lord is always there, coming in the form of His Spirit or in the form of people He has placed on our paths to help us. Even in our moments of weakness, He has the strength to help pull us through any trial.

This memoir is the journey of my life, seen through my eyes and perspective. Others may see things differently, but I can only speak for the events as I see them and how they, individually, have affected my life. We all have our own journeys to live and experience while we are here on this earth, and I know that we have all experienced heartache in one form or another. This book outlines the journey that I have been through, where I was, and where I am now. My journey is not over, as I know there will be many more things for me to learn as I go along in my life. My hope is that through reading my story, you will find something useful in its pages that will be of benefit to you in your own journey on this earth.

For the sake of certain individuals that are mentioned in the book, some of the names and identifiable details have been changed and/or altered for the sake of their privacy and protection. Although certain details have been altered, the stories that are written herein are true and are based upon my memories as I remember them.

Chapter 1

A NEW START

Stepping back onto the Ball State University campus in Muncie, Indiana, at the ripe old age of twenty-nine, to complete my Bachelor of Music degree was not in the forefront of my mind, but the fear of being destitute certainly was. I had recently found myself sitting in a courtroom across the aisle from Michael, the man I thought I was going to spend the rest of my earthly existence with, but unfortunately, after two and a half years of marriage, it was not to be. Because of my naïve nature, divorce was something that never crossed my mind. However, sitting across the aisle from the man that I thought would be my future caused my heart to ache in a way I had never experienced before. I felt like a complete failure, but strangely, I felt relieved at the same time.

We didn't have any assets, nor were we blessed with children, so that allowed us to file a simple divorce. The problem with that belief was that there was a quick turnaround for simple divorces, like ours, because there were no major legal issues that had to be dealt with, like child custody. That put our case on the docket about thirty days later from the filing, which was not enough time to sort out our affairs, so we crazily decided to continue living together in our home and split the rent until we could both raise enough money to move out of the house. We did not have an exact plan as to how or when either of us would move out, so the choice to continue living together was one of the many bad decisions I made during that period of my life; and it nearly destroyed me.

At the time of our divorce in 1998, we were living in Central Florida. I had a job with a ticket-and-tour company, only making $8.00 per hour, and working thirty hours per week. That amount was definitely not enough money to pay my rent, car insurance, and other living expenses. I didn't know what I was going to do to survive, but I knew I couldn't continue living in the house with Michael for much longer. I was starting to develop emotional issues because I was living in the same house with the man I loved who didn't love me anymore. He had moved on with his life and started dating again. Michael was doing that secretly while we were married, but now he had his "Get Out of Jail Free" card, so he openly flaunted his newfound freedom in my face, with no regard for my feelings.

I knew I needed to get out of there, but I didn't have a viable exit strategy. Also, the stress of everything was really starting to get to me, and then one day, the thought of Dr. Irwin Mueller, the assistant director of the Ball State University School of Music, popped into my mind. I had not thought of him since I was a student at Ball State years earlier. My memory opened to the conversations that I used to have with him on campus. I was a music performance major at Ball State, and every time he passed me in the music building hallway, he would always say,

"You're supposed to be a teacher, girl!" and I would always reply, jokingly, "Never! I'm never going to teach those bad kids!"

We would smile at each other in recognition of the ongoing conversation and keep walking. It was our little inside joke … or so I thought. Now that I was single again and needed to find a way to support myself, my mind went back to those conversations with Dr. Mueller, and I realized that he just might have been onto something. While in school, music performance was my major, but Dr. Mueller always felt that I should have chosen music education instead. I started doing a little research and found out that if I finished my music performance degree, I could apply for a temporary teaching license in Florida, and the state of Florida would give me two years to take the education courses that I needed to be certified in K-12 music education. That temporary license would allow me to teach at the same time I was completing my coursework. I would then receive a teacher's salary and be able to survive on my own. It would have been convenient to finish my schooling in Florida, but because I only had one semester left, I would have been required to take additional classes, and I would potentially lose credits in the transfer process, so back to Ball State I went to finish the Bachelor of Music degree that I started back in 1986.

When I arrived back on the Ball State campus, I drove around and looked at some of the changes to the campus since I was last there taking classes two summers earlier. Many things were the same, but there were some nice, cosmetic changes to the campus. Luckily, while I was driving, a car pulled out from a parking space close to the music building, and I was able to pull right in. I was happy about that because it prevented me from having to park out by the football stadium and take the shuttle into campus. It was January and the dead of winter, so I started to put on my winter battle gear before getting out of the car. I put my favorite red scarf on my head, making sure my ears were covered, and I tied the scarf under my chin. I then grabbed my earmuffs and placed them on top of my scarf, over my ears; that gave my ears a double layer of protection. I then grabbed my gloves and exited the car.

Once outside, I took a few steps along the side of my car to reach the front of the car and then took a step up to get onto the sidewalk. The moment I stepped onto that sidewalk, I started to slip. I hadn't noticed the clear sheet of ice that had formed on the sidewalk before stepping, so I quickly flung my arms out to the side of my body, squatted down slightly, and controlled my balance so I didn't fall, but that was an immediate reminder of where I had returned to. I was born and raised in Indiana but had moved to Florida and had acclimated to the warm, snowless Florida winters. Returning to the cold, snowy winters of Indiana was a shock to my warm-blooded system.

Even though I had lived in snow my whole life, the Ball State campus was the most dangerous place that I had ever lived in the wintertime. Most of the time, the snowplows would not make it out to remove the snow before the students came out to classes. So, the students would walk on the snow and pack it down, which would turn the snow into slick ice. The plows would then come out, but these were no ordinary snowplows. These were Ball State specials, and they didn't have big shovels that were typical for the front of a plow. Those shovels were replaced by big, black, bristly brushes. The plows would come along with the brush on the front, spinning top speed, and that brush would shine that ice up until it was extra slick. It looked like a perfectly clean mirror on the sidewalks, and the sun rays would bounce off it to create gorgeous spectrums.

However, that was the deception; the glistening ice was beautiful, but that was how it got you. It would draw you into its beauty, all the while camouflaging its danger of causing you to fall. Some patches of ice were completely invisible, while other patches were noticeable but ignored. Metaphorically, this was the story of my ex-husband Michael and me. He was the ice, and I was the one that chose to ignore the danger.

When I started walking and began to slip on the campus sidewalk, the memory of what I needed to do came back immediately. I jumped over into the snow-covered grass where there was no ice and walked in the snowy grass as long as I could until it was absolutely necessary to go back on the sidewalk. There were many places where the snow was knee-high, but it was much safer than walking on the ice. When I ran out of grass, I'd look for an unplowed area around the edges of the sidewalk that I could walk on. That was the technique I used all the years I was at Ball State, and with this approach, I never had a fall while I was there. I wish I had developed the same protective instinct when it came to Michael, as it may have saved me a lot of heartache.

I safely made my way into the music building and down to the student lounge to take a seat. As I sat on the wooden bench, I looked around at the students as they were laughing and talking to their friends. It brought back memories of my friends and I when we were together during lunchtime or after classes. However, these students were very different than my friends and me. They were young and quirky. Don't get me wrong; we artistic people have varying levels of quirkiness within us, but these kids were loud and much more obnoxious. They were an entirely different breed of student, and I didn't really fit in with them. I am sure the older kids in my day felt the same way about us when we were freshmen.

All my friends were long gone now from Ball State, having all graduated many years earlier, so I felt alone on the campus. I was about thirteen years older than the typical freshman, and, surprisingly enough, it felt like I was in a completely different generation. I was at a different level of maturity than I was years earlier, young and crazy back then, and I didn't have any real, meaningful goals as a freshman. I wasn't sure if I wanted to get my degree in music or business or accounting. I had taken three years of accounting in high school, so a degree in accounting was a consideration. I also pondered pursuing a degree in business management so I could potentially run my own music business, but I did not know what type of music business I wanted to start. I was confused, just like many other freshmen who were trying to figure out this thing called life. However, this time around, I had a purpose and a focus, and that outlook was all about survival! I didn't have a choice but to finish up my education; it was my only option if I was going to provide for myself.

I had another reason for wanting to finish my degree. My little sister Alberta was attending Brigham Young University in Utah, and she was close to finishing her degree in community health, so I made it a goal to finish before she did. I could not let her graduate first because she would have taken the title of *First Grandchild of James and Garnette Pegues to Graduate College*. My grandmother finished her bachelor's degree and eventually went back to school and received her master's degree in elementary education, but none of her children had finished a four-year degree at that time. My older brother Tommy did not go to college, so I was the next grandchild in line to go to school. Going to school was an issue of pride for me, and it made me feel a sense of validation in the work that I had put into it. There was no way on this good, green earth that I was going to allow Alberta to take that title from me.

I worked too hard to achieve that, so I made sure I completed my schooling by June 1999, one year before she finished. I was so proud of myself because, for the most part, I put myself through school. My parents, for their own personal reasons, didn't help me financially with school, so that contributed to my thirteen-year stretch between semesters. I would go in and take classes, and then drop out to save money, and then go back and drop out again when money wasn't there.

However, this last semester was different. My dad stepped in and helped me, paying for my housing, and I received a $500 scholarship from the School of Music to play in the orchestra. With the money that I saved already, the scholarship, and the money from my dad, my last semester of school fees was completely covered, and I finally finished that phase of my life, kicking that huge monkey off my back that had been there all those years.

Fast forward to the year 2020, and I was back in Florida. A lot of changes had happened in my life since going back to school. I got married again, this time to an amazing man named Jonah Matee Nganga, who later changed his name to Chuma Nganga Matee. (He will be referred to as Chuma hereafter in the book.) The other big change was that I had been a teacher for twenty years. I was working as an itinerant teacher in my own orchestra classroom, traveling around and teaching students at two elementary schools and two middle schools. That school year of 2020 was very difficult because we were in the height of the Covid-19 pandemic. Because of Covid, I was teaching a hybrid model, with some students online and some meeting me face to face. It was a very challenging year to say the least, but contrary to my joke with Dr. Mueller years before, I actually loved my job and the kids. Ironically, had I not experienced my divorce, I probably would never have considered going back to school and becoming a teacher.

My time with the kids was always precious, and it brought me joy. Of course, there were always students that tried my patience, and still do, but I was dealing with children from many different backgrounds and struggles. As a teacher, I learned to work my way through all the challenges that emerged and was able to reach most of the kids to help them work through their struggles, like frustration over completing assignments in my class or other classes, problems at home, and/or lack of acquiring basic school supplies or clothing. However, one day, my perfect world in teaching came crumbling down. It was as if I had been living in a glass house, and someone threw a stone. That stone shattered the beautifully fabricated walls of the house that I had been living in, uncovering the bruised and battered walls of my real life that had been buried deep within the house. The reality of my true life was now exposed, and it shook me to the core to see it out in the open.

Chapter 2

CASSIE

I picked up the phone and dialed the ten-digit number of the Employee Assistance Program (EAP). A female voice answered the call and gathered the required information that she needed from me. She then asked me to tell her a little bit about what prompted my call, so she could assign me to the correct counselor. I took a deep breath and said the following:

"I am a teacher, and several days ago, one of the students in my classroom threw a tantrum and started pushing me and hitting me. I'm okay physically, but I am struggling emotionally. I start crying at random times, and I can't seem to pull myself together."

She empathized with me and said, "I am so sorry that you experienced that. Let me get you assigned to a counselor."

She placed me on a brief hold and came back with the information.

"Here is your counselor's contact information, and here is your case number. You will need to give it to her when you call."

I thanked her, and we hung up.

I hesitated to call the assigned counselor for several reasons—I guess pride would be the first one. Sometimes it is difficult to admit to ourselves that we are having a problem beyond the scope of our understanding. I knew something was wrong, but I thought I was smart enough to manage whatever was going on inside of me. The other reason that I hesitated to call was my schedule. Between my regular job, my private music studio, and upcoming concerts, I just couldn't imagine adding one more thing to my schedule. I knew that it would be difficult to try and create extra time for counseling sessions. On the other hand, deep down inside, I knew I was having some sort of emotional breakdown that made it almost impossible to keep my emotions in check. I couldn't focus on the things that I needed to do … like teaching my classes full of students. I would be teaching and laughing with the kids one moment, and the next moment, I would have to turn my face away from them because I had just randomly started crying. I kept asking myself, *What Is Wrong With You?* But I just couldn't seem to figure it out, and the fact that I had no control over my emotions was even more frustrating.

The day before I made the call, I had just experienced a crying spell at one of my elementary schools. The kids were playing a song, and I just started crying. Now crying randomly is not uncommon for me because I am a musician, and I can easily be drawn away by the beauty of a piece of music and start crying. However, this was something completely different, as this type of crying came about whether there was sound or silence. The tears came about randomly, with no positive or negative emotions preceding them, but I could feel myself getting ready to cry for no apparent reason. I used all my will to hold the tears back, but I couldn't do it. Unprovoked, the waterworks came, and when the students stopped playing, I quickly dried my eyes and gave them feedback when they finished.

The class period then ended, and it was time for them to go back to their classes, so they packed up their instruments and lined up at the door to walk out and head toward the PE area, where their teachers could pick them up. After they all exited the classroom, three of the students stopped, turned around, and ran back to me: it was two girls and a boy. They looked up at me, and I looked down at them. Unlike many of the other elementary students in my class, these particular students were not the hugging type, and because of the Covid-19 pandemic, we generally didn't touch the students to avoid spreading germs. We four, at first, just kept our distance, but these three students somehow knew I needed to be comforted. So, they opened their arms and gave me a great big group bear hug. I knew at that moment my efforts to conceal my inner pain had failed. They knew something was wrong, so without uttering a word, they hugged me and quickly left to catch up with their line. I thanked them and turned around quickly, stepping back into my classroom to cry.

When I got home that evening, I talked to my husband Chuma and told him what had happened that day; we discussed the struggles I was going through. He asked me if I thought I needed to talk to someone about it. At that point, I wasn't sure if I needed to or not and was still under the illusion that I could work through this issue myself. The following day, I had several more crying bouts, so I called my friend, who was a secretary in my department in the school district. She was aware of the incident and asked how I was doing.

"I am struggling. I am an emotional wreck," I said.

"Have you considered using the EAP to talk to someone?"

"No. I hadn't thought about it." With concern in her voice, she said, "You should really make the call. The service is there for this very reason, and it's free. I'll text you the number." I thanked her, and we hung up.

Later that afternoon, I was sitting in my car, getting ready to go home for the day, and I decided to make the call. When the counselor answered the phone, I could tell by the sound and timbre of her voice that she was African American. This would not have even been a concern to me in the past, but for some reason, at that moment, I felt comforted by her ethnicity. She was a sister like me, and I could tell that she had a strong personality that was the opposite of mine. Her sense of strength made me feel optimistic that she would be able to help me get through this.

Our first appointment was set for the very next day. She used an online medical streaming platform for our virtual meeting. This was different, but I liked the setup because I didn't have to go into her office; I could talk to her from anywhere I chose. She handled all the shopkeeping questions first, like, "What is your name?" "Age?" Blah, blah, blah. She needed to build a clinical portrait of who I was before she could start counseling. After all of that was done, she told me to tell her what happened at school. So, I started relaying my story:

I have a student in my class named Cassie, who has some diagnosed behavior issues. She has been struggling in my class and wanted to quit, but her parents would not let her because they wanted her to learn about commitment and responsibility. This was a huge struggle because the sound of the instruments, at times, really bothered her; it seemed like it had something to do with the frequency of the pitches. A couple of days ago, Cassie came to school, and her behavior was completely off that day. She came to my class very agitated and would not come inside the room. She sat down on the ground outside the door, and as the other kids came into the class, they told me that she was outside the classroom and refused to come in. So, I took a deep breath and said to myself, *Oh no! Here we go!* I got the other students seated and started them working on an assignment. I then went over and opened the door to talk to her.

"Cassie, please come inside."

"No!" she said.

I tried to reason with her.

"You don't have to play today; just come in and take your seat."

She then screamed, "No! I don't want to be here. I want to go to art."

She was escalating, but I tried to remain calm, so I said, "I'm sorry, but today is string day, not art day. You have to come inside."

Cassie reluctantly came in and immediately started screaming once inside the room. She dropped to the floor and started rolling around, kicking, and yelling. Cassie was throwing the worst tantrum that I had seen her exhibit all year. Worse yet, she was doing it right in front of the door and was blocking the doorway. I asked her to please take her seat, but she would not get up. She was literally screaming at the top of her voice. The other kids were used to this behavior, so they continued working on their music and tried to ignore what was going on. I asked her several more times to get up, but she outright refused and continued screaming, so I silently turned around and started to head toward the phone to call for help.

As I took about two steps away from her, Cassie realized I was headed toward the phone, so she jumped up and ran toward me. She started pushing me from behind, so I walked faster to get to the phone. She ran around me and started grabbing my arms and pushing me in the stomach to stop me from walking forward, and when I got close to the phone, she saw the lanyards that were hanging around my neck. One lanyard had my employee ID on it, and the other had my school keys on it. She was determined to stop me from making that call, so she grabbed both lanyards in one hand and yanked downward on them with all her strength. This pulled my neck and torso downward. Though I remained standing, the force at which she yanked my lanyards caused me to bend harshly at the waist. I felt like I had just gotten a sucker punch to the back of my neck. I was completely in shock because I had never, in my entire teaching career, been assaulted by any student.

Everything happened so fast that it didn't give me time to think. All of a sudden, I felt the immediate pain in the back of my neck, so, with my right arm, I grabbed the lanyards directly above where one of her hands was holding the lanyards, and I tightened my bicep and pulled my arm in against my body to gain leverage so she couldn't yank my neck downward again.

I yelled out, "Don't touch me!"

She had one hand on my lanyards, while the other hand was swinging at me. So, I yelled out again, but louder and firmer this time.

"DON'T TOUCH ME!!"

The volume of my voice was loud, and it startled her. She released my lanyards, stood still, and looked at me. I backed up a couple of steps toward the wall to put some distance between the two of us. She continued to look at me as if she were in a trance, and the sound of my voice forced her out of it. Suddenly, she moved toward me, as if she wanted to hug me, but because of what had just happened, I moved backward and lifted my hands up with my palms facing her, as if to say, *Stop! Don't touch me.* My rejection of her hug upset her, and she started crying and ran out of the classroom.

At that point, I told the counselor that I felt bad because Cassie wanted to be consoled, and maybe I should have … but the counselor stopped me in mid-sentence.

"Nope! You do not get to take that guilt or that responsibility! She had just battered and injured you. That was not the time nor the place for you to try and make that child feel better."

My typical response to adversity was to always look out for the other person before I looked out for myself. I knew the counselor was right, but I still felt guilty because Cassie was a child. However, the counselor told me I had done the right thing in protecting myself. I heard what she was saying, but my heart still felt bad for Cassie. She asked me to keep going, so I continued:

I canceled my next class and went up to the administration office and reported the incident. After I did that, I went out to my car and sat there for a moment. I was rattled and was not emotionally capable of going into another classroom that day, so I called in sick to my next two schools and went home. When I got home, I crawled into my bed and cried. I felt completely violated, and I didn't know what to do with those feelings. I was at home all alone, so the only thing I could do was cry until I fell asleep.

It just so happened that I had a chiropractic appointment already scheduled for later that day, so I went to the appointment. It had been several hours since the incident, and my neck was really sore. I told the chiropractor what had happened, so he checked my neck. Sure enough, it was out of alignment, as was my upper back. After the adjustment, he told me to go home, ice my neck and back, and rest for the remainder of the day.

I told the counselor that something else was bothering me.

"I feel frustrated because I have never felt afraid to be in my classroom. I have never had this type of experience before, so I'm completely in a new, emotional territory. It's unfamiliar, and it's frightening. My eyes are open to the fact that I can be injured, and I don't know what to do with those feelings. I just know that this fear is real and very scary. I keep running that scene of violence through my mind, blow by blow, over and over again, so the fear is starting to become more intense.

"Another problem that has come from that situation is the fear of wearing my lanyards. I have not put them back on my neck since the morning of that incident. I am carrying them either in my bag or in my pocket. I just cannot bring myself to put them back around my neck."

As I discussed this situation with the counselor, she said, "The fear that you are experiencing is a typical response to trauma. You have just been through something violent, and the experience is still very raw, but with time, you will be able to work through it."

Cassie's mother was notified about the incident and at her request, Cassie was immediately withdrawn from my class, but that was exactly what Cassie wanted in the first place. In my mind's eye, withdrawing her felt like a reward and not really a punishment for her behavior. At the same time, I didn't want her back in my class either. The vindictive side of my personality didn't want her to go to art either because that seemed to be a reward at my expense. *Why should she get rewarded and be allowed to go where she wanted to go in the first place by doing such a violent act against one of her teachers?* It just didn't seem right, but she got exactly what she wanted. That news was a bit disturbing to me, but I had to keep reminding myself that she was a child with a mental disability.

My emotions were all over the place after the incident, and for the most part, I was pretty much left to deal with that situation on my own. No one at the school came to check on me, and when I reached out for their help, there was silence on the other end. This was one of the reasons why I called the EAP. I needed help, but no one at the school seemed to be able to help me through it, as though it got brushed under the rug. Everyone went on about their lives, but I couldn't. I was stuck.

I continued my conversation with the counselor and talked to her about my concern for the random crying, to which she explained that I had just been through a traumatic experience so the crying was understandable and could actually be therapeutic. However, what came next was shocking.

She started asking me about my music career. I told her that I was a violinist. She then asked me how long I had been playing the violin, to which I told her that I started playing in the fourth grade. This line of questioning seemed harmless, because people often sparked a conversation or asked me questions when they found out that I was a violinist; however, the conversation took a turn in a different direction. She then started digging into what made me start playing the violin, which brought up some memories that I was not really prepared to think or talk about. However, she asked, and because I promised Alberta that I would be open to this process, I knew I needed to respond.

"The violin came to me at a time of my life that I absolutely needed it. I was going through some difficult times, and playing the violin gave me a safe place to go away from my life," I stated.

She then said, "It seems that music has been a safe haven for you since you were a little girl. This incident happened in your safe space, and it has made you feel unsafe. It sounds like you have some unresolved issues from your life where you have felt unsafe. These are issues that you have not dealt with. This incident was just the catalyst that brought those issues to the surface, and the tears are your body's response to that. You have locked away some things that need to come out."

I do not know how she figured all that out with the few questions that she asked, but somehow, she did, and she went right for the jugular. After she said that to me, a tear dropped and rolled down my cheek. I wasn't sure

THE EYES BEHIND THE VIOLIN

if I felt sadness or relief at that moment, but whatever the case, my body responded with a tear.

After we talked a little bit more, she told me that this first session was to help pull me back from the edge, which was exactly what it did. She validated my feelings and my frustration about the incident, and I felt better. She also said that we needed to deal with the other issues that were hidden, so we needed to continue to meet to work through what was behind the tears.

After juggling our schedules, we scheduled a weekly date and time for our video sessions. Having to add these weekly visits to my schedule was a source of stress for me because I had so many things going on in my life. Just trying to find a day and time to schedule the sessions really made me anxious, but I reluctantly agreed to meet with her. After the session was over, I called Alberta, who was aware of what I was going through and was waiting for my call. She wanted to know how the session went, so I told her.

"Everything went fine, but she wants to go through my past, so she wants to schedule a bunch of sessions. I have several music performances coming up and a bunch of other stuff going on. This is very stressful. I don't have time for this right now!"

"Kyeni, do you hear yourself?" she said.

"Yes, I do, but it's true. I have a lot of stuff going on."

"Well, I think she's right. This is exactly the right time to deal with this," she rebutted.

Of course, I added another excuse to the conversation.

"This is too much for me to deal with."

As usual, Alberta pulled out her trump card.

"Kyeni, you are always focused on everyone else. It is time for you to focus on yourself."

I let out a huge sigh because she tells me this all the time, but this time, I listened to her because I knew she was right. *She is always right.* She is seven and a half years younger than I am, but she is wiser in so many ways. That is probably why I have leaned on her for my emotional support all these years.

As we were talking, and I gave her every excuse that I could think of to cancel, or at least postpone, the counseling sessions, I realized that my excuses had landed on deaf ears this time. So, I quietly said, "Okay. Fine! I'll do it."

I promised Alberta that I would go through this process, and although it felt scary and made me nervous, I knew she would be there for me and would catch me if I started to fall. In addition to Alberta, I had a circle of really close friends that I could rely on as I was traveling down this path. Some were near and some were far, but they were all only a phone call away. That gave me a lot of comfort because I knew in my heart, I was getting ready to go through hell and back. I could feel that my body had buried a bunch of stuff inside, but it wasn't like a complete loss of memories. My thoughts just seemed fuzzy, so I didn't think about anything. At that point, I realized that all those thoughts and memories were hidden away for a good reason. My body must have known I was not strong enough yet to deal with those things at that time, so it buried them deep within so I could continue to function.

As I was driving home from work one day, my concern about what was going to happen in opening my emotions was very real to me at that moment, but as I pondered it, I came to the realization that the Lord's hand might be involved. This whole situation happened in the one place that would rattle me enough to unearth the sleeping demons that lay beneath. It happened in my place of refuge, my place of solace, my place of peace: my music classroom. I don't believe I would have responded the same way if it had been in a different setting. Music has always been my safety net, and that safe space had now been violated. It was as if the Lord spoke to my mind and said, "It's time, daughter! You are spiritually strong enough now. Let's deal with these things together so you can continue to grow."

Today, when I look back at that moment right before I took my inward journey, I knew that God would be there and walk with me through that trial. I also knew that it would be a huge struggle for me because I would have to be willing to give up my sense of power to control my life so I could walk that path. I needed to learn what it meant to surrender, not just to that situation but to learn to surrender to God entirely. I needed to give up my perceived power and put my faith and trust in Him. I thought I knew this truth, but I immediately realized that knowing and doing were two very different things. The journey reminded me that God knew who I was and how important I was to Him.

Chapter 3

THE JOURNEY INWARD BEGINS

I promised myself I would walk through this process no matter how dark it got, but I have to admit I was concerned about what would be uncovered in my counseling sessions. It was clear to me that my issues were filled with guilt and shame. I didn't know what the issues were, but I felt a sense of sadness and felt like I was going to be uncomfortable talking about them. So, I started to prepare myself for the experience I was getting ready to have. The next few weeks were going to be difficult, but they would also provide me with an opportunity to re-live some things in my past, looking at the good, the bad, and the ugly. On a different note, the sessions would also give me a chance to look for lessons I could learn from those experiences. There had to be something positive that I could gain from them.

On our next visit, my counselor started asking me more questions. The first question she posed was concerning my relationship with my parents during my childhood years. I thought to myself, *Boy, she wastes no time. She jumps right in there!* I closed my eyes and took a few deep breaths to try and calm myself before answering. When I opened my eyes, I began my journey back down memory lane. She would ask me guided questions, and I would answer them as honestly as possible. As I responded to the questions, things started coming to my recollection; lucky for me, the memories that were surfacing were collections of good and bad memories. That made things much easier because my big fear was only the dark and scary stuff would come up, but that was not the case. I started remembering a variety of positive things, like how my childhood home looked.

My mom, dad, brother Tommy, and I lived in a two-story, three-bedroom gray house on Dubail Street in South Bend, Indiana. It was the typical style of house in our middle-class, multicultural neighborhood in the late 1960s, with nice, big windows in the front of the house and a triangle-shaped roof. It was a good house with a lot of space for our little family of four (at that time). Out of all the houses that I have ever lived in, it was my favorite. It had a nice, big porch in the front of the house that was great for sitting outside and watching what was going on in the neighborhood. Upon entering the house, there was a small breezeway where we placed our shoes and wooden floors throughout the entire house, except for the kitchen, the bathroom, and the basement. The kitchen and the bathroom had vinyl flooring, while the basement flooring was a cement slab.

On the main floor, there was a large entryway, and through this room, you could access all parts of the house. To the left of the entryway was a large, arched opening that led into our living room, where we spent most of our family time. We had a couple of comfortable couches in there and a large, floor-model, color television that was in a big, brown, wooden cabinet. I remember the day when Dad brought that TV home. We were so excited and were amazed to see the vibrant colors because they were a stark contrast to the black-and-white shows we were used to watching. That was the top-of-the-line technology for the early 1970s, and we had one in our very own house. Dad bought the color TV as a family gift to replace our smaller black-and-white TV.

Through a doorway on the right side of the living room, there was a smaller attached family room. Dad spent a lot of time in there, reading the newspaper and magazines. By buying us the new color TV, he was able to put the black-and-white TV in there so he could watch his favorite country/western shows and serials like *M*A*S*H*, which my dad loved because he was in the military. That room was like his man cave, so he spent much of his free time there. In the back, right-hand corner of the family room was a doorway that led into the back, left side of the kitchen. You could access the kitchen from the family room or straight through the main entryway. There was a table in the kitchen where we ate all our meals and rarely ate in the living room, unless it was popcorn for movie-watching.

To the right of the main entryway was a staircase that led up to the second floor where the three bedrooms were. There was a bedroom for me that was forward and slightly to the right of the stairs, one all the way to the left for my brother Tommy (who was one and a half years older than I), and my parents' room that was directly to the right of Tommy's room. We had one bathroom, which was right next to my bedroom.

Visualizing that bathroom brought back a lot of memories. One of the most important memories was remembering not to go into the bathroom right after Dad had been in there, unless it was an emergency.

One year, we were having a birthday party for Tommy, and many of our extended family members were there. Everyone was gathered in the kitchen around the table, as we were getting ready to light the candles on Tommy's cake and sing, "Happy Birthday." All of a sudden, water started pouring out of the round tubes of the fluorescent light in the ceiling directly above us. Of course, the water splashed down on the beautiful birthday cake that was sitting on the table directly beneath the light. Tommy was so upset because it ruined the party for him; come to find out my uncle Jimmy had been in the bathroom upstairs, and he clogged up the toilet. The sewage line traveled right above the kitchen light, and it somehow burst to where all that sewage water fell onto his cake. Yuck! Tommy was so mad, but to me, I thought the whole thing was disgustingly funny.

Right next to the bathroom was a door leading up to the attic. We used the attic stairs as a makeshift storage space, but I didn't go up into the attic because it was spooky. One year, the attic became the home of a colony of bats, which we didn't know were there until someone opened the attic door, and a bat flew out into the house. When that bat flew downstairs, I ran outside. I didn't know it was a bat and thought it was a bird. At the age of six, I knew that it wasn't supposed to be inside our house, so I removed myself from the situation and let Dad deal with it. I absolutely did not do creatures in enclosed areas; well, for that matter, other than dogs and cats, I didn't do creatures. Period!

When they called an exterminator, they found a hole in the attic window where the bats got in through there and took up shop. Even when the window was sealed and the bats were gone, I never went up to that attic again. I had similar spooky feelings about the basement, so I only went down there when someone else was with me.

However, this was home, and it was very comfortable. It had plenty of space for my brother and I to play, and plenty of hiding places for hide and seek. We had a nice-sized, fenced-in backyard that housed a beautiful, mature black walnut tree off to the left side of the property and a large, white garage at the far end of the property out by the alley.

I was your everyday, run-of-the-mill six-year-old girl. The only real difference between my neighborhood friends and me were the schools that we attended. I went to a private church school called Calvary Temple, and they went to public school a few blocks away. Both of my parents worked at the time: my dad was a plumber and certified journeyman in the states of Indiana and Michigan, and my mom was a telephone operator at Indiana Bell. So, the main reason we were sent to the private school was because it had extended hours. We stayed after school until our parents got off work and could come and pick us up.

Despite the fact that we went to a church school, we were not a very religious family and very rarely went to church. I knew who God and Jesus were, and I knew some of the Bible stories. Most of what I learned about God and religion came from my grandmother, Garnette Pegues (Mama), and from my school. We periodically went to church with Mama and sometimes received invites to go to church with one of my mom's friends, but that was not very often. My dad was not religious in those days. He was not resistant to it; he just didn't engage in it. As a child, I prayed to God when I needed help, but it wasn't until many years later, during my early adulthood, that my relationship with God became stronger.

Calvary Temple was a pretty decent school, which I was there for kindergarten and first grade. When I was in kindergarten, I remember my mom going to school to meet with my teacher because I had developed a strange way of pronouncing some words. My mom was concerned about it, so she set up a meeting with the teacher to discuss it. As she started talking to the teacher, she immediately understood why some of my words were spoken weirdly. I don't know where my teacher grew up, but she was the cause of the problem, as she would pronounce words that ended in "er" with a long "e" sound before the "er."

So, this was most noticeable in my speech when I pronounced the names of the months. They sounded like: "SeptembEE-er, OctobEE-er, and NovembEE-er." When my mom heard my teacher pronounce November, she knew what the problem was. She also knew that she could not change the teacher, but she could definitely change me, which was exactly what she did. My mom worked with me on my pronunciation until I made the correction on my own.

Getting ready for school was always a little stressful for me because I had chronic nosebleeds in those early years. The doctor said that there was nothing physically wrong with my nose, and I would eventually grow out of them, but that didn't make things better for me in the meantime as there was nothing that could medically be done about it. I was just one of those children that was plagued with childhood nosebleeds, and I had no idea how long it would take for my nose to decide that it was old enough and didn't need to bleed anymore. I had to learn to keep my head slightly elevated in the morning because blood would just randomly start dripping from my nose and land on my shirt or my dress, which would then force me to change clothes before I left for school.

My mom always kept a supply of cotton balls in the house so she could shove one up into my nose until a clot formed. Right before we left for school, she would remove the cotton ball, and as she slowly pulled the cotton ball out, there would be a big, long, black clot that had attached itself to the end of the cotton. Sometimes the clot was so long that it activated my gag reflex when it came out; I hated that. When the clot was removed, she would check to see if the bleeding had stopped, and then we would run off to school.

One day when I was in the first grade, my nose decided to be extra naughty that day. We went through my regular nosebleed regimen of putting the cotton ball in before leaving for school. This almost always worked, but not that day. My nose bled, bled, and bled some more. We finally had to leave, or Mom would have been late for work. So, Mom replaced the bloody cotton ball with a new clean one, packed a little baggie of cotton balls for me, and we jumped in the car and hit the road. When we got to school, the bleeding had slowed down a bit, but it had not finished bleeding. Mom decided to put a fresh cotton ball in my nose, and I went into school and sat down at my desk.

Class started, and we all began to work on our assignments. My teacher noticed that I had a cotton ball in my nose, so she walked over to me and told me that I could not have a cotton ball in my nose at school. She then told me to take it out. I tried to explain to her that my nose was bleeding and it had not quite stopped yet, but she refused to listen to me. She told me to get up, and she walked me over by the bathroom. She reached up to my nose, removed the cotton ball, and threw it away without even checking to see if there was any blood on it that would corroborate my story. She was just offended by the fact that I had a cotton ball in my nose, so she removed it. Her action upset me because she was employing what I call "Adult Syndrome"; that's when adults think they know everything and don't listen to kids because they think that kids are stupid and know nothing.

The frustrating thing about this whole situation was that she didn't understand my plight with nosebleeds and was unwilling to listen to me. I tried to explain it, but she did not want to hear what I had to say and did not care. So, I decided to let my mischievous personality come out against my teacher. I usually kept it under wraps at school, but somebody was gonna learn a lesson that day.

The teacher sent me back to my desk, and with a little smirk on my face, I kindly obliged. I sat down and started working on my assignment again, but this time, I made sure that my head was tilted downward. The bleeding had almost stopped, but that would have messed up my plan for my teacher, so I started to covertly rub, squeeze, and wiggle my nose from side to side. I was sneakily doing everything that I could to dislodge that clot and make my nose start bleeding again, and bingo, the blood started to flow. Drip … drip … drip onto my desk the blood went. I let it flow until one of the students next to me saw the puddle of blood all on my desk and got the teacher's attention, saying, "She's bleeding!" The teacher started walking toward me, and what happened next could not have been timed more perfectly.

When she approached me, a drop of blood came out of my nose and slowly started rolling onto my upper lip. When she reached me, she saw the blood all over the desk, and then I raised my head up and made eye contact with her. When she looked at my face, the blood started rolling down my lips. "Oh, my goodness!" she said.

She grabbed my hand and quickly walked me back over to the bathroom, grabbed a paper towel, and started wiping my nose. She told me to hold my head back and hold the paper towel against my nose. Back then, we didn't have anything like HIV or any other blood-borne pathogens that people were afraid of, so she just grabbed some paper towels and went over to my desk and cleaned up the blood. After that, she called for the nurse, who came to the classroom and grabbed a chair. She told me to lean back in the chair, so my head was pointed upward, and then she pinched the bridge of my nose. After a minute or so, she made me pinch my nose for a few more minutes until the bleeding stopped.

The teacher told the nurse that I had come to school with a cotton ball in my nose and that she took it out. The nurse didn't say anything then, but when my mom came to pick my brother and I up later that afternoon, the nurse told her that I was not allowed to come to school with a cotton ball in my nose. Mom told her that I had nosebleeds all the time, but the nurse said that my nose could not be bleeding when I came to school, and cotton balls were not allowed. Why that was a rule, I do not know, as my cotton ball was not bothering anybody but me. So, I did not understand what the big deal was.

Lucky for me, my nose went back to its normal morning flow, and I never had a bad one like that again. Slowly but surely, within the year, the morning bleeds became fewer and farther between until they eventually stopped. I was happy when that day finally came. Besides that one incident at school, I only had to deal with the nosebleeds at home, and only my family knew the extent of the nosebleeds. The bleeding didn't hurt; it was just annoying, and the cause of some extra laundry when the blood got on my clothes. I was very grateful when the bleeding finally stopped.

* * *

Through the eyes of my five-year-old self at that time, my parents seemed normal and like any other parents. However, I didn't notice that my parents were having trouble. They argued, but that was a normal occurrence. My dad talked loudly, and he would yell whenever he got mad or if we did anything that displeased him, like squeezing the toothpaste in the middle of the tube; that was an absolute no-no. They always bought the big tubes of *Crest* toothpaste, so we had to learn how to balance that toothpaste in our little hands and squeeze it from the bottom. When we were done brushing our teeth, we had to go back to the tube and push all the contents upward in the tube, flattening the tube at the bottom as time went by. To this very day, I have issues with people using my toothpaste, especially my husband, because he squeezes it in the middle. For that reason, we use our own individual tubes of toothpaste because I cannot deal with that.

Sometime in 1974, after I turned six years old, I woke up one morning and heard rustling and bustling downstairs. I got up, got dressed, and went down to see what was going on. I saw some bags and boxes that were packed and sitting in the entryway. I then saw my mom come in from outside, grab some of the things that she had packed, and then go back outside. I followed her out and watched her put the things into her car. I was very confused because we had not talked about going anywhere. So, I looked at her and asked, "Where are we going?"

As she passed me to go back into the house, she said, "We're leaving your dad!"

When she went back into the house to get some more things, I stayed outside in the yard and stood there in shock. I didn't know how to respond to that news, but I said what any six-year-old would probably say.

"I don't want to leave Daddy!"

My mom passed me and put the next load of stuff in the car. She turned and headed back toward the house and, in her anger and frustration at what was going on in her current situation, she said four words that would emotionally and mentally damage me up through my early adulthood.

"WELL, STAY HERE THEN!"

She projected all her anger, hurt, and frustration onto me, her daughter. I know now, as an adult, that it wasn't intentional. She was dealing with the pain and frustration of my dad's infidelity, and other adult issues I was not privy to, but I certainly didn't understand her hurt when I was a child and didn't know what was going on between them.

I stood still and tried to process what she just said; however, what she said and what I understood her saying were two very different things. Her words made me feel as if I had to choose between going with her or staying with my dad, so in my young mind, I thought, *Which one do I pick? I love both of them.* These thoughts kept rapidly running through my head. She knew that I was going with her, but I didn't. I was weighing my options between the two of them, but I quickly decided that I needed to stay with my mom. Unfortunately, this decision haunted me because it set me up to become a victim, in the worst kind of way, and it placed me on a path of self-destruction, down the road of low self-worth.

My parents divorced eventually, and I felt an immense sense of guilt for picking between my parents. I felt that somehow, I must have done something to cause their breakup. There, of course, was nothing that I could possibly have done to cause their problems, but six-year-old minds can have the uncanny ability to come up with some interesting things. I dealt with a huge sense of guilt over their breakup, and it affected my sense of self-worth. I felt like I was a bad person, and because I wasn't a good girl all the time, I somehow was to blame for their breakup. Our parents never talked to us about what was going on or explained to us why they were getting divorced. It was like the topic was taboo, so my understanding of the situation was left completely to my own interpretation and imagination.

Those feelings were too heavy for me at that young age to process, so this is the first memory that I remember of my mind burying hurt feelings. It protected me so that I could continue to thrive and never deal with those feelings of guilt. I never talked to my mom about these feelings, as my mind just buried them, and I moved along as if nothing had ever happened.

My counselor and I discussed this scene in my life in great detail, because this was where the blame game started for me and continued through my adulthood. Placing blame on myself, when it wasn't warranted, was a form of guilt for me, and feelings of guilt can be very dangerous if gone unchecked. My mind may have hidden away the act, but the emotional damage that resulted from the act remained and became part of my own self-destruction. The more I started destroying myself, the lower my sense of self-worth became. This, in turn, brought about depression that went unchecked and unnoticed, up through the middle of my college years.

Chapter 4

AFTER THE FALLOUT

I was amazed at how all my memories started jumping into my mind during my counseling sessions. It was like my memories were all in a single-file line, waiting for their opportunity to come out and tell their stories. Most of my younger childhood was completely blocked, but when the memories came, I thought to myself, *Oh yeah. I remember that.* Some of the memories brought a smile to my face, while others made me sad, like remembering what happened after Mom had finished packing her car that fateful morning. Mom, Tommy, and I got into the car, and I cried as she drove away from our home. Half of my heart was left at that house that day for my dad, and tears rolled down my face as we drove away because I didn't know when I would see him again.

Mom secured a nice apartment for us to live in that was just a few miles away from our house, but it wasn't home; it was very different living there without Dad. Tommy and I went over and visited with him periodically, and sometimes he would come and pick us up from school. Over time, Mom and Dad started to work things out, and low and behold, a miracle happened. They got back together and eventually married again. All was well with the world ... for a minute. Unfortunately, it was all too good to be true, and they divorced again. I didn't find out until I was an adult that there were issues of infidelity that crept into their relationship, which was the reason for their first divorce, and those old behaviors crept back into their relationship during their re-marriage. Eventually, a second divorce occurred between them, and Mom got custody of us while Dad got visitation rights. We lived with Mom full time and generally went to Dad's house every other weekend. That was the end of that chapter of my life.

* * *

During my parents' separation, my mom started seeing another man, and by the time the divorce date came, she was pregnant with my sister Alberta. The man's name was J but was not spelled J-a-y. It was just the letter J. He was suspect to me, but I was just a kid and thought any man other than my dad would have been suspect. However, my instincts were right about J. He was not a very good person, but Mom was all in for their relationship. I had never met a man like J before. He had long hair and used to get his hair done by a lady named Vera. She used to come to the house and bring her hot comb and curlers that would be heated up on our gas stove. My mom and my grandmother used to straighten my hair using a hot comb, but I had never seen a man with straightened hair before.

After Vera straightened his hair, she would use the curlers. When she was curling his hair, all you could hear was the "click, click, click" sound of her opening and closing the curlers. You had to do that because they were very hot, and if the curlers were left in the hair without opening and closing them like that, they would burn the hair off. However, used correctly, they would create nice, tight curls that would stay in the hair for at least a week.

J was the first man that I had ever seen have his hair curled like that, and I guess my mom liked it, and him, because we eventually moved in with him. He was not particularly kind to Tommy and me, and he wasn't always nice to Mom either, but she stayed with him anyway. They would get into very bad arguments where they would scream at each other, and, from time to time, the arguments would turn violent, and J would beat my mom up. That was a very scary time for me, and I was worried about her. Because I didn't know what went on behind closed doors between my mom and dad, I didn't understand why she would leave my dad and start a relationship with a man that beat her. My dad might have yelled a lot, and he might have had some other weaknesses, but he did not physically hurt my mom; he did not believe in that.

* * *

One day, my mom dropped Tommy and I off at my great uncle and aunt's house, where we were going to be staying overnight. Right as Mom was leaving, I walked up to her and asked her where she was going. She told me that she and J were going to get married; that was a shocker, to say the least. I couldn't understand why she would want to marry him, but to each their own, I guess. When she came back and picked us up, we went back to the house as a "family." It wasn't really a family but more like the May family (Mom, J, and Alberta, who was still inside my mom's belly) and the two Bryants. Tommy and I were never fully integrated into that family unit but just lived in the house with them. We were not J's kids, so he never treated us like we were. However, Tommy and I understood that reality and never questioned it. Occasionally, J would do something nice for us, but those times were few and far between. Mom was aware of his treatment of us, and she would confront him sometimes about it, but there wasn't much she could do to stop it.

Daddy also re-married, marrying a beautiful woman named Marjorie Lynne, but called herself Lynne. She was nice to us and had a daughter named Sandra Trunae. I was a year older than Trunae, so we got along very well. She became like a regular sister to me, treating me with love, kindness, and respect. For that reason, I loved going to Daddy's house because I enjoyed spending time with Trunae. She never judged me or put me down, and we were just like sisters.

Mom and J rented a house on Cedar Street, which became one of my two "Houses of Horror." The only good thing that came out of this house was the birth of my younger sister Alberta, who was a breath of fresh air for the family. J had produced quite the brood of children from previous relationships around Indiana and other states, of whom my mother was unaware of until after they got married. Shortly after we moved into the Cedar Street house, J's daughter Trina, who lived in town and was in high school, was having problems at home with her mother, so she came to live with us for a time. Eventually, another daughter, Paris, from another woman in Mississippi came to stay with us for a while too. These two were like two peas in a pod. They were close in age, so they did everything together once they were living under the same roof.

Unlike my relationship with Trunae, these two stepsisters tormented me. They picked on me, made fun of me, and played practical jokes on me all the time. Since we were now family, and they were now stepsisters, I thought we were supposed to be loving to one another, but nothing could be further from the truth. They were the exact opposite of what I imagined, as they were like the stepsisters in the story of Cinderella. Paris wasn't as bad as Trina and even stuck up for me sometimes, but that didn't stop Trina from picking on me. She was a teenager, so I guess I was her daily entertainment. On top of all of that, she had a bad attitude; that behavior was probably why she and her mother were not getting along.

I was in second grade while they were in high school. Their cruelty toward me was part of their daily routine, and they went out of their way to humiliate me regularly. One day, I was at home with them as they babysat us, or more like tormented me, while Mom was at work. It was almost 5:30 p.m., and Mom would be home any minute. One of the things that Mom asked us to do before she left that morning was to clean our bedroom. I don't know what they were doing all day, but I played outside and played games all day. We forgot to clean the room, and when they noticed that Mom would be home any minute, they sent me upstairs to clean everything up before Mom arrived.

My blood started boiling because most of the mess in the room was theirs; I just needed to make my bed because I didn't do it when I got up that morning. As usual, I was their little slave, and I couldn't do anything about it because they were older than I was. I got up and quickly ran up the stairs that led to our room in the attic. The attic was like a loft, carpeted and spanning the entire upstairs of the house, so there was plenty of space for the three of us.

I was up in the attic, rushing to get the room clean, when the two girls came upstairs. They knew that Mom would be home any minute, so they should have jumped in and helped me with the cleaning, but no! This was another opportunity for them to torment me, so they seized the moment. I started making up my bed, and they walked over to me, leaned over, and started sniffing the bed. They then said, "You peed in the bed!"

"No, I didn't!" I said, but Trina kept going,

"Yes, you did. We can smell it. You better fess up or we're gonna tell your mom that you peed in the bed, and you are going to get in a lot of trouble."

With more fervor, I yelled out, "I didn't pee in the bed!"

Then, they looked out the window and saw my mom and said, "Look! Your mom just pulled up! We are going to go and tell on you."

They turned around and started rushing toward the stairs. I don't know why I believed their lie or was afraid for them to tell my mom that I had wet the bed, but I cried out and said, "Ok ... wait! I peed in the bed!"

Then they both busted out laughing.

"Ha ha ha! No, you didn't! Why did you confess to that?" Trina said.

They found ways to tease me all the time, and it was so frustrating and hurtful. Since we shared a room, they had constant access to me while Tommy's room was downstairs, so they rarely picked on him. Because they were older than I was, and because they were J's daughters, I felt alone and like a nobody in that house. It seemed like Trina and Paris were treated more like family than I was by both Mom and J, like I was on the outside looking in. This was the period of time where my sense of self-worth started to wane, just before the self-destruction started.

Mom's relationship with J was very shaky, to say the least. One day, we were all at home, and Mom and J got into a really bad argument. I didn't know what it was over but just heard them yelling. It carried on for a while and kept escalating, becoming more and more aggressive until J hit his boiling point and started beating up my mother. I was outside in the backyard when it happened, so I didn't see what was going on, but I could hear the blows through the window. As these beatings came to my recollection, I had not realized how much anxiety I felt as a little girl when she was being beaten. It was so stressful for me because I was helpless and could do nothing to help her.

When J started beating my mom, she started screaming and crying. I was young, so I didn't understand what they were fighting about, but the moment my mom started crying, I was terrified. When the beating finally ended, my mom cried out for Tommy and me. We ran to her, and she told us to leave and walk together to my grandmother's house. It was about a half-mile or so away, so we quickly headed to the front door and exited the house. Trina and Paris were sitting on the porch, and when we passed them, Trina started laughing and chiding us, saying, "Ha ha! Your mom got beat up!" That infuriated me so much! She picked on me all the time, so I was used to that, but she went too far when she started making fun of my mother's pain. I looked at her and, with all the rage that a second grader could muster, I yelled out, "You shut up! I hate you!"

She just looked at me and kept laughing. I knew I could do nothing, so I turned around and started walking down the street.

Mom left J after that beating, and we ended up staying at my grandmother's house for quite a while. Over time, Mom and J eventually made up, and we moved back home. Both Trina and Paris went back to their mothers, and it was just us again. I was so grateful for that because I would no longer have to deal with their cruelty.

On a side note, Paris lived in Mississippi, but I never saw her again. Trina grew up and became more mature, eventually getting married to a man named Carter. We became cordial and more sister-like toward each other, and she even drove down to Ball State for my college graduation. I was surprised that she came, but I was grateful that she did because I was able to spend some time with her. We were able to talk, and through our conversation, she showed me that she actually did care about me, which helped me see her in a different light.

*　*　*

Living on Cedar Street caused a change in our education as well. We started attending public school for the first time, as Mom enrolled us in McKinley Elementary School. I really liked that school; it was different than Calvary Temple. There were a lot more kids, and the school was bigger. I was enjoying my time there until some of the kids started picking on me for my weight. I was an average-sized girl when I first started attending McKinley, but I started gaining weight; when that happened, the name-calling began. Tommy's friends, who we walked to school with daily, were some of the biggest offenders, but Tommy never stopped them. He just let them make fun of me and, sometimes, he would join in with them, not realizing how much that hurt me.

I didn't understand why I was gaining weight, not relating eating a bunch of candy to gaining weight. When we walked to school, there was a fire station right across the street from McKinley. All the kids would stop there because the firefighters sold cheap candy, with most of the candy being ten cents and below. Tommy and I would look around the house for loose change for candy, and when we couldn't find any, we started going into J's pockets and taking his change. When his change was gone, we started taking his folding money. He caught on eventually, and we got a whooping and were no longer allowed to go to the fire station. This, it turned out, was part of the reason that I started gaining weight. The other reason was much more tragic.

Now that we were attending a public school, our school did not have extended hours, but we were too young to stay at home by ourselves. Trina and Paris were no longer there, and both sets of parents worked during the day, so Mom did not have a babysitter. So instead of going home after school, we started walking to the house of my mom's cousin; this is when things started going really wrong. Most of the time her cousin was there to watch us, but sometimes, her cousin would leave us with her son Auggy, who was an older teenager at that time. He was involved in sports, so he was a big guy. Tommy and I did everything he told us to do because he was like a giant to us, and we were afraid of him.

On one of the days he was watching us, his relationship with me changed. I was only about seven years old at the time. He started to request things of me that I first thought were innocent but really turned out to be his form of grooming. He would ask me to sit next to him on the couch, and then, over time, he would ask me to sit on his lap. If I declined, he would grab me and put me there, and then he would start to move and gyrate his hips around me. His requests slowly became more and more sexually inappropriate, so he told me not to say anything about what we did. Since I was only in the second grade, and because I was afraid of him, I didn't tell anyone.

Tommy was with me in that house when these things were going on. He did not react to anything that was going on with me because he was afraid of Auggy also. Tommy would just go into another room, or Auggy would take me to another room. Auggy was very mean to Tommy and did cruel things to him, like run over him with his bicycle. One day, when Tommy and Auggy were outside, Auggy was riding his bike, and he began to chase Tommy. Tommy was running until he tripped and fell down. Auggy rolled completely up Tommy's behind, up his back, and over his shoulder blade, and almost ran over his head with the tires of his bike.

Tommy and I were both struggling in that house, but because of Auggy's threats, we were afraid to say anything. We both suffered in silence and internally dealt with Auggy's cruelty in our own ways. I dealt with it by finding comfort in food, which was when I really started to gain weight.

Mom would complain about my weight, but she never investigated why I might possibly be gaining weight. She was so caught up in her own issues with her abusive relationship that my issues flew completely underneath her radar. But she never would have imagined that Auggy would be doing bad things to her daughter and being cruel to her son.

At this time, Tommy and I were in awkward positions in my mom's household. She had started a new family with a man that acted as though he did not like Tommy and I, and, for whatever reason, Mom was unable to do anything about it. Therefore, I didn't trust that she would believe me about Auggy's abuse, so I just kept quiet about it. I couldn't discuss anything with her and even though Tommy was aware of my abuse, we never talked about it either. So, food became my friend, my source of comfort, and my confidante.

When I was over at Auggy's house one day, I saw Auggy's parents go into his room and close the door behind them, which was strange to me. I had never seen both of his parents go into his room at the same time like that before and knew something was going down, so I needed to get closer to hear through the door. Right next to his room was a small bureau that had a shelf on the bottom. I crawled over to it and climbed up on the bottom shelf to listen to their conversation through a vent in the wall. They were doing an intervention, of sorts, with him.

My friend Marcy told her mom that Auggy tried to do something sexual to her when he babysat her and her brothers a few nights earlier. She told him no, and he eventually left her alone. However, Marcy told her mom what happened, and her mom told Auggy's mom, so now Auggy's parents were confronting him about the situation. I shared my situation with Marcy, so she was aware that Auggy was abusing me, but Auggy's parents only talked about what he had done to Marcy, never mentioning me in that conversation at all. They chastised him about Marcy and told him never to do it again. I could hear that they were ending their conversation and coming back out, so I crawled out from under the bureau and ran back to the back bedroom, pretending like I didn't hear anything.

I was so proud of my friend, as Marcy did what I couldn't do. She told on Auggy, and he never approached her again. I thought I was in the clear because he stopped messing with me too. It was a miracle. Marcy had saved me … or so I thought. Neither my mom's cousin, nor Marcy's mother, ever told my mother what Auggy had done, and both knew that he was babysitting me regularly. That information was swept under the carpet and hidden away with the other family secrets, with the hopes that they would never be discovered again. However, that hiding of the family secret eventually allowed Auggy to continue his abuse of me unchecked. He just waited for things to settle down, and when the coast was clear, he came back to me and started again.

Since he was caught, he threatened me and warned me not to ever say anything about the abuse, so my fear of him was much stronger this time than it was the last time. I tried my friend's tactics and said, "No! I don't want to," but for some reason, that didn't work for me. He didn't take no for an answer and would just grab onto me tighter and become more forceful. Because of his strength, I could not fight him. Auggy told me that I better not say anything, so from that time forward, he interfered with me on and off for the next eight years. I was so mad at myself for staying silent and would say things like, *Why didn't you have the courage to tell on him? Why couldn't you have been strong like Marcy?*

I completely blamed myself for the abuse, telling myself that I was weak, which was why he was able to mess with me. *If I had just been stronger, I could have fought back.* This negative self-talk was something that we addressed in my counseling sessions, as I didn't realize how damaging those thoughts were to my mind and body. Those thoughts kept me stuck in a giant hamster wheel in my mind that I couldn't get off from. My counselor continued to work with me on the fact that I always blamed myself for the inappropriate actions of others. I completely blamed myself for my parents' divorce, and I blamed myself for Auggy's abuse. Because I was getting fat, the negative self-talk going on in my head was its own level of abuse, in and of itself, toward myself. That alone was probably more damaging than the abuse I was experiencing at the hands of Auggy.

In one of our conversations, I told the counselor, "I felt like it was my fault because if I had chosen to stay with my dad instead of going with my mom, I would not have come into contact with Auggy. So, I chose wrong, and because of that, it was my fault."

"No ma'am!" she said.

"You don't get to claim that; that is absolutely not yours to take. He was an abuser and a pedophile. His actions were his choices! You were a child, and you had no fault in that situation."

She stopped me every time I tried to take the blame for something that I had no control over, and it was during that conversation that she informed me I was showing signs of post-traumatic stress disorder (PTSD). After she said that, my brain started thinking, *Wait! How can that be? Isn't that for people who fought in a war?* I never realized PTSD can come from a myriad of things that are non-combat-related, like sexual abuse and car accidents. I had only heard of it mentioned in relation to war and soldiers, so hearing that I might be suffering from PTSD was very shocking to me, but it helped me to realize the extent of my trauma.

I was holding on to so many negative thoughts and hurt feelings, and the random bouts of crying were results of some very painful memories that were being unearthed in these sessions. They had not fully come to the surface yet; it was more like the thoughts had come up to a location inside of my mind that only my spirit could sense and feel. My brain had not grabbed hold of them yet, which is why I was so confused as to why I was having these uncontrolled bouts of crying, even during the counseling period.

When my memory started to kick in, I was completely overwhelmed by grief and guilt, as if everything started coming out at once. The flood gates were open, so I started recalling everything that happened in my life. Talking with this particular counselor was just what I needed, for she helped me process my feelings while I was reliving some of the dark memories that were being uncovered. She walked me through them, one by one, and helped me navigate them in a healthy way. I didn't have the tools to do that before, and some of the memories were just too painful, hurtful, or embarrassing for me to walk through alone. I didn't have any family members or friends that I could talk to about this when I was young, so they were hidden away until I was strong enough to deal with them, which was at age fifty-two when that finally happened.

Chapter 5

OH NO! THE STUTTER!

We lived on Cedar Street for about a year. Mom and J were still having a rough go at it, as their relationship continued to be volatile. So, Mom decided to leave him and buy a house across town on Johnson Street, and they decided to separate. It was just going to be us, Mom and her three children, but J had other plans in mind that he did not share with Mom until later. He waited until Mom purchased the house on her own, and then he decided he was going to come and live with us instead of separating from Mom as planned. I am sure she was very frustrated with that decision, but she just dealt with it because they were still married, and I guess, in her own way, she still loved him despite the beatings from him. This new house would end up becoming my second "House of Horrors" and, in many ways, was even more destructive than the first house on Cedar Street.

Tommy and I were enrolled in a new school named Marquette Elementary, but I continued to struggle emotionally as new trials were placed upon me. Sometime in the beginning of the third grade, I developed a speech impairment. I began to stutter, which wasn't there before and just spontaneously started. That was one more thing to be embarrassed about, as I was already dealing with the fact that I was gaining weight, and the kids were making fun of me. Now, my stutter just gave them another dagger to throw at me. Even at home, it was frustrating because Tommy started to make fun of me, and so did Auggy.

Auggy would molest me, and then turn right around and make fun of my weight or my stutter. He would say, "Don't cry when people make fun of you. Just laugh along with them." I thought that was the stupidest thing I had ever heard of and could never laugh while I was the butt of their jokes. It was hurtful, so life was absolutely miserable for me at that point.

My stutter was most noticeable when I was at home, and that was because I talked more freely at home. I was an introvert when I was at school because when I opened my mouth, the kids would mock my stammer, so I just chose not to talk a lot. When I was talking at home, and I would get caught up in a very repetitive stammer, my mom would say, "Slow down!" I didn't know it then, but my mom's chiding and telling me to slow down is what helped me later on. I would stop and then start over at a much slower pace.

My problem was that my brain was thinking faster than my mouth could utter the words, so I would stutter mostly when I was excited, or when I was trying to tell a story about something that happened to me. The letters that I struggled with the most were M, W, S, T, I, A, C, and K. The letter M was the worst one.

I hated reading during this period of my life because my stutter really affected my self-esteem and sense of self-worth. I didn't even like to read leisurely and only read when I had to, so my reading skills started to lag. That gave me more reason not to want to read, especially out loud during class. One day, my teacher called on me to read during the English portion of class. I declined at first, but she insisted. I knew it was going to be bad, but I slowly started to read. I tried to be ever so careful because I didn't want to stammer on anything; unfortunately, that dream was not in the cards for me that day. The repetitive stammer came out in full force. My old faithful letters, which plagued me on a regular basis, reared their ugly heads that day, and, of course, the kids started laughing. The thing that made it worse was that the teacher didn't even stop them but let them mock me.

For that very reason alone, I despised my teacher. She forced me to read, and then she didn't protect me when I did and had issues. She told my mom, in a parent/teacher conference, that my reading skills were behind. *(So, I guess her way of trying to make me get better was to humiliate me in front of my peers?)* My teacher knew I stuttered, so in my little kid's mind, there was no excuse for her throwing me to the wolves. I obviously didn't care for her too much, so I avoided participating in most activities after that conference.

Fast forward about thirteen years, and I was a music major at Ball State University. I finally decided to focus on music as my major because I had engaged in music for the majority of my life, and it was the area that I was the most proficient in. We had to take multiple music theory classes as music majors. The music analysis and composition portion of the class met three times per week on Mondays, Wednesdays, and Fridays. The ear training portion of the class met on Tuesdays and Thursdays, but it was taught by a different teacher, a doctoral student. (He was pretty cocky if I might add.)

While we were sitting in the first class of the semester, he was going over the syllabus and the requirements for the class. He began to tell us about rhythmic dictation, where we had to count out rhythms verbally at a specific speed. As he was talking about how fast we had to count these rhythms, I realized I might have trouble because of my speech impairment, which was still present. For years, I never talked about my speech problem because I learned how to control it, for the most part. Most people, outside of my immediate family and close friends, didn't even know that I was speech-impaired. My mom's counsel on slowing down was part of my strategy to avoid stuttering, so I spoke slowly and methodically, thinking about every word before I said it.

When I got ready to say "A" or "I," I snuck a little "h" sound at the beginning of the word, which smoothed out the entrance of that word. I put a little accent on my "M" words, and this helped me to control the start of the word as it came out of my mouth. I don't really remember how I figured all of that out, but I personally think my heavenly Father had something to do with it. As a kid, there was no way I could have figured out all the different techniques that I used all by myself to prevent from stuttering.

At the end of that first class, I decided to stay back after everyone else left and do something I had never done before. I chose to disclose my speech impairment to the teacher, telling him that I had a speech impairment where I stuttered. I explained to him that most of the time I had my stutter under control, but when I started to speak too fast, I sometimes lost control, and the stutter would come out.

I said, "I know that you want us to be able to count the rhythms at a specific speed, and I will do it as fast as I possibly can, but I might not be able to speak it at the speed that you would like because I stutter."

I thought this was a reasonable explanation, but boy was I wrong! The next thing that came out of his mouth shocked me to no end.

"Don't use your speech impairment as an excuse!" he said.

I looked at him in utter shock and said, "I have never used my speech impairment as an excuse. As a matter of fact, most people don't even know that I stutter. I do what I can every day to try and control it, but in the end, speed is what brings it out and makes me lose control."

He then interjected, "Well, I don't accept that, and I will not slow your tempo down. I have the same expectations for you that I have for every other student." *What a jerk!* I thought to myself.

I started to get really mad at him and finally, after standing there trying to plead my case to him, tears started to drop because I was so frustrated at his rudeness. Even seeing how frustrated I was, he still dug his heels in and refused to hear what I was saying, so I picked up my things and walked out of the classroom.

As I walked down the hallway, the tears were freely flowing down my face. My little heart was hurt, and I started having a conversation with myself. (This was a frequent event in my life.)

How could someone be so cruel and inconsiderate? He wouldn't even listen to me!

Right in the middle of that conversation, I saw a sign on the wall that was advertising free speech therapy classes. The Speech Pathology and Audiology (SPAA) department in the building offered free speech therapy to students so the SPAA students could practice their trade. Now that I look back at that time, I am amazed at the perfect timing of those signs that I saw. I had been in that building many times before, because a lot of our ear training classes were over there, and never noticed those signs before or any advertising about the SPAA department for that matter. When I saw the sign, I walked down to the basement where I found the secretary of the department. We discussed my speech impairment, and she scheduled me with a student therapist for the next day. I met the therapist and explained the incident that occurred with my teacher. I told her I was there to get help with my speech impairment.

She asked, "Have you ever worked with anyone for your speech before?"

"No. I just kind of dealt with it on my own, but now I think I am going to need help in order to pass this class," I said.

After she filled out the intake forms, we started working on my speech. She pulled out a storybook and asked me to start reading. I read through it perfectly—no stutter. I was proud of myself. She took some notes and asked me a few questions, and then the appointment was over. I came back for the next appointment, and the same thing happened. She asked me to read, to which I read the book perfectly. *Score!* The next time I met with her, she showed me a video of multiple people stuttering. They all had very severe stutters and were much worse off than I. She then asked me, "Is your stutter like any of these individuals?"

"No," I said. "It is definitely not that bad."

We talked a little more, and I left. We met again, and, as usual, she asked me to read from the same storybook. As I was reading, I had the distinct feeling that someone was watching me through the two-way window in the door of our room. (The practice rooms in the music building had the same two-way windows, so I was aware that people could see into the room.) No sooner had I thought that to myself, there was a knock at the door, and a middle-aged man entered the room. He identified himself as one of the speech professors and that he was the therapist's supervisor. He asked me to start reading in the book, so I did. Then he said, "Faster!"

I started again and read a little faster, and he stopped me and said, "Faster!" As I was reading, he kept saying,

"Faster!"

"Faster!"

"Faster!"

Finally, I got to the word "mechanic," and it happened. The loss of the control over my mouth occurred, and the word came out, "Meh, meh, meh, meh, meh, meh, mechanic!"

I put my face in my hands and started crying.

"Why are you crying?" he asked me.

"I am so embarrassed," I said.

He then said something that completely changed the way I thought about my stutter.

"You shouldn't be embarrassed at all. I needed to push you so we could figure out what your stutter pattern is. You control it so well that we could not even tell that you stutter. Everyone stutters to some degree or another. The amazing thing is that you figured out all the different tools that we use to teach our clients, but you did it on your own without anyone to guide you. That is amazing! You are doing just fine and don't need our help. Just keep doing what you have been doing."

That experience was a blessing to me, a confidence-booster that made me realize the Lord had shown me how to control my stutter. He taught me so well that even a professor, a trained practitioner, could not figure me out. This was a testimony that the Lord knew me and loved me. I received the confidence I needed to help me get through that class and nailed all the rhythmic exercises that were given to me in that class. I even got an "A" in the ear training portion of my theory class that semester. Because my attitude was indifferent toward the teacher, I only spoke to him when I was called upon, or to take my tests, and he never had a conversation with me either.

Looking back at that period in my life made me realize that I didn't give myself credit for anything, never once realizing the stutter was no longer a problem. The Lord had already helped me fix that problem, and I never gave Him thanks because, in my mind, I still saw myself as a stutterer. I was so used to looking at all my flaws and condemning myself for them that I was completely oblivious that my stutter only came out occasionally and usually when I, mainly my brain, was tired. When I was awake, I always stopped myself and slowed myself down before a repetitive stammer came out. I was fully aware of the stutter, but no one else knew unless I told them. It was only part of my identity between me, myself, and I.

* * *

Finding my identity was an area that my counselor and I talked about a lot in my counseling sessions. I didn't really know who I was at that time and only knew myself by the flaws I was still carrying around. Those flaws were the very things that were governing and guiding my life, but not anymore.

Chapter 6

THE DAY THAT CHANGED MY LIFE

My fourth-grade year turned out to be a major turning point in my life when I was placed in Mr. Rupe's classroom. Mr. Rupe had been teaching for quite some time; even my uncle Jimmy had him as a teacher when he was a boy. He was a very strict teacher, but we knew that he had high expectations of us. He was a very tall man with big feet and very large ears. Of course, some of the kids made fun of his ears, and we could always tell when he was getting upset at us because his ears would start to turn red. When they turned all the way red, we knew we were in trouble. He would start yelling at us, and then he would start shaking his head from side to side. When he started doing that, the loose skin on his cheeks would flap, and his voice would shake right along with his cheeks and head.

It was October of my fourth-grade year, and we were sitting in class when there was a knock at the door. It was a middle-aged woman with reddish hair at the door. I didn't know who she was, but she started calling out names of specific students that needed to come with her. Even though I didn't know her, or where she was taking the kids, I really wanted her to call my name. However, I never got called for anything and was just one of the rank and file. I never got in trouble at school, but I also was not one of the super smart kids either. I was just a regular girl that never stuck out for anything, except with my weight and my stutter; I was pretty much invisible.

The woman called a couple more students, and I began to accept that the usual would happen. The popular kids would get called, but not me. That didn't stop me from hoping to be called though, so I sat there wishing she would call me. Miraculously, my name escaped from her lips that day.

I was shocked, but I was also extremely happy. I got up, pushed my chair in, and lined up in the back of the classroom with the other kids that she had called. We left our room in a single-file line and started walking down the hall. All the kids were excited about being in the line. We didn't know where we were going, but we were excited, nonetheless. She went into every fourth-grade classroom and called out names. After she collected all the students that she needed, we walked to the end of the hallway and started descending the stairway. We were up on the second floor of the school building, so I thought we were going down to the first floor, but no, we continued down to the basement. This was a new adventure because I had never been down there before.

When we got to the bottom of the stairwell, we exited the door, and she led us into a classroom that was across from the stairwell. We went into the room, and I could immediately see that it was a music room. There were chairs in the middle of the room and instruments around the perimeter of the room. On the right side of the room, there were storage shelves and racks that housed a bunch of instruments of varying sizes that looked like violins. I was extremely intrigued by what I was seeing. We played pitched instruments like bells and drums in our music class, but this was the first time I had ever seen string instruments.

We all sat down, and the lady introduced herself as Mrs. Kearns, the orchestra teacher. She explained to us that in May of the previous school year, she came into our classrooms and administered a music listening test. *Oh yeah, I remember that,* I thought to myself. She said that we were all sitting there because we scored in the top 10% of all the third graders at my school, and because of our scores, we were allowed to play in the school orchestra if we chose to. I was surprised, but it made me feel good to know I scored one of the highest scores in our school.

Mrs. Kearns took out the four different instruments that we could choose from to play: they were violin, viola, cello, and bass. We learned about each of the instruments, and then we needed to choose an instrument that we were interested in playing. I really liked the violin, so I chose that one. She gave us an information sheet and a permission slip to take home to our parents to sign up for the orchestra class. I was so happy! We would get to attend orchestra class twice per week during our elective classes. After school was out, I went home quickly. Mom was still at work, but I wanted to tell someone about my good news, so I called my grandmother. I told her about what we did in the orchestra class and that I had chosen the violin. She then told me, "Your aunt Marilyn used to play the violin too. (Marilyn was my mom's sister.) She stopped playing when she graduated from high school. I still have her violin, so you can have it."

I was so excited. Not only was I going to learn the violin, but I would also have my own instrument as well.

When my mom came home, I told her my good news. She congratulated me, signed the paperwork for me, and I returned it to Mrs. Kearns at the next class meeting. Unfortunately, it ended up that Marilyn's violin had been sitting for a long time, and some damage had set in: it had some open seams and also needed a new bridge and a new set of strings. My mom didn't have the money to pay for the repairs at that time, so she signed me up to use a school violin. I used the school violin for one year, and then my mom took Marilyn's violin to a shop to be repaired.

According to the labels inside Marilyn's violin, the violin was made in Arlsbach, Germany in 1957 by Karl Heirmann. It was then shipped to the Scherl & Roth company in Cleveland, Ohio, where it was assembled in November of 1957. My grandmother bought it for Marilyn at a local music store in Indiana. It was brand new when my grandmother purchased it, so Marilyn was its only owner and played on it all the way up through high school until she graduated.

Once my mom had the violin repaired, and it was given to me, I no longer referred to it as Marilyn's violin. I named him "Meechy," and he was mine. He was like my alter-ego, but Meechy was a gift from God. The Lord brought him to me at the exact time that I needed him the most, as he became a helpful distraction from the trials I was going through at the time.

I would come home from school and do my homework. After that, I would spend the rest of the evening upstairs in my room playing on Meechy. It was a great opportunity for me to leave my dark reality and find a happy and beautiful alternate place in my own, little music world. When I was sad, I could pour all my hurt feelings into my music. I was so depressed as a child and had no one to turn to until Meechy came into my life. He was my best friend. I could tell him anything, and he would listen to me and help me express my feelings through the music I played. I don't think I would have emotionally and mentally survived my childhood without him.

My next year in orchestra brought change. Mrs. Kearns was no longer there, so we got a new teacher named Mr. Fisher. He was Marilyn's teacher when she played, up through high school. He was happy to hear that I was her niece, and from what everyone told me, Marilyn was a good violinist. She was not upset when my grandmother gave me her violin and actually encouraged me to play. Marilyn wanted me to be great, so I was determined to be as good as she was or better. I worked hard and put my heart into playing.

My grandmother was my biggest fan and loved to hear me play. She encouraged me to keep working at it, and I did exactly that. The darker my world got, the harder I practiced and the better I became. I loved practicing. I would get duet books and would record one part of the duet with my tape recorder. After it was recorded, I would press play on the cassette player, and I would play the second part of the duet along with the recording. That was so much fun, as Meechy and I were our own, little band, creating beautiful music together. Finding music literally changed my life; it protected me and gave me hope for the future.

* * *

This was another area that I discussed thoroughly with my counselor. Music had become such an important part of my life, as I literally relied on it to survive. As a kid, I did not have enough understanding of who God was and His role in my life. What I needed to understand was that He was the giver of my gift of music. He was the one that I needed to turn to for help and guidance during those dark times. I was using Meechy and my music almost like idols, and almost replaced God with Meechy because I did not truly understand who He was. Meechy was who I turned to for everything: my comfort, my peace, my joy, and my happiness.

As I got older, my understanding of God changed, but my reliance on music was still active in my life. When I had to deal with the Cassie situation, my counselor opened my eyes to the reality that music was something that I did, but it was not who I was. My identity was completely enshrined in music, so learning to separate the two things was a necessary step in my evolution of understanding my true spiritual identity.

Chapter 7

TOMMY

During my sessions, my counselor asked me many questions about the different members of my immediate family, because she needed to figure out where many of my issues stemmed from. She asked me about my siblings, so I started with my older brother Tommy, because he is the closest in age to me. He is one and a half years older than me.

Tommy and I had a decent relationship when we were younger, but we had the typical sibling issues of fighting and arguing. Most of those issues were just petty things, like who was better than the other in our sibling competitions. He was around for much of the trauma that I experienced, and he was the only one that knew what was going on with Auggy. He was my big brother, but he could do nothing to help me.

Despite our sibling rivalry, we loved each other, and seeing my pain was a huge source of pain for him too; and through our conversations, I can see that the pain torments him even today. Our story is filled with periods of love and frustration, but in the end, love conquers all. A lot of my early years were locked away with some of the dark things that I was experiencing, so many of my memories with Tommy were locked up until I started to open up and talk to my counselor.

* * *

When my mom, Claudia J. Pegues, met my dad, James T. Bryant, she already had an infant son. She had been dating a man named Archie and got pregnant, but they broke up before the child was born so she gave the baby her last name. She named him Thomas Tyler Pegues; we all knew him as Tommy. My grandmother was acquainted with my dad and thought he was a nice man, so she introduced him to my mom. After about a year of dating, Dad asked my mom to marry him. My grandmother encouraged my mom to marry him, though my mom had a lot of trepidations about marrying my dad. She really did not want to be with him, but despite her better judgment, she followed her mother's counsel and married him.

Archie's family caused a lot of problems, arguing with my dad over visitation rights concerning Tommy, and then one day, an altercation occurred. Daddy decided that he had had enough, so he went down to the courthouse and filed the paperwork to adopt Tommy. Since Archie was not on Tommy's birth certificate, and DNA testing was not a thing back then, the process was fairly simple. Tommy was then known as Thomas Tyler Bryant. This one move should have ended the fighting between the families, but there were still occasional squabbles. However, if Archie's family wanted to see Tommy, they had to try and act right.

When Tommy and I were very young, we had a great relationship, playing together all the time because it was just the two of us, and we were so close in age (a year and a half apart). As we got older, our relationship got a little bit more complicated. I think the change happened when Mom enrolled us in McKinley Elementary School. We were now in public school and needed to make new friends. Tommy was a boy, so he navigated this period in a completely different way than I did. Unfortunately, I got the short end of his transition stick because with his need to make friends, he met some not-so-nice boys that lived in our neighborhood. Those boys picked on me and made fun of me, and instead of Tommy sticking up for me, he joined in on the fun. That was very frustrating and upsetting for me. I knew he still loved me, but he was just strange at times. He was my brother, but he was also a typical boy, so his behavior was very hard for me to deal with at times.

One example of his weirdness occurred one winter day when we lived on Cedar Street. My mom asked the two of us to go out and shovel the snow off the sidewalk on a typical winter day in northern Indiana. It was cold outside, and the snow had finally stopped falling; the sidewalks were laden with fresh, fluffy snow. Mom sent us outside to shovel the snow off the sidewalks before it got packed down. The snow was fresh, so it would be easier to shovel. We put on our winter coats, hats, scarves, boots, and gloves, grabbed two shovels, and went out the front door to start shoveling.

Our house sat up on a hill and had a small cement slab for a porch. From there, you then had to take three or four steps down in order to get to the main sidewalk in the yard. At the end of the sidewalk, there was another set of four or five stairs that you had to go down in order to get to the sidewalk at street level. I was shoveling at the end of the upper sidewalk and was moving toward the house. Tommy started at the porch and was working his way down toward me. Our backs were toward each other. Suddenly, Tommy started acting silly. (This was the new boy behavior I was talking about.) He started swinging his shovel wildly and throwing snow everywhere. He was annoying me, so I said, "Stop it, Tommy!" He started laughing but kept acting crazy.

We had gotten fairly close to each other while shoveling, and he was still swinging the shovel around, so I turned around to tell him to cut it out, and wham! He hit me dead in the center of my upper lip with the pointed edge of the shovel. I dropped my shovel, grabbed my mouth, and started screaming. Blood was all over my face. He tried to apologize, but I just continued screaming. Mom heard my cries and opened the front door to see what had happened. She stepped out onto the porch, and I ran over to her. I removed my hands so she could see the damage. The wound was deep, so deep that you could see the white meat under all the blood. She freaked out!

Immediately, Mom took me into the house, and we went straight to the bathroom. She started rinsing the blood off my face, grabbing a washcloth and holding it up to my mouth for a few seconds. She gently wiped the blood off my lip so she could get a good look at how deep the cut was. The wound was deep, and the blood kept flowing. She realized that I needed stitches, so she began to get dressed and ready to take me to the hospital. J heard all the commotion and came out to see what was going on. He looked at my lip and told my mom that I didn't need to go to the hospital. Mom told him that it looked very deep, but he wouldn't listen and would not allow her to take me.

He went into the bathroom, opened the medicine cabinet, and found the bandage box. He pulled out a butterfly bandage that was designed to close wounds and put that on my mouth. He said that it would pull the two sides of the wound together, and my mouth would be fine. *Wrong!* It did pull the sides of the wound together, but the wound was too deep. It didn't heal correctly on the inside and needed some stitches (which I never got). With all the commotion going on and the debate about whether I needed stitches or not, Tommy never got in trouble. Mom forgot that he was the cause of the injury.

That wound would become another source of ridicule for me. For some reason, two to three times a year, my upper lip, at the site of the wound, would fill up with fluid and puss. It would become huge and heavy and was so embarrassing because there was no way to hide it. I could always tell when it was coming because my injured lip would start to get numb. From the first numb feeling until it was completely gone usually took about two to three weeks. Just imagine going to school with a giant, puss-filled ball on your upper lip. That big ball was saying, "Hello world. Look at me!" Without a doubt, everybody did!

Having to endure all the jokes and name-calling for two to three weeks, several times a year, was just downright brutal. I didn't figure out what was going on with my lip until I was an adult. The center of my lip would swell into a big ball after I would get sick, usually with a cold or a sinus infection. The tail end of my illness resulted in the big puss-sack on my lip. It was as if my body was pushing out the dead stuff it had killed during my illness, sending it to the weakest location of exit that it could find; and that was my lip. The big lip flare-up still happens to me even today. I was never taken to a doctor to have my lip checked out as a child. So, I just learned to deal with it, but as an adult, I found a medicinal oil to put on it that stops it from growing, if I address it right when it starts becoming numb.

Before I found the oil, I still dealt with the big lip even after I started teaching. One year, I was in my classroom, and one of my elementary students came over to me and said, "There's something on your lip." Elementary students are brutally honest about everything, as they haven't learned about tact yet. If they think it, they say it. I don't know how many times the Pre-K and kindergarten kids have walked up to me and said, "You're fat!" I'd usually just smile, say, "Yes I am," and keep walking because how do you respond to that statement when it is posed by a four- or five-year-old? They are not trying to be mean; they are just stating the obvious. These were just kids making an innocent observation to a teacher.

* * *

Living on Cedar Street, Tommy and I were pretty competitive. Tommy was older, faster, and stronger than me, but we would do things that were competitive. We would periodically have races outside in the front of the house. When I was a kid, I had a special pair of sandals that were white and had five white straps across the top of my foot, with one white strap in the back. It also had a small, silver buckle on the side. I wore these sandals all the time, as they were my special lucky sandals. When I raced Tommy, I would always use these sandals, not my sneakers, to run. I lost every race that Tommy and I did, and he would beat me by a large margin every time. He was older and he was a boy, so he had that advantage over me. He also knew he could beat me and was cocky about it until one summer day.

I guess I had a growth spurt that summer, and we went outside to do our regular "Tommy beat Kyeni at racing" date. We lined up on the lower sidewalk, and Tommy said, "Ready, set, go!" I took off running top speed down the sidewalk and, to my surprise, I was slightly ahead of him. I could hear him breathing and panting hard as he tried to pass me, but I kicked it into high gear and took off and crossed our finish line first. I was so happy and couldn't believe it! I just beat my brother, Mr. Cocky, at a foot race. He couldn't believe it either, so of course he said, "That was just winner's luck." Because he thought it was a fluke, he challenged me to another race, and I accepted. We walked back to the starting spot in front of our house. I was glad because I had used up most of my energy in the first race, so walking back gave me a minute to catch my breath and regain energy.

We got back to the starting line, and I could see the determination on his face this time. His pride was on the line, but so was mine. I couldn't let the first race be a fluke. I had to beat him again, or the first race meant nothing. He counted us down again. "Ready, set, go!" I took off just like I did the first time, but I ran with all my might. We both huffed and puffed our way down the sidewalk, and I started to lead again; and would you believe it, I crossed the finish line by a body length. I finally truly beat my brother at something. I had so much pride in that win because I was overweight, but I beat him. I will not claim that victory completely because there must have been some angels behind me pushing me down that sidewalk, because it seemed like such an impossibility.

I beat him one other time that summer, but by the end of the summer, Tommy had a major growth spurt, and I never beat him again. That was okay though, because I will always have the memory of beating my brother with my special sandals, and that can never be taken away.

* * *

Back to the incident with my lip, one would think that Tommy had learned his lesson from that horrific snow shovel incident on Cedar Street, but no, he certainly had not. Several years later, after we had moved to Johnson Street, I was in the fifth grade, and my dad was sent to Norton Air Force base in San Bernardino, California. He was in the air force reserves, but this particular assignment required him to go out to live on this base for about a month. He decided to bring his family out there for a week. So, the plan was for Lynne, Trunae, Tommy, and I to fly into Los Angeles, and Daddy would pick us up from there. It was so exciting because this trip happened in the middle of the school year, so we got to skip school for a whole week.

We flew to the Los Angeles Airport (LAX), which the size of LAX was absolutely insane. It seemed like we had to walk miles to get from our gate to baggage claim; it looked like a small city. Daddy picked us up at LAX and gave us a little tour around Los Angeles. I had been to Chicago many times and the traffic was bad there, but the traffic in Los Angeles was completely ridiculous. It was on a whole different level, as the traffic was bumper to bumper on the highway that was at least four lanes. After we toured around for a while, we drove to San Bernardino. Because of his length of duty, Dad secured housing on the base. He was staying in a small apartment at the time, but it was nice. Staying on the base was pretty cool, and it was bigger than Grissom Air Reserve base in Indiana where Dad was working. We never stayed overnight at Grissom because we only lived about one and a half hours away from the base.

Norton Air Force base was big and sat at the foothills of a beautiful mountain range. I loved sitting outside looking at those mountains while there. I was born in the Midwest where there were no mountains, so this was my first time seeing mountains. They were so peaceful and majestic and helped me to get a view of the workmanship of God's hands. I didn't know it then, but mountains would become a place of refuge, faith, and strength for me later in my life. I could have spent the entire trip just sitting and looking at those mountains, while watching the military airplanes continuously take off and land on the base. I really loved it out there.

One afternoon, we decided to stay on the base and relax at the apartment. Tommy and I went to the playground that was right by our apartment. There was a nice, big swing set there, so we ran over to it. We were racing each other to try and be the first one to arrive at the swing set so we could pick the swing we wanted. He got there before I did, of course, so he picked the swing on the right. I got on the swing on the left. Me, being the "normal" child, started swinging in the usual way: back and forth, back and forth.

However, my brother chose to be different that day. He started swinging side to side, side to side. Because the swings were designed to go back and forth, he had to put some extra effort on the swing to gain momentum. I was in the swing right next to him, so one could probably use their imagination and figure out what happened next.

"Tommy! Stop swinging like that. You are going to hit me!"

"Ha ha ha!" he laughed, and then…

Bam!

The big, metal chain that connected the seat to the top frame of the swing made contact with my mouth and fractured my big, right front tooth. I fell off the swing and started crying. I do not know what his fascination with my mouth was, but now he had broken the tooth that was in the front of my mouth, which he had already injured. My two front teeth were already proportionally huge compared to my face, so they were already an object of many cruel jokes from the kids. This just added insult to injury; it would give the kids another thing to tease me about. This was a permanent tooth, but neither my mom nor dad wanted to pay to have it fixed, so I kept my mouth closed as much as I could and avoided smiling when I was at school to help limit the mean jokes. To this very day, I still have that fractured tooth in my mouth. It is less noticeable now because it smoothed out over time, but it is a reminder of my first and only trip to California and my brother's silly antics.

* * *

That was my last, big, physical injury caused by Tommy. The other injuries were emotional, but they were just as painful, or even more so, than the physical ones. I guess between Tommy's friends and Auggy, Tommy developed a habit of picking on me and making fun of me. His friends and Auggy were the worst culprits, but he would occasionally join in; I suppose it was peer pressure. The old adage, "If you can't beat them, join them," must have become his mantra, which was especially true when he was around

Auggy. The most challenging time between Tommy and I occurred when we moved to Johnson Street in Indiana. Tommy had a friend named David, and David made it his business to come to our house after school on a regular basis. Unfortunately, he would harass me while he was there, making fun of my weight and anything else he could think of. He would start saying mean things, and then Tommy would jump in and join him in teasing me. Except for my room and my violin, I had no place of refuge: not at home, not at school, and definitely not at Auggy's house.

With all that craziness going on, Tommy and I used to fight and argue all the time. He would always win all our physical fights because he was stronger than I was, pinning me down or deflecting any hits that I tried to make; this went on for years. We would tell on each other and try to get the other one in trouble, or we would argue long enough where we both got in trouble with Mom. It was a constant back and forth between us, just typical sibling banter. When one of us got in trouble, my mom would often send the other one outside to get a switch off a tree in the backyard so she could whoop that person. The tree was right up next to the house, and it had good, flexible switches on it. When Mom would send me out to get a switch so she could whoop Tommy, I would always get the biggest switch that I could find. But then, I realized that the big, hard switches were not the best ones because they were more brittle and would break easier. The smaller, more flexible switches were best.

Mom tended to use switches or electric cords to whoop us, but Dad used belts. We didn't get whooped by him very often because he was Dad. We didn't want to make him mad because he would get loud when he got mad and was in the military, so we knew not to push his buttons too much. One week, we were across town at Dad's house on Dubail Street for a visitation. Dad had just put a fresh coat of white paint on the garage. The next day, he went to work, and we stayed home. Tommy and his friend from across the street were outside in the backyard playing until they decided to pick up the black walnuts from off the ground and play baseball with them. Black walnuts have a dark green or black flesh that covers the actual nut, which is in the middle. When it is really ripe, that flesh turns black. These two crazy boys thought it was a good idea to throw those black walnuts into my dad's freshly painted white garage. Talk about brain damage.

I told them that they had better stop because they were going to get in trouble, and they eventually did, but not until they covered that whole door of the garage, and some parts of the broad side of the garage, with round, black circles from the walnut strikes.

Daddy came home, and I guess he went straight out back to check on his freshly painted garage. The next thing I heard was him yelling at the top of his voice for Tommy and me to come downstairs. I was thinking in my mind, *Oooh … Tommy's gonna get a whooping!* We were upstairs in our bedrooms, so we jumped up and met him down at the bottom of the stairs in the entryway. I had never seen him so mad before!

"Who threw those walnuts into the garage after I just painted it?" he yelled out.

Knowing that I had nothing to do with it, I said, "Tommy did it!"

Tommy then said, "No, I didn't! Kyeni did it!"

Absolute horror flashed across my face because I could not believe that he just lied the biggest lie in the history of the world, well … my world … and included me in his foolishness.

"No, I didn't! Why are you lying?" I said.

"You know you did it, Kyeni !" he screamed back.

We yelled back and forth at each other, and in the middle of this shouting match, Dad said,

"Shut up! Since you can't decide which one of you did it, you both are going to get a whooping!"

Dad walked over to the closet in the corner of the room. He kept his military uniforms there, and he removed a belt from his military pants and walked toward me because I was the closest to him. He grabbed my arm, turned me around, and started swinging; I cried out with every blow. When he finally finished with me, he grabbed Tommy, but Tommy immediately dropped to the floor. Dad whooped him while he was on the floor anyway. When he was done, he sent us up to our rooms. Later on that evening, I snuck into Tommy's room and asked him why he lied. He told me that he would get in less trouble if both of us got in trouble. It was like he had played me in a game of chess and check-mated me in a couple of moves. He then told me that I didn't know how to take a whooping and said that I was dumb because I stood up and took my licks. By doing that, the entire momentum of Dad's swing made contact.

"Did you notice that I dropped to the ground?" he said.

"Yes, I did," I said.

"The reason I did that is because when Dad swung, the upper portion of the belt hit the ground first and slowed the momentum down before it made contact with me. Because of that, it didn't hurt that much."

I thought to myself, *How in the world did he figure all of that out?* I realized that day Tommy was much more intelligent than I gave him credit for.

* * *

I might have admired his intelligence that day, but when we were at Mom's house, we still argued a lot because he continued to pick on me. However, the day came when the tables finally turned in my favor. I had grown taller and stronger, while growing weary of Tommy's teasing. On this particular day, he made me so mad that I started crying out of complete anger and went after him. I started swinging, but this time I was making contact with him. I chased him out the back door and around to the front of the house where our fight ensued. I just about beat him that day, but he finally got the upper hand and threw a few, quick blows. I gave up, and that ended the fight. My strength shocked him, and he then knew that I was just about as strong as he was. From that day forward, we never got into another physical fight again. We still got on each other's nerves from time to time, but the physical fighting was over.

My relationship with Tommy is very different today. We are very close and talk to each other regularly on the phone, easily talking for three to four hours. The two of us have been through a lot together, so we are a support system for each other. We can talk about any and everything, and often talk about our childhood traumas because we are the only ones that truly understand what happened to both of us. I have had the opportunity to open up and work through my trauma with a counselor, but also having my brother there to talk to was very therapeutic in my healing process.

Chapter 8

ROBIN

The time that we spent on Johnson Street in Indiana proved to be the most difficult time of my youth. As I started to unpack this period of time with my counselor, I realized that I was what we now openly call depressed. I don't even remember anyone talking about depression back in the 1970s. It was not a topic of typical conversation among people, but now that I look back at what was going on, I can see that I was very depressed. I was so unhappy, but I could do nothing about it. I had no sense of self-worth, and because of the constant name-calling and hurtful jokes from others, my sense of identity was non-existent while my level of self-hatred was extremely high. Unpacking this part of my life caused me to shed many tears because of the pain I felt as a little girl. Even though I lived in a house with other people, I felt alone because of some of the trials I was going through at that time.

Marquette Elementary School was the bane of my existence. Outside of my orchestra class, I was miserable at that school. I was bigger (meaning fatter) than all the other kids, so I was the source of their daily entertainment. They constantly picked on me and bullied me with either fat jokes, jokes about my large front teeth, or jokes about my stutter. Between the kids at school, my brother and his friends, and Auggy, I had probably heard all the possible fat jokes that had ever been thought of.

My sixth-grade year at Marquette was, by far, the worst year in elementary school for me. My size had caught the eye of a bully named Robin who lived in the projects about six blocks north of the school, along with all her cronies. Her little "gang" went out of their way to make my life difficult, constantly mocking me about my size, my teeth, and my stutter. I couldn't stand her. She was a little shorter than me, but she was thick and muscular. She looked strong and was definitely a scrapper, beating up anybody, boy or girl, in the entire school. Because of that, I never defended myself when she teased, taunted, and called me mean names. I might have been a big girl, but I was soft-spoken and an introvert. I was definitely not a fighter by any stretch of the imagination.

* * *

One day, we were in gym class. The class had just finished, and the teacher sent us to the locker room to change clothes. Because of my size, my breasts had started to grow, and they were bigger than any of the other girls in the sixth grade. Robin and her girls were standing across the room from me, and I had not noticed that they were checking me out. They waited until I took off my shirt, and then they started laughing out loud at me.

Robin said, "Look at her breasts. They're not even real breasts; they're just fat!" Everyone in the locker room looked at me and started laughing. I was so embarrassed, so I quickly put my shirt on, and a moment of what might have been insanity came over me. I looked at Robin and yelled out, "Why don't you just leave me alone!?!"

After I spoke up, I thought to myself, *Oh no! What have I done?*

I had just defended myself and stood up to the biggest bully in the whole school. Before I could finish rationalizing what had just happened, she said, "Oh! You want to talk back, huh? Well, you just wait until after school!"

I was terrified and unsure what I was going to do next. I quickly finished getting dressed and got in line, and our teacher came and picked us up and took us back to class. I was so scared. I didn't know how to fight because the only person I had ever fought was Tommy. However, Tommy was my brother, so we never seriously tried to hurt each other. We would punch each other here and there, but never to the point of serious injury. A real fight was something that I had never experienced before, and she was going to try to hurt me for real. *Why did I say anything? I should have just kept my mouth shut. What am I going to do now?* I thought to myself.

All those thoughts kept running through my head. When we got back into the classroom, I watched the clock relentlessly through all my afternoon classes. I was aware of every minute as it passed by because that was one minute closer to my beating. Every time I looked at the clock, it seemed as if time was speeding up faster and faster, and then to my horror, the dismissal bell rang. I sat there frozen for a moment, and then I slowly began to pack up my things. Tommy was in middle school now, so I couldn't even go and get him to help. *What am I going to do?*

All of a sudden, a solution came to mind. *I could ask my teachers if they needed any help, and then I could stay after school a little longer.* Robin and I had physical education together, but we were in different classes. Because of that, she wouldn't be able to see what I was doing. So, I went up and asked my teacher if I could clean her blackboard, and she said, "Yes!" *Perfect! I could drag this out for at least five minutes.* So, I grabbed the eraser and slowly started cleaning the board. My next-door neighbor Stevie walked into the classroom while I was cleaning the board. We walked to school together every day, so he came in and waited for me to get done. I stalled for as long as I could, talking to my teacher about random things while I slowly cleaned her board, and then my teacher finally said, "Okay, Kyeni, finish up because I need to go." I wiped off the rest of the board, grabbed my backpack, and left the room with Stevie, killing about fifteen minutes. I walked down the hall and asked a couple of the other teachers if they needed help with anything, but they were all preparing to go home. After my help had been rejected by the last teacher, I discovered I had killed about ten more minutes.

I had done a good job stalling because all the kids were gone, and the hallways were completely empty, so I started to feel a little more optimistic about my situation. Stevie and I walked out the side door that led onto the playground. It was completely empty, and all the bikes were gone. I released a sigh of relief because I felt like I had dodged a bullet. We walked through the playground and turned to the left onto the sidewalk that ran along the side of the school. We came to the street in front of the school and looked both ways before crossing the street. All the kids and crossing guards were gone. *My plan must have worked*, I thought to myself. When we got across the street, we turned to the right. At that point, I told myself, *Robin must have forgotten about me.* So, I was able to relax and started telling Stevie about Robin and why I stayed so late after school, which we talked about as we walked home.

We walked up one block, and then we turned left onto Johnson Street. We then needed to walk about three blocks down to get to our houses. We got about a quarter of the way down the first block when we started hearing sounds of a bunch of people talking. I turned my head and looked over my shoulder to see where the noise was coming from, and shockingly, Robin was walking quickly toward me with a large group of kids behind her. I thought, *Where did they come from?* The streets were completely empty, so I didn't know where that many kids were hiding out, but when I saw them, my heart sunk! Before I could get too caught up in my situation, I remembered that Stevie was walking with me. Robin and her cronies were all African American kids from the projects. Stevie was white, and he was on the larger side like I was. My biggest concern at that very moment was for his safety, not my own. I knew that I was going to get beat up; that was now my reality, but he didn't have to get hurt. Because he was white and an introvert like me, he was in danger, so I turned to him quickly and said, "Run home, Stevie! Don't stay here!"

"No! I am not leaving you!" he said.

I pleaded with him to leave, but my faithful friend stood firm and would not leave my side. In my heart, I was grateful, but in my mind, I knew he was in trouble.

The mob of boys and girls caught up to us and encircled us. Stevie told them to just leave us alone, to which Robin walked up to him and punched him in the mouth. His mouth started bleeding, and he started crying. He stepped back out of the circle and held his mouth to cover the blood, but he still did not leave. There was absolutely nothing that he could do to help me, and if he had said anything else, they would have beaten him up. So, he stepped back and watched the carnage unfold. Robin moved closer to me and said, "So, you want to talk smart?"

The next thing I saw was her fist coming at me. Her fist missed my face because I dodged her swing, but everything else she did after that was cold and calculated, hitting its mark. She threw blow after blow, and then she grabbed my hair. I had about shoulder length hair, and she went right for it. Robin yanked my head down by my hair and started hitting my head with her knee. All the kids around were yelling, screaming, and laughing, egging her on. "Ooooh, OOOH" they yelled after every hit. Hit after hit, her knee slammed into my head and my face, and on the last hit, she pulled out a plug of my hair from the left, front side of my head. I could feel the individual hairs ripping out of my scalp, and I screamed out with pain. I could hear Stevie yelling from the side, "Stop! Please stop! Please!"

I was completely helpless at that point. The louder the kids yelled, the harder Robin fought, and I could do nothing about it. Because of the barrage of hits that she landed, I was caught off guard and distracted. I never imagined that she would grab my hair like that, and she positioned herself in such a way that when she yanked my head forward and downward, I couldn't reach her. All I could do was try to protect my face from her knee, but not even that could stop her knee from making contact with my nose. When one blow met its mark, my nose started bleeding.

The next thing I heard was a man's voice. All the kids stopped yelling, and Robin released my hair. It was a teacher from my school. He saw the gang of kids and drove down our street to see what was going on. I had seen the teacher at school before, but I didn't know him. Nonetheless, I was so happy that he showed up when he did. I don't know what would have happened to me had he not come. He broke up the group and sent all the kids home, except for Robin and me. Even Stevie started walking very slowly up the street. The teacher wrote down our names and sent us on our way. I caught up to Stevie, and both of us cried as we started to head home. I was crying because I was hurting, but I also felt extremely bad that she punched Stevie in the mouth when he stood up for me. His mouth was still bleeding a little bit because the punch caused his lower teeth to puncture the inside of his bottom lip. The one thing I did know was that Stevie cared about me so much that he was willing to put himself in harm's way to protect me; that is true friendship.

When I got home, I went into the bathroom to take care of my bloody nose and to look at my head. My nose was sore, but it had just about stopped bleeding. I put a cotton ball in it, just like we used to do when I was younger, and waited for a clot to form. The most shocking sight was my hair. The bald spot in my hairline was right up in the front. The hole was about the diameter of a fifty-cent piece. I cried so hard when I saw that, realizing the kids would now have something new to bully me about.

When my mom arrived home, my nose had stopped bleeding, but there was swelling on my face, and a huge, circular spot in the front of my head that was missing hair. I told my mom the whole story of what happened and told her that I was not fighting Robin; she was fighting me. I didn't get one hit on her at all. So, Mom said that she would contact the school the next day. I pleaded with her to let me stay home, but she would not let me and said I had to go.

* * *

I woke up the next morning, and my face was still a little puffy. I started begging my mom again to let me stay home, but she refused each request. She grabbed a comb and brush and started brushing my hair over to the right side of my head. She was trying to cover the bald spot with my other hair, but it didn't really work. You could still see my white scalp poking through the strands of hair. I was so embarrassed, but there was nothing I could do about it because I was being forced to go to school. I finished getting dressed and reluctantly left. I met up with Stevie, and we walked to school. He had recovered from the punch with no visible marks, and we talked about the fight from the previous day as we walked. When we arrived at school, all the kids were talking about the fight, and Robin was gloating over her achievement. I just tried to ignore her as much as I could.

My class and Robin's class had a combined art class that day, and while we were in class, the principal called and sent for Robin. A little while later, he called for me. When I arrived at his office, the secretary told me to have a seat, so I sat in a wooden chair right outside of his office. I could hear the muffled sounds of the principal talking to Robin. It got quiet for a minute, and the next thing I could hear was three swats. Hearing those swats brought back memories of a conversation that the kids were discussing in our art class a few weeks earlier, talking about the principal's paddles. The kids that were discussing this were some of Robin's buddies, who were well acquainted with his paddles. They said that the principal had three different paddles. One was solid wood, which they said was the one that hurt the least. They said that he also had a fiberglass paddle, which hurt more than the wooden one. It was thinner, so it stung more.

The worse one was the wooden one that had three holes down the center of the paddle. They called this one the "meat sucker" because when he hits you, the meat from your butt cheeks would suck up inside of the holes and would leave round circles on your butt cheeks. I was never worried about the paddles before because I never did anything to get in trouble. Now, there was a good chance that I would soon be getting acquainted with one of those paddles. After the third swat, Robin came out of his office. She saw me sitting there, and she smiled and snickered at me. There were no tears or anything; she took those swats like a champ!

As Robin left the office, the principal called me in. I got up and slowly walked into his office. "Take a seat, please," he said, as he pointed to the wooden chair directly in front of his desk. He started talking to me and told me that the teacher had reported that he broke up a fight that Robin and I were in the previous day. I told him my side of the story, but he told me the teacher said that we both were fighting. I told him that it wasn't true and that I didn't hit her at all, but he wouldn't listen to me. Even though I pleaded my case and told him that they were picking on me, he was determined to log a few more miles on his paddle that day. He had "Adult Syndrome" and didn't care about my situation. He told me that he called my mother at work and talked to her, saying that my mom gave him permission to paddle me.

I was absolutely dumbfounded. In my mind, I thought, *How could she let him paddle me? She knew that Robin had beat me up badly and pulled my hair out, and she still gave this man permission to hurt me some more? How could she do that to me?* That was the first moment in my life I could actually say I hated my mother. I already had frustrations with her because of some choices she made pertaining to Tommy and me, but I just dealt with those. This was her opportunity to protect me, and I felt like she completely abandoned me in this situation. This incident turned those previous frustrations with her into pure hatred for a while.

The principal stood up and walked around the desk toward me. He told me to stand up, and he pulled my chair backward away from his desk. He turned the chair parallel to his desk and told me to lean over and put my hands on the seat of the chair. As I leaned over, I watched him walk over to a table on the other side of the room, which had three paddles on it. I thought to myself, *Hmm … the kids were right. He did have three paddles, and they looked exactly like they described them.* He leaned over the table and grabbed the solid wood paddle. When he grabbed that paddle, I was relieved, and I thought to myself, *Well, at least he didn't pick the "meat sucker."* He walked over and stood behind me. He positioned himself, raised the paddle high in the air, and swung. The paddle landed with extreme accuracy, as he hit me right in the middle of my butt. The sting of that impact made me clench my butt cheeks together, and the pain was instantaneous. Unlike Robin, I started crying immediately. One reason for crying was because of the pain, but the other reason was because of pure anger. I felt like my mom, the teacher, and the principal had all betrayed me that day.

Before the tears could leave my tear ducts, swing number two made contact. The second swing hurt more than the first, and I think that is because I squeezed my butt cheeks together after the first swat. The muscles were engaged when the second hit arrived, so he made contact with my tight muscles. As soon as I started feeling my cheeks throbbing from the second hit, bam, the third strike hit its mark. He walked over to the table and put the paddle down. He came back over to me and told me not to fight anymore. He opened the door and sent me back to class.

When I exited the office and stepped into the hallway, Robin was standing outside the door waiting for me, and she started laughing because I was crying and then walked away. She made a point to put more salt in the wound. Of course, when we got back to class, she told everyone that I was crying, so the kids were laughing at me. I looked at her, and in my mind, and with clenched teeth, I said to myself, *I CAN'T STAND THAT GIRL!* I had to endure her taunting for the rest of the school year, but change was coming.

Chapter 9

BROWN MIDDLE SCHOOL

Moving from elementary school to middle school was a breath of fresh air for me. The kids were older, so they were more mature and a lot nicer. Having multiple teachers every day and moving around to different classrooms was a huge blessing for me as well. I was no longer sitting in one teacher's room and dealing with the same, mean kids all day. The incoming seventh graders came from multiple elementary schools in the area. I fortunately did not have Robin or her crew in any of my classes, so the bullying almost completely stopped ... almost.

The move to middle school did wonders for my sense of self-esteem. In elementary school, I felt like I was a piece of dirt in the corner of the room. However, in middle school, most of the students in my classes came from other schools. They didn't know me when I was in elementary school, so they had no prior knowledge of the drama that went on there. I was much more at peace, and I no longer felt like I was walking on eggshells but was starting with a clean slate.

Now that I was in the seventh grade, I had elective classes, which met every day instead of once or twice a week. My mom signed me up for home economics, which I really liked. The teacher was amazing and taught us how to cook and how to sew. We all had to make a jar of grape jelly and sew a pair of pants, or a skirt, in that class. I did well on both projects and was so proud of myself. I received a B+ on my jelly. I had a few issues with the cleanness of the paraffin that we had to put at the top of the jar, so I lost a few points.

When the teacher finally returned our jelly so we could take it home and eat it, I put my jar in the pocket of my jacket and proudly carried it home.

I was so excited for my mom to see and taste my creation. When I got close to home, I decided to cut through the alley and go up the back walkway of the house. There were about four steps that I had to go up to get into our backyard. I started jogging up the steps just like I had done many times before. However, this time, I had forgotten that I was carrying precious cargo in my pocket. Right when I jogged up and landed on the fourth step, I heard a big crash on the ground. Without looking down, I knew the travesty of what had just happened, and my heart sank. I slowly looked down, and my beautiful jar of jelly had bounced out of my pocket and hit the ground. The impact shattered the top of the protective glass jar and rendered the delicious spread inside of the jar inedible. My little heart was broken.

My mom looked at the jar when she arrived home, and even though I pleaded with her to just eat the bottom part of the jelly where the glass didn't break, she told me that it was in glass, and it could have shards of glass in the jelly that could hurt us if we ate it. She told me how beautiful it looked and congratulated me on my hard work, but she lovingly let me know that we had to throw it away. Watching that jar fall into the garbage can was gut-wrenching, but I was still proud of my effort.

My other elective was orchestra, my favorite class of the day. The kids were awesome, and there was no contention. Everyone loved music, and we all got along. It was my little piece of paradise away from home. Mr. Fisher from Marquette Elementary School was also the orchestra director at Brown, and he instilled in us a love of music. He was always kind and attentive, offering suggestions to help us get better. He made us feel like he cared about us, and his class made me want to be a better person and the best violinist that I could be. Playing gave me such peace of mind and confidence in music. It brought me joy in something that was bigger than myself.

In orchestra, all the instruments were divided into different sections: violin, viola, cello, and bass. In a typical orchestra, the violins are divided into two sections: first violin and second violin. The first violin section usually plays the higher notes. Mr. Fisher put all the eighth graders in the first violin section and all the incoming seventh graders into the second violin section. I was sitting in the last stand of the second violin section with my new friend, Debra. We became friends right away, as she understood me, and we could talk about anything. She was not offended by my size or my stutter because Debra cared about me, and I was grateful to have her as a friend.

Every so often, we would have seating challenges. A challenge was a type of playing test, but the difference was that you could challenge someone in front of you and take their seat. Mr. Fisher would pick a short excerpt from our music. Each person would play the excerpt, and the person that made the least number of mistakes would win the chair. So, if I beat someone in front of me, I would move into the new chair that I won, and everyone else, starting with the person that I beat, would move down one chair until my vacant chair was filled. It was just a little, friendly competition that kept everyone on their toes. The top goal was to get into the first chair because you would become the section leader. I never challenged anyone because I chose to sit in the back with Debra. Debra's technique was not as developed as some of the other students. It wasn't for lack of trying. She just had to work harder in order to accomplish the same things. I figured she was in the last chair, so I was okay with sitting back there next to her, as long as I wasn't in the last chair.

One day we had challenges, which always started with the last chair player and then moved forward. So, Mr. Fisher started with me.

"Kyeni, do you want to challenge?" I replied, "No challenge."

That was my usual reply. He then went to Debra.

"Debra, do you want to challenge?" She replied, "No challenge."

That was her usual reply. I hadn't noticed that he called my name first. I just knew that I was not going to challenge because I was going to stay in the back with Debra. He went through all the challenges, and then he came back to me so I could play my excerpt for a grade. I played very well and would have beaten several people in front of me, but I was okay with where I was.

When the dismissal bell rang at the end of class that day, I was packing up to leave, and Mr. Fisher walked back to me and said, "Why are you not challenging? You are sitting back here in the last chair when you could be sitting way up there in the front."

I was completely shocked by what he had just said, so I asked for clarification.

"Wait! I thought Debra was sitting in the last chair!"

"No! You are sitting in the last chair," he replied.

Wow! I was shocked. I was fine sitting back there as long as I was not sitting in the last chair. I guess the idea of me sitting in the last chair was a sign of weakness, and since I was always treated in a way that made me feel weak, I didn't want to feel weak in orchestra. So, I started practicing really hard and prepared for the next challenge.

The day before the next challenge, we had sectionals. Each section of the orchestra divided up and went into different practice rooms to work on their music together as a group and correct any problems. While we were together, we were working on a particular spot in the music. I noticed that Stephanie, the girl who sat in the second chair, was playing that particular spot incorrectly and wasn't counting it correctly at all. We worked on it for a while, but she was still playing it wrong. This was my chance to get her chair.

A big part of a challenge was strategy. You had to analyze each other's strengths and weaknesses, then choose your challenge wisely because you can only challenge one person. Maybe the others didn't take it as seriously as I did, but my pride was bruised from the moment I learned I was sitting in the last chair. I had to get out of there, but I didn't want to challenge the five people that were directly in front of me, even though I knew I could beat them. They would be the obvious choices, but I didn't think Stephanie would ever expect me to challenge her. She would probably expect the third chair player, but not me because I had never challenged her in the past. Actually, I never challenged anyone. Anna was in the first chair, and she and Stephanie were both very good. They played at about the same level, but Anna had a slight edge over Stephanie. I didn't think I was ready to beat

Anna yet, so I kept my eyes focused on Stephanie. I just hoped that luck would be on my side, and Mr. Fisher would pick that specific piece for my challenge. If she didn't practice that piece, and I played it correctly, I could beat her and take her chair.

The next day came, and challenges were upon us. Because I was sitting in the last chair of the section, I was the first person asked to challenge.

Mr. Fisher said, "Kyeni. Do you want to challenge?"

"Yes! I'd like to challenge Stephanie," I confidently said.

Because I always said no, several people in the orchestra made a quiet gasp. I waited for him to tell us which song we needed to play, and to my utter joy and delight, he picked the song I wanted and the exact section that she was messing up on. Now the question was, did she practice that section last night? Because I was challenging her, she had to play first. Off she went, and *yes!* She made the same mistakes that she made the day before. I couldn't believe it; here was my shot. I started playing, and I played without error. I won the chair, and everyone was shocked. I did a silent assassin move on her, and it worked out perfectly. I gathered my things and moved up to second chair while she moved down to the third chair. Everyone else in the section behind her moved down a chair, and Debra was now sitting in the last chair by choice and stayed there for the rest of the year.

My time in the second chair was short-lived because when it was time for Stephanie to challenge someone, I just knew she was going to challenge me back, but she didn't. To my surprise, she challenged Anna and beat her: this moved me down to the third chair, Anna to the second chair, and Stephanie to the first chair. When it was Anna's turn, she challenged Stephanie back, but she lost the challenge. I remained in third chair for the rest of the school year, but I was okay with that. I had learned a valuable lesson that I should not accept mediocrity. I sat back there with Debra because we were friends, and I could just coast my way through. However, I needed to do better because I was capable.

Before this challenge, music came very easy to me, and I was getting by on sheer talent. This challenge forced me to start having more deliberate practice sessions and was the period of time that my skills as a violinist started to really develop.

* * *

During this time, my mom worked hard to support her family. She didn't have a lot of help from J, so the finances were very tight. When I started attending middle school, I was able to secure a job as a volunteer in the cafeteria. When we were scheduled to work, we got a free lunch. I worked almost every day, so Mom generally only had to pay for Tommy's lunch because mine was free. Our main jobs were serving food on the line and working in the dish room. Food was placed on real plates back then; we also drank out of real cups and ate with silverware. We did not have disposable containers then.

There were usually two of us in the dish room. One of us loaded the dirty dishes into square racks, which were then fed into an electronic dishwashing machine that cleaned and sanitized the dishes. The other person unloaded the dishes when they came out of the other end of the machine. Most of the kids liked working on the front line, dishing out food because they could see their friends and serve them as they passed by. But I didn't have very many friends, so I was perfectly fine working in the dish room.

One day, after all the workers were finished serving, and the dishes were done, we went up and got our lunches, then we went and sat in our private dining area in the back of the kitchen. They served my favorite lunch that day: pig in the blankets. They were hotdogs cooked inside of a crescent roll and so yummy. As the students were talking and eating their lunches, I unrolled the top part of my crescent roll, broke off a piece of bread, and ate it. Next, I bit the exposed hotdog, and, somehow, the chunk I bit slid right down my throat and got stuck. The speed at which it moved into my throat caught me off guard. I tried to cough it back up, but it wouldn't move up or down. It was a pretty, big chunk, so it was really stuck and extremely painful. The position in which it was sitting completely blocked my airway, so I couldn't get any air in.

My eyes started watering uncontrollably, and I started to panic. None of the kids noticed what was going on, but just kept right on talking and laughing. So, I stood up and started banging on the table to get their attention. They finally looked at me, and I pointed to my throat. They then realized that I was choking.

One of the kids ran to the front to grab one of the cafeteria ladies, and all the other kids got silent and started staring at me. At that very moment, I immediately became aware of my mortality. I couldn't breathe, and I realized that my life was hanging in the balance, that I was close to death. So, I closed my eyes and said in my mind, *Please help me.* I didn't really have a relationship with God at that point in my life, and I didn't really know how to pray, so I did the best thing that I could; and the Lord was listening. Within seconds, the hotdog slid up and out of my throat all by itself. It was as if someone reached into my throat and pulled the hotdog up. When it got up to the back of my throat, I reached in, grabbed it, and pulled it out of my mouth.

Moments later, the cafeteria lady showed up. Everyone relaxed, and I sat down and took a few big, deep breaths. I sat there and pondered about the fact that I almost died of hotdog asphyxiation; that would have been an interesting obituary. Needless to say, I didn't eat hotdogs again for quite some time after that.

* * *

Everything seemed to be going well for me at Brown. I loved orchestra, I was working in the cafeteria to help my family, and I was doing some cool stuff in my home economics class. I was happy and enjoying life until an unfortunate incident in my math class temporarily changed that. I had a good friend named Patty, and we were in a couple of classes together. One day, we were sitting in our math class, and the teacher wanted us to grade each other's papers. She told us to exchange papers with another student, so Patty and I chose to exchange our papers like we had done many times before. This particular teacher made us draw a line down the right side of the paper, with the area to the right of the line being our answer column. We would work out the problems in the center area of the paper and when we arrived at our answers, we needed to write the answers in the column that we drew to the right. This way, all we had to do was grade straight down the column; this made grading much easier because we didn't have to look through all their work to find the answers.

The teacher gave us instructions on how she wanted us to mark the papers, saying, "All answers must be in the column. If the answer is not in the column, mark it wrong." She was very strict about how we did our work in her class. If we did not follow her instructions perfectly, she would take points off our grade; we all knew this. So, she started calling out the answers, and we started grading down the column. When we were done, we handed the papers back to each other so we could see our scores before the teacher collected them. One of Patty's answers was not in the column, so I marked it wrong. She looked in the center of her paper to see if the answer was correct, and it was, but I followed the teacher's instructions and marked it wrong. That one, little act was some sort of betrayal to Patty, and it, unfortunately, ended our friendship from that moment forward.

I tried to explain to her that I was just following instructions, but she was not hearing that at all. Over the next few days, she started hanging out with some other girls and told them that I was a traitor. They all started saying mean things about me, and the girls were instigating and escalating the situation between Patty and me. One morning during homeroom, they were being mean to me, but I just tried to ignore them. The bell finally rang, and I started walking toward my first period class, which was up on the second floor. They started following me and egging Patty on to fight me. I tried my best to keep going and ignore them, but I started to get nervous because it brought back memories of the Robin incident the previous year.

I needed to go into the stairwell so I could walk up to the second floor, but when I went through the door, a big group of kids had overheard the instigation and had gathered behind Patty and her group of friends. As I started to walk up the stairs, I noticed that there were no teachers monitoring the stairwell, and I was all alone with a big mob of kids behind me. I was in big trouble. Because I was overweight, it generally took me a little longer to walk up the stairs than the other kids, so that extra time was plenty of time for a lot of things to go very wrong for me.

The stairs were in three sections. The first section was just a few stairs, and then there was a landing. Then, you needed to make a quarter turn to the left, go up about ten steps, and then there was a larger landing. You then needed to make another quarter turn to the left and go up that last section of stairs, which put you onto the second floor.

As I walked up the stairs and got to the larger second landing, I was pushed from behind and slammed into the wall. I don't know what came over me, but I lost it. Maybe it was because of all the bullying that I experienced in elementary school. Maybe it was the memory of being beat down by Robin, but something snapped in me, and for the first time in my life, I decided to physically defend myself. I threw my backpack to the ground, turned around, and came out swinging. I didn't really know how to fight, but I just tried to make physical contact in any way I could. I grabbed Patty's hair at one point and landed a punch to her face. She got a few hits on me as well, but her hits were not damaging at all. My punch bloodied her nose, and that made her really upset. She said, "Look at my face!"

Right after that, I heard the voice of a teacher. She must have heard all the commotion and came into the stairwell to investigate the situation. This was happening during our passing period between classes, so the stairwell was completely full of kids yelling, screaming, and instigating the fight. The teacher finally got to us and separated the two of us. She led us back downstairs and into the principal's office, sitting us down across the room from each other as we waited for the principal.

The principal brought both of us into his office and closed the door. He asked us what happened, and we both gave our sides of the story. I spoke first.

"Patty got mad at me in our math class because I marked her answer wrong because she didn't follow instructions. After that, she and her friends started picking on me and calling me names. I tried to avoid them today, but they followed me into the stairwell, and when we got halfway up the stairs, she pushed me into the wall."

Patty then interjected, saying, "I didn't push her. One of the kids in the crowd did it to try and make us fight. That is how the fight got started. After she was pushed, she turned around and started hitting me."

The principal lectured us about respect, treating each other kindly, and all the typical principal mambo jambo. He then said, "You have two options for your punishment: you can choose to be paddled, or you can choose suspension for three days."

Considering what happened with the whole Robin incident, one would think that I would never choose to be paddled again, but I didn't want to miss orchestra for three days. That was the most important class for me at school, and I couldn't imagine missing it for that length of time. So, I said, "I'd rather be paddled."

That fight must have done something weird to my brain because I was shocked that the request came out of my mouth. He looked over at Patty and she said, "I would rather be suspended."

The principal sat and thought about it for a moment, and he finally said, "You both have to have the same punishment, so I am going to suspend both of you for three days."

We were not allowed to go back to class and had to sit in the office until they contacted our parents. Because this fight happened at the very beginning of the school day, I missed orchestra that day and the next three days. That was brutal for me, but I was allowed to go and pick up my violin from the orchestra room before I left school. I thought my mom was going to be mad at me, but she wasn't. She didn't yell at me or anything like that. She did make me call my dad and tell him what happened, but he wasn't mad either. Of course, they both lectured me, but they knew I was not the kind of kid to instigate a fight. I stayed home for those three days, watching TV and chilling out. I enjoyed my time at home and was glad that I didn't needlessly take those swats from the paddle.

When Patty and I returned to school after the suspension, we eventually apologized to each other and were cordial to each other, but our friendship was never the same again. Her mother requested that we not sit by each other in our classes, so she was moved away from me, and when we exchanged papers for grading, I never graded her paper again.

Besides that incident, I loved Brown Middle School. I learned so many amazing things there. The real work toward my musical development began there, where I was really locked into music at that point. Music was my security blanket and is what kept me grounded. It is what kept my mind turned away from the dysfunctional things going on in my household. Mom and J were still fighting. J was still not nice to Tommy and I, and Tommy and his friends were still picking on me. The more emotionally destructive the household became, the more dependent I became on my violin, Meechy. He kept me distracted.

Chapter 10

MARC

My eighth-grade year brought change, as the school district decided to shut down a couple of schools in our county, and Brown was one of them. All the Brown students that lived on my side of town were bussed to Dickinson Middle School, which was the sister school to Brown. The schools looked alike, but they were architecturally built in reverse, and the color of the masonry was different too. Just like Brown, Dickinson was also a good school for me, and I thrived there because I didn't have to deal with bullying at all.

Mr. Fisher was the orchestra director at Dickinson too, so I was able to stay with him and his teaching. He became a very important figure in my life, so it was great to know that I would still have that support system. I was an eighth grader by then, so I was placed in the first violin section. However, all the Brown students were placed in the back of all the sections because we were new to the school, and all the returning Dickinson musicians were placed in the front. As I made my way over to the first violin section, I saw the most gorgeous boy that my eyes had ever beheld. He was tall, thin, bow-legged, and light-skinned. He had beautiful, thick, black, wavy hair, and thick, black eyebrows that were almost a unibrow, but they were cute. I had a crush on him immediately. His name was Marc, and he was the first violin section leader. I was in the fifth chair and was the highest-seated first violinist from Brown, because Stephanie and Anna were bussed to Clay Middle School on the other side of town.

Marc sat next to a girl named Debbie. She was nice, but I knew that I would have to beat her in a challenge if I wanted to sit next to Marc, and I definitely wanted to. I would need to use strategy and learn the strengths and weaknesses of the Dickinson kids so I could devise my plan of attack. I had several weeks to observe the violins in front of me. The two girls directly in front of me in the second stand were not an issue. I knew I could play better than them, so my focus was on Debbie, who actually played well, but I felt like I had an edge over her. Marc played better than she did, so he would be much more difficult to beat. I would have to work hard if I planned to beat either one of them. In the meantime, I tried to develop a friendship with Marc, which was very easy because he was a great guy. He talked to me all the time but also talked to Debbie … a lot! I eventually found out that they were dating. That was such a sad day, but it wasn't the end. I could still be good friends with him.

The day of challenges came, and I used a little strategy and chose to challenge in stages. So, I challenged the girl in the third chair and beat her with no problem. This moved me to the chair directly behind Marc. I was now in striking range and could better observe Debbie, who challenged Marc but lost. When the next challenge came along, I beat Debbie with no problem at all. She challenged me back, and I beat her again, so I maintained my chair and was now sitting next to Marc. That was probably one of the best things that had ever happened to me at that point in my life. We became great friends, laughing and joking around all the time. He was so nice to me and treated me like I was a human being and was special; that did wonders for my self-esteem. I was so used to being talked down to that I didn't really know how to respond to his acceptance of me. So, I just tried to be the person that I wanted to be.

Challenges were coming up again, so I had to decide if I was going to challenge Marc or not. Not challenging went against my newfound competitive nature, so I decided to practice really hard and challenge him. If I lost, I would still be sitting next to him. Then I realized that Debbie was breathing down my neck in the third chair, so if I wanted to keep sitting next to Marc, I had to be prepared to defend my seat. On the day of the next challenge, no one challenged me. That was a relief, so now I knew that no matter what, I would be sitting next to Marc. When it was my turn to challenge, I challenged him. It was competitive, but I came out on top. I beat him! He challenged me back, and I beat him again, so I was now the section leader. I couldn't believe it, realizing all my hard work was finally paying off. I sat in that chair the whole first semester, but he eventually beat me in the second semester. He regained his chair and stayed there for the rest of the year, while I maintained my second chair for the rest of the year.

However, I really didn't mind because I was sitting next to the most gorgeous guy in the world, well, in my eyes, and that was my ultimate goal anyway.

* * *

The next school year, we went to La Salle High School. Mr. Fisher was also the orchestra director at La Salle. He was an itinerant teacher, so he taught at all the schools that fed into La Salle High School: that was three elementary schools, one middle school, and one high school. (Ironically, I currently have the same type of orchestra job that Mr. Fisher had, where I am an itinerant string teacher.)

The orchestra was amazing, and the proficiency level was much higher than middle school. The first violins were incredible and could play anything. They were juniors and seniors, so that showed me where I could potentially be in a couple of years.

Marc was also a basketball player, so he was even more sought-after by many girls at school. I wasn't surprised by that because he was gorgeous. Meanwhile, I started going to basketball games so I could watch him play. I had never gone to any basketball games before, but Marc gave me a reason to go. I also went to the games to hear the pep band play and watch the cheerleaders dance to the music. La Salle had the best pep band in the city. Mr. Willie Keys was the band director, and he was amazing. He taught the pep band all the popular music that was on the radio at the time, so when they played the songs at the games, everyone in the stands got up and danced to the music; it was so fun.

Attending high school helped me to come out of my shell a little bit. I was still an introvert, but I started to take a few risks that I wasn't accustomed to doing before.

Marc still dated Debbie for the first part of the school year, but they eventually broke up, and she stopped playing in orchestra class after middle school because she was also in band. She chose to do band full time in high school and play the bass clarinet. I had to admit I was kind of happy to find out that they were no longer together. Marc and I were great friends, but that was about it. He wasn't really interested in me romantically, and because he had all these girls after him, I knew I didn't have a chance with him, so I just focused on school.

* * *

The time of the year came when we needed to start preparing for the district solo and ensemble assessment. We would prepare solos, or we could do duets or larger ensembles, performing our pieces on a Saturday before a judge to get a rating. If we scored a Superior and/or Excellent, we would earn a medal. I was definitely going to do a solo, but I also wanted to play a duet with Marc. I wasn't sure if he was interested, but I figured that it wouldn't hurt to ask him.

Marc and I had the same language arts class, and I sat in the next aisle over from him, one seat back. I passed him a note and asked him if he wanted to do a duet with me at Solo/Ensemble. I saw him writing his response, but he didn't give the letter back to me until class was over. As we started to walk out of the classroom, he handed me the letter. I noticed that he looked a little nervous, but I shrugged it off, and we left and headed to our next class. I didn't read the note until I sat down in my class. When I read the note, he wrote me that he would love to do a duet with me. As I continued reading the letter, my jaw hit the floor. I could not believe what I saw. He wrote, *I better just tell you now. I am falling in love with you, and I have been for quite a while. If you are dating someone, let me know and I will not bring this up again.* My heart started beating fast because my one true wish had just been granted. The sad thing is that after I read his words, my lack of self-worth immediately crept into my thoughts. *I can't believe he has the same feelings as me. Why would he want to be with me when he could have picked any of the girls at school that he wanted?* I knew this to be true because when I walked down the hallways, I could see the cheerleaders checking him out and drooling over him.

However, I replied to his letter the next day, and I told him that I was not dating anyone and that I had feelings for him too. After that, we officially became boyfriend and girlfriend. Love was in the air. The day after we became a couple, Marc motioned for me to come and sit in the empty chair that was behind him in our language arts class, so I moved. I always put my feet up on the back legs of the chair in front of me when I was sitting in my classes. When I moved behind him, I carried on with that tradition. One day while we were in class, we were working on a writing assignment, and I put my feet on the legs of his chair. He reached down and rubbed my left ankle and held onto it while he was writing. It sent shivers straight up my leg and right to my heart. He was very romantic and affectionate, and he wrote me love letters all the time.

One day, Marc wrote me a letter and asked me to meet him at the orchestra lockers at lunchtime. We met up and talked for a little bit. As we were standing there, I had the strongest feeling that I was going to receive my first, real kiss. I was super nervous because I had never been kissed by anyone before, so I wasn't really sure what to do. However, I had nothing to worry about because he knew exactly what to do, and he went right in for it. In my mind, I thought my leg was going to pop up like it did in the movies when the men kissed the women, but it didn't work out like that. Marc was a lot taller than me, so when he was leaning over me, my back leaned backward really far. Because of the awkward position that my back was in, my leg never would have come up anyway. It wasn't until later that I realized the leg pop was just movie magic.

My understandings of relationships, love, and intimacy were completely warped because of the emotional and physical trauma I had experienced earlier in my childhood. So, this relationship was something very new to me, but the problem I was struggling with was the question in my mind of, *Why would Marc want to be with me?* In my mind, that question was validated one day when Marc and I were walking to class. We were holding hands, and I walked him to his classroom first and said goodbye there. I then left to go to my class. As I turned away and was walking toward my class, one of the cheerleaders walked up to me and asked, "Is he your boyfriend?"

She had this perplexed look on her face, but I responded, "Yes, he is."

I looked at her and walked away. Negative self-talk was a regular thing for me, and that interaction really added fuel to the fire of my insecure mind. I started thinking things like, *He is so handsome. He should have someone prettier than I. I am ugly and fat. I'm just dragging him down.* Marc didn't feel that way at all. He was very genuine, kind, and loving. He showed me every day that he loved me, but it was my negative self-talk that kept me from believing I was worthy of him.

We were doing well as a couple until one day when we met up at the lockers. We spent our lunch together, and right before we got ready to leave, he embraced me and gave me a long, passionate kiss. He looked in my eyes and said, "I love you, Kyeni."

I could feel his love for me. I hugged him, and I looked back up at his eyes and said,

"That's interesting."

Oh no! I just ruined the moment, I thought to myself. He looked at me with a confused look, and then the bell rang. We started walking hand in hand toward our classes. As I sat in my next class, I felt bad that I did not tell him my true feelings. I should have told him how much I loved him and appreciated him. I don't know why the words didn't come out when they should have, but when I received a letter from him the next day, I knew that

I had hurt him. He wrote, *I love you, Kyeni, but I don't think you love me as much as I love you. I don't want to hold you back, so I feel that it is best that we break up.* I was absolutely devastated. I had just lost the one man that truly loved me and showed me kindness. My heart was broken.

When I look back at that memory, I am reminded of a hurt little girl that was very lost. I loved him, but his love scared me. I also loved several male family members and close friends, but their love brought pain into my life. Although I loved Marc, I couldn't truly show him love the way he deserved to be loved because I didn't love myself. I couldn't give him what I didn't have to give at that time in my life. As painful as that realization might have been, it was my reality.

We eventually got back together for a short time at the very end of our senior year in high school. Unfortunately, it was a little too late for us. We graduated in June of 1986, and we both went off to college. I went to Ball State in Muncie, Indiana, and he went to school somewhere in Albuquerque, New Mexico; that was the last time we physically saw each other. We did have the opportunity to talk on the phone a couple of times over the years, but we both eventually got married and went our separate ways. He passed away in 2016 from cancer, leaving behind his parents, his sister, his brother, his wife, and his son. Rest in peace, my friend! Rest in peace!

Chapter 11

LOW FLYERS

In my sophomore year of high school, I started babysitting for people around the neighborhood and for some of my mom's friends. Babysitting was another opportunity to get out of the house, as the more time away from the house, the better for me, or so I thought. Low flyers, people that are easily manipulated by the adversary/the dark one, come in many shapes and sizes, and they can be very deceptive. I had already encountered many low flyers in my life, and unfortunately, I was going to encounter many more.

My stepdad, J, went to church regularly; that was very interesting to me because the way he behaved at church was very different than the way he behaved at home. He was like "Dr. Jekyll and Mr. Hyde." He would be cruel to us at home, and then he would go to church and be the most spiritual person in the world at church. He started going to a new church, and, shockingly, he made us come with him. Interestingly enough, when we arrived at church, he didn't sit with us but sat across the aisle from us as if he was single. I guess he was too embarrassed to be with us because we weren't dressed "fancy" like he was.

Mom worked super hard to support J and the household. He rarely contributed financially to anything in the household, so she didn't have much money to spend on "fancy" church clothes for all of us. We had decent clothes, which were basic with no frills, but they were good clothes. She spent her money making sure that we had the clothes we needed for school, but she rarely bought clothes for herself. That is one of the reasons why we didn't go to church very often. The wearing of fancy clothes and hats was pretty much compulsory in many of the churches that we attended; wearing basic clothes would often be met with judgmental eyes. Mom didn't want to be judged, so she just chose not to go to church at all. I didn't understand all the drama behind all of that. We weren't poor; we just didn't have any "fancy" clothes and had what we needed: no more, no less.

I saw the situation like the story I learned in one of the children's Sunday school classes that I had attended. We learned about the widow who gave all that she had, and the Lord accepted her offering. It wasn't about the amount; it was about the heart and the faith behind the giving. I felt like God would understand our financial situation, and if we wore the best that we had, He would understand and would still love us. Mom didn't feel that way, so it was just easier not to go to church rather than have her feeling embarrassed.

* * *

It was at J's new church that I met the pastor and his wife. My mom was friends with the pastor's wife, so she asked me to start babysitting for them, and I agreed. They had two amazing kids, a young boy and an infant girl. They were very easy to take care of, and the baby hardly ever cried. One day, I was asked to babysit for them. The parents would be returning late, so I put the kids to bed and waited for their parents to return.

The couple had gone to two different events. The pastor returned home first, sat down in a chair, and started talking to me. He then got up, walked across the room to the stereo system, and put on some slow music. He asked me to dance with him, but I declined. He did not take "NO" for an answer, so he walked over to me, grabbed my hands, and pulled me up off the couch. I told him that I didn't know how to dance, so he said, "I'll show you." He put his hands around my waist and pulled me close to him. Because of my past, this made me feel very uncomfortable. When I said no, and he forced me to dance anyway, he reminded me of Auggy; that made the situation even more awkward for me. However, I didn't think he would do anything bad because he was the pastor at the church that we were attending. He was a "man of God."

He started moving side to side, and I tried to follow his movement. Then, he pulled me closer to him, and my body was now completely against his. He kept moving, but I started to feel anxious. We kept dancing, and then he raised his hand up from my waist to my chin to raise my chin up so he could see my face. The next thing I knew, he was kissing me on the mouth. I was completely shocked. My instinct told me that he was getting too familiar, but I guess I just didn't want to believe that he would do something inappropriate. I pushed back and moved away from him.

Strangely, my mind was giving me mixed signals. On the one hand, I felt a little flattered that he was interested in me, but on the other hand, I knew it was very wrong because one, he was the pastor; two, I was a teenager; and three, he was married. I started thinking to myself, *How could he do that to me? He is married, and he is my pastor.* I was so confused. He looked at me, and I guess he immediately saw the confusion on my face. He went over, turned off the music, and apologized to me. Shortly after that, his wife returned, paid me, and took me home. As usual, just the way I had been trained by Auggy, I didn't tell his wife or say anything about the pastor's inappropriate actions. I just sat quietly in the car as she drove me home.

I could hardly sleep that night because my mind started telling me that I had done something to cause him to do that. I was doing my normal thing again, blaming myself for the bad things that people did. I kept telling myself that I must have done something to make this pastor come on to me. It never crossed my mind that he was a man making some bad choices in his life. I immediately blamed myself like I always did. I never babysat for them after that, which was probably for the best. It wasn't until a little later I realized that the fault wasn't mine. Later on, the pastor got caught up in an affair, and his inappropriate choices caused the breaking of his marital union. He was a low flyer.

* * *

In my junior year of high school, I was babysitting for a family right down the street. The wife was out of town, and the husband worked a swing shift, getting home around 2 a.m. We talked for a little bit when he got home, which we often did when he and his wife returned after their dates, so this was nothing out of the ordinary. It was super late, so he told me that I could stay the rest of the night and go home in the morning, but I didn't feel comfortable doing that when his wife wasn't there. I just lived down the street, so I wanted to go home and get into my own bed. He walked up to me and said, in a very intimate kind of way, "Stay with me tonight. I want to be with you. I have never been with a Black woman before. I want you to be my first." He was a middle-aged white male, so I started to think, *Do Black people do that differently than white people?* I really didn't know because I was fifteen years old. I said, "NO! You are married!" He did not care about that at all because he begged me to stay. I finally said, "I have to go now."

I turned around and walked to the door and said goodnight. As I was walking home, I started asking myself, *Why do I keep attracting men like this?* This time, I didn't feel any guilt because I knew I had done nothing to illicit that response from the married man. I could tell that he must have stopped at the bar on the way home because he was drunk, a low flyer as well.

These two men were definitely low flyers, and because of my warped sense of intimacy, and my failed relationship with Marc, I think these two men were sent to me to pull me over to the dark side. For the most part, music kept me flying high, but I was continually being bombarded with low-flying men in my life that would either injure me or tempt me to do things that were bad. These types of temptations would continue with multiple men well into my adulthood.

Chapter 12

JUST "J"

After I left from babysitting that night at the home of the drunken man, I made it home and got into bed. I had to emotionally deal with another grown man's inappropriate interaction with me. My mind was racing because I was trying to decompress what had just happened, but I eventually fell asleep. It was about 3 a.m. when I finally drifted off, and at about 7 a.m., I heard J yelling downstairs. He woke up the entire house because he was going to have a poker party with his friends down in the basement later that evening and wanted the house to be cleaned, from top to bottom.

I had only slept a few hours when he started his tirade. Tommy, Alberta, and my younger brother Corey (he was born shortly after we moved over to Johnson Street) got up and went downstairs to start cleaning. I was exhausted so I didn't get up right away. A little while later, I guess he didn't see me come downstairs, so J yelled up to me, with his southern Georgia drawl.

"Alright, Kyeni, I done told you to get down here now!"

I said, "I got home late from babysitting. I have only gotten a couple hours of sleep."

"Don't argue with me! Get down here," he said.

Needless to say, I was mad at him. I put on some sweatpants and a T-shirt and went downstairs. (I did take my time going downstairs because I thought his request was unfair, and because I was mad at the situation.) When I got downstairs, the house was very clean, and J was helping with the cleaning. He wasn't doing it for us, though; he was doing it to impress his friends. He started yelling at me because I wasn't moving as fast as he wanted me to, so I walked into my mom's bedroom to find out what she wanted me to do.

She was sitting on the side of her bed because she had a cast on her leg. (She stepped on a broken stair at one of the houses that J was remodeling and fell down the stairs and broke her leg.) She told me to go downstairs to the basement and put a load of laundry in the washing machine. So, I did what she asked me to do, and I came back upstairs and went back into her bedroom to find out what else she wanted me to do.

A few moments after I stepped back into Mom's room, J walked in behind me and was holding an extension cord. He started yelling at me, and then he swung the cord and hit me. I moved away from him and fell backward onto the end of their bed. Mom stood up, with the cast on, and yelled at him, saying, "You don't come in here and hit her like that!"

He then walked over to Mom and hit her with the extension cord too, and she fell back down onto the bed. He walked back over to me and started whipping me with the extension cord. The next thing that happened is nothing short of a miracle, and to this very day, it is hard for me to fully explain it, or even talk about it, but here is my attempt.

At the moment that he swung the extension cord for the second time, my spirit left my body, literally. It moved up to the left-hand corner of the room and just hovered up there above my body. I was then looking down at the scene of him hitting my body, but my spirit was not inside of my body. Because I was watching what was going on from above, I didn't feel any of the hits, and that was a blessing because he was swinging with all his might. From above, I could see my body sitting there motionless on the edge of the bed. I can't explain how this situation was accomplished, but all I know is that the Lord somehow protected me from feeling those blows. After a few moments had passed, my spirit went back into my body, and I looked up at J and said, "Don't you hit me again!"

He swung one more time, and I looked him dead in his eyes and said, with all the strength and courage that I had within me and the power of the Lord above me, "DON'T ... YOU ... HIT ... ME ... AGAIN!"

That caught his attention, and he stopped swinging, but he kept yelling at me because he felt that I wasn't moving fast enough; then he walked away. Mom was yelling at him for what he had just done. It was all too much for me, so I got up from the bed and went upstairs. At that time, I didn't feel any pain. I was full of adrenaline and was mad at him for what had just happened.

When I got up to my room and sat on my bed, the pain finally kicked in, and the throbbing commenced. The pain was so bad that it shocked me, and I started crying uncontrollably. I first looked at my arm. I had a T-shirt on, so one of the strikes made direct contact with the skin of my upper left arm. The strike broke the skin of my arm right above the inside crease of my elbow. The wound had a big, puffed-up welt around it and was bleeding from the middle of the welt. I could feel both legs throbbing, so I pulled down my sweatpants to see the damage, and that sent me emotionally over the edge. Most of the contact that he made with the extension cord was directed at my legs. (I think that is why my spirit was taken out of my body.) The pain of each blow would have been excruciating if I was in my body, as the amount of force that he used was an indicator of the rage he was in. I could see that he was hitting me very hard, but because I couldn't feel it, I didn't realize the amount of damage he was doing to my legs.

Right after I saw my legs for the first time, Tommy walked in to check on me. He was downstairs and had listened to the entire scene unfold. I showed him my wounds, and he was horrified. I showed him my arm first, and then I said, "Look at my legs. They are deformed." The welts that had formed on my thighs made my legs look double in size. I was lucky that I had chosen to put on pants that morning and not shorts. Looking at the state of my legs sent me mentally and emotionally to a place that I had never been to before, and I knew I had to get out of that place. I pulled my pants up, put my shoes on, and ran out of the house. Mom heard me crying and heard the door slam, so she got up, went to the door, and called for me. "Kyeni! Come back here!" I heard her clearly, but I kept going and walking. I was enraged, and I just could not go back into that house. She called again, but I just ignored her and kept walking. I didn't know where I was going to go; I just knew I had to get out of there.

I walked around the block to my friend Georgia's house and asked her if I could use her phone. She saw that I was crying and asked me what happened, so I told her and showed her my arm. She was shocked and immediately led me to the phone. Calling my dad was not an option because he was out of town on reserve duty that weekend. So, I called my grandmother. I asked her to come and get me, and she told me that she was on her way. I thanked Georgia and headed back home.

When I got back home, Mom yelled at me because I didn't come back when she called me. I showed her my arm and my thighs. She cleaned up my arm and put ice on my thighs to get the swelling to go down. A little while later, my grandmother and my mom's sister Marsha showed up at the house. They came in and talked to my mom and begged Mom to let them take me to my grandmother's house for a while until things settled down, but my mom said, "NO! It was partly her fault anyway, so she cannot go!"

That was the second time in my life that I could honestly say, *I hated my mother!* After seeing the damage that J inflicted on me, she made me stay in the house with that evil man! I hated her. I just wanted to run away and never go back.

When I look back at the situation now, I can truly see how hurt people often hurt other people. My mom had been beaten by him so many times that I think it became the norm for her. I witnessed him beat her multiple times, and that was emotionally damaging to her and to her four children. Alberta was seven and a half years younger than me, and Corey was one and a half years younger than her. J was their biological father, so to see him beat their mother that way had to be horrible for them. He never beat them, but they witnessed him beat Mom up and hit her on the head with a hammer while they pleaded with him not to do it. These types of things don't just affect the abused; they silently affect the witnesses as well, because it can create a sense of helplessness and fear within them.

Tommy and I suffered emotional abuse from J as well. We were the two Bryants living in the May household, so he treated us like outsiders. When Alberta and Corey were mischievous and did bad things, he would say that they were too young to do it and would blame it on Tommy and me. Even when Mom would tell him that Alberta and Corey had done it, he would not believe her, so Tommy and I would get in trouble for things that his children had done. J was just downright cruel during the ten years that we lived on Johnson Street, and it took some more fights between him and my mom, physical fights between him and Tommy, and threats from our family for Mom to finally separate from him. He moved out of the Johnson Street house, and a little while later, my mom decided to sell the house and move to Indianapolis, Indiana.

I didn't want to move with her because I had a chance to do a concerto (a solo with an orchestra accompaniment) with our high school orchestra the following year. I had worked so hard on it, so I didn't want to miss that opportunity. I asked my grandmother if I could live with her for the rest of my junior year, and my senior year, to which she said yes. Next, I had to convince my mom to let me stay, and with my grandmother's help, she agreed to let me stay in South Bend. Tommy also stayed in South Bend, but he went to live with my aunt Marsha.

During my senior year, Mom and J got into an argument over the phone, and J drove all the way down to Indianapolis, which was about two and a half hours away, and started beating my mother at her house. Tommy was there at that time, having graduated from high school the year before. I don't think J knew Tommy was there, but Tommy came out, and they got into a terrible fight. Mom tried to stop Tommy from fighting J, but Tommy had just had enough of J's behavior, and he was not going to allow J to beat Mom up that day. Tommy was beating him at first and knocked out one of J's teeth. But after a few moments, J got the upper hand and injured Tommy. J had really thick, strong nails, and with those nails, he grabbed Tommy's face like you would palm a basketball, and he intentionally closed his hands inward. When he did that, his nails ripped through the skin on Tommy's face. After he did that, he was able to get free from Tommy. J then ran out of the house, got into his car, and drove back to South Bend. Mom took Tommy to the hospital to get his wounds cleaned. The wounds did not require any stitches, but they would eventually leave some minor scars on his face. After eleven years of marriage, this incident is what finally gave Mom the courage to divorce J.

I thought that was the end of the J chapter, but boy was I wrong. Mom was single and started her new life in Indianapolis. She was dating and was in a pretty serious relationship at the time; it was dysfunctional at best, but it appeared that she had moved on from J. I was in college, and Tommy, Alberta, and Corey lived with her. J had moved to New York, and it appeared that he had moved on with his life as well. One summer, Mom told me that she was taking Alberta and Corey to New York to visit their dad. I told her to just send them on an airplane so she wouldn't have to go there and deal with him. Their relationship had a volatile ending, so I didn't think she should go, but she insisted on taking the kids herself. So, she drove them to New York, and they were there for a while. The next thing you know, she called me and told me that she and J were getting back together again.

"What? Are you serious?" I said.

"Yes," she said.

She came back and packed up her house in Indianapolis. She pretty much put Tommy out on the street and moved to New York. The relationship between Tommy and my mom was very strained at that point. Tommy was emotionally damaged because of our childhood, so he made some bad choices as well. He was drinking and doing drugs, and Mom and my siblings saw Tommy's decline firsthand, so the breakup of that family unit was pretty brutal for them but didn't affect me directly because I was in college. Mom and J were together for a while, but the same old things returned in their relationship. He was never faithful to her, even in South Bend, and she finally made the decision to leave him for good but decided to stay in New York. Mom got her own place and got a job to support herself and the kids, starting her new life in New York.

*   *   *

What did I learn from that period of my life? It was hard for me to see any positives that came from that time in my life. I didn't have a spiritual practice to help me look at what was happening in a spiritual way. However, when I was older and more mature, I learned that every trial in life is an opportunity to learn something. Oftentimes, we judge people by our experiences with them. However, when we do that, we don't provide them with an opportunity to change and to grow. We completely judge them by their past behavior, leaving them no room to live in the present and no opportunity to grow in the future. I believe that part of our purpose for being here on this earth is to learn, to grow, and to become more like the Savior. When He walked upon the earth, He loved everyone, even the sinners. He may not have liked the sin, but He loved the sinner. His example teaches me that we must forgive, as forgiveness provides us an opportunity to show love, even in the midst of extreme adversity.

Anger, fear, and hatred are emotions that have lower and slower wavelengths. These are the emotions that the adversary likes to encourage people to keep in their hearts and minds. This is why I call people that function in these wavelengths low flyers. That is because when these emotions are present, the adversary can use that darkness to manipulate people. We all, at times, behave in ways that encourage us to use emotions that fall in the slower wavelengths. Contrary to these slow wavelength emotions are emotions like love, peace, and joy. These all come from God, and they have higher and faster wavelengths. These are the emotions that we should be striving for in our lives because they bring light and true happiness into our world.

We, as humans, move in and out of these different levels of light and darkness. The dichotomy between the two is ever present, but our goal should be to stay in the light as long as we can because when we do, it makes it more difficult for the adversary to manipulate us.

In the end, I chose to forgive J, because that enabled me to rid myself of those dark emotions. Yes, he did some very bad things, but in the Lord's eye, sin is sin, and I have chosen to let the Lord handle that. It took me about six years to choose to forgive him, and that only happened at that time because of the Gospel of Jesus Christ. It taught me that the Savior had already paid for all our sins, including everything everyone had ever done to hurt me. So, when I was baptized, I chose to let all of that go. I don't know if J has tried to repent for the things that he has done, but it is not for me to get involved in that. I have my own sins that I need to deal with daily and cannot be worried about his sins. What I do know is that people can change if they choose to, and J has shown me that change in a couple of instances.

When my sister Alberta was graduating from college, she wanted us to come out to Brigham Young University in Utah for her graduation. So, several of us, including Mom and J, flew out there, all hanging out together to celebrate Alberta. On one of the days, we went to a theme park called Lagoon. I love theme parks and rides, but over the years, my body has grown to a size that the rides could no longer accommodate. I walked around with everyone, but I couldn't ride anything; I was just too big to fit in the seats on the rides. So obviously, this made me sad. Halfway through the day, everyone went on one of the big-ticket rides, but I couldn't go so I found a seat and sat down to wait.

J noticed my sadness, and he asked Alberta what was wrong with me. She explained the situation to him, and it made him feel sad. He didn't like rides and wasn't riding anything, but he made a point to try and make me happy. So, he walked me over to some of the games, and he paid for me to play them. He carried on a conversation with me to try and distract me from my sadness. I may have had issues with him earlier in life, but that simple act of kindness softened my heart toward him. It helped me to see that, despite his many foibles, he did have kindness in his heart. I also see that kindness toward me even today. I have not seen him in about twenty-five years. He is in a nursing home now, and when he first went in there, I got his phone number from Alberta and decided to call him and see how he was doing. When he answered the phone, I said, "Hi J! It's Kyeni."

He couldn't hear me very well, so he asked, "Who is it?"

I repeated my statement, but louder this time.

"It's Kyeni."

To my surprise, he said, "My daughter Kyeni?"

I paused for a moment because I was shocked. He had never called me his daughter before.

"Yes! It's me!" I said.

He was very happy to hear from me and asked me how I was doing and wanted to know about my life. He was very kind to me and even quoted some scriptures of encouragement. When we got ready to hang up, he thanked me for calling and said, "Bye bye now." He displays those same feelings every time I call him. People can change. They must choose to do it, and we should allow them the opportunity to make the change. We can't control what they do and how they do it; we just need to get out of their way and let them do it at their own pace. Of course, we must use prudence in how we interact with people that are or have been involved in dangerous types of sin, or people that have caused us great harm or injury. How one chooses to interact or not interact with those people is completely up to the individual, but for me, forgiveness of my offenders has been a huge blessing in my life. It has given me peace and allowed me to heal.

Chapter 13

THREE AMAZING MEN

Although I struggled in my relationships with men in my life, there were some men that greatly influenced the trajectory of my course through life. I believe all three of the following men were placed in my life exactly at the times that I needed them most. Each of them helped me develop specific aspects of my musical gifts and because of them, I am the musician that I am today.

ZEAL FISHER

Mr. Fisher was like a dad to me, as he nurtured me and helped me develop my musical gifts, just like he did with my aunt Marilyn when she played the violin. He always showed me kindness and was in my life from fifth grade through twelfth grade. He was my teacher, but I could tell that he cared about me and wanted the best for me. He cared about all the kids in our orchestra, and we all loved him too. We gave him Christmas gifts, and he graciously accepted them, even though he was Jewish. He never complained about it or corrected us but just accepted them and said thank you. I didn't know that he was Jewish until I was in middle school, and then out of respect, I stopped giving him gifts and started saying, "Happy Chanukah."

During my senior year of high school, Mr. Fisher pulled me aside and told me that the orchestra director from Ball State University was recruiting in our area and was coming to visit our school the next day. I had not decided on what I was going to do for college. We had never talked about it, but being the father figure that he was, Mr. Fisher somehow knew that I was indecisive about college. He stepped in and intervened on my behalf, telling the visiting director about me and asking him to recruit me.

I didn't play the violin at school during my senior year, as we did not have a string bass player in the orchestra. I started learning the string bass five years earlier when I was at Brown Middle School. Mr. Fisher would leave the orchestra door open for me so I could go in at lunchtime and practice on the days that I wasn't working in the cafeteria. I practiced the violin, but I also started practicing the bass. I eventually got really good at it. In fact, I was so good that I qualified to compete at the state level for Solo/Ensemble on the violin and the bass during my junior and senior years of high school, receiving Superior ratings on both instruments both years.

Because our orchestra was in need, I made the sacrifice and moved over and played the bass for my entire senior year at school. I was okay with that because I was still taking private lessons, and I had auditioned, got into, and was playing the violin in the IUSB Philharmonic.

Mr. Fisher's plan for the college visit was to have me play through the first movement of Bach's "Double violin concerto in D minor" with Marc, and then go back and play the first movement of Mozart's "Haffner" symphony on the bass. This would show the director both of my specialties, and the plan worked. At the end of class, the director came up to me and told me, in his very British accent, "I was very impressed with your performances today, and I would love to have you come to Ball State and audition to attend the School of Music next year."

His presence at school that day made me realize that I needed to get on top of my plans for college because I was procrastinating on the whole thing. He gave me the date of the audition and the number to call and schedule my audition time. That evening, I discussed the audition with my mom, and we decided that I should do the audition. She drove me down to Ball State, which was about one and a half hours away, on the audition date, and Mr. Weintrob, the violin professor at Ball State, accepted me right on the spot, but he could not officially offer anything to me because I had not filled out a Ball State University application yet. Before they could accept me into the School of Music and potentially offer me a scholarship, I had to be accepted into the university first. So, I immediately filled out the required paperwork, and a couple of weeks later, they sent me my acceptance letter, along with a $500 per year scholarship to play in the Ball State Symphony.

It was because of Mr. Fisher that I ended up going to Ball State. He was watching out for me, and he did all that he could to help me succeed. He was one of the most important male role models in my life, from elementary school all the way up through high school. It was his love for me that set me up to be where I am today.

GEORGE ZIGMONT GASKA

Mr. Gaska was a character, an older gentleman with snow-white hair. He had plump fingers and a big, round belly. Mr. Gaska kind of reminded me of Santa Claus, but without the beard. I enjoyed studying with him. He was a violinist and a luthier, so he repaired instruments and had a workshop in the room next door to his studio. We did a lot of my learning by playing duets together. He always made me play the first violin part while he played the second violin part, using the duets to teach me technique; that was the perfect way for me to pick up levels very quickly. The duets got more and more challenging and required new techniques in order to master them. I played duets all the time at home, so playing them with my teacher was a treat. I always wanted to make sure that my part sounded great when we played together, so I practiced a lot during that period of time.

Taking lessons from him helped me to pass my audition for the Youth Orchestra. All the best players in town played in that orchestra. Marc and the other top violinists in the county had been in the group for a couple of years, but because I wasn't taking lessons, I didn't know about it. When I started studying with Mr. Gaska, who Marc also studied with, I found out about the orchestra. I was at the end of my eighth-grade year when I started preparing for the audition to play in the Youth Orchestra during the upcoming school year. I would be a ninth grader in high school, and that was the last year that I could play in that particular group. After that, I would have aged out, but there was another orchestra I could audition for, the Indiana University at South Bend (IUSB) Philharmonic. It was a college-level orchestra, but it was open to the top high school students in the area. If I auditioned well, I would have a chance of getting in.

I got the audition requirements for the Youth Orchestra and worked on the audition material with Mr. Gaska, and low and behold, I got in. Not only did I get in, but I was placed in the first violin section my first and only year; that was the section where all the top violinists were. I was in the seventh chair, and Marc was in the third chair. Another student, Mari, was in the first chair of the first violin section, so she was the concertmistress, and she was amazing. Since I was new, I did not know her well, but I loved watching her play because she made me want to be better.

Halfway through my eighth-grade year, my mom told me that she did not have enough money for me to continue taking private lessons, so I would have to quit studying with Mr. Gaska. My technique had gotten so much better studying with him, so this was a big blow for me, but I didn't question her decision because I knew my mom was struggling. She was financially taking care of everything while J was not helping her the way he should have, so that made her life very difficult. When my last lesson was over, I said to Mr. Gaska, "Mr. Gaska, this will be my last lesson. I cannot come back because my mom cannot afford to pay for the lessons anymore."

He looked at me with compassion in his eyes and said, "You are too good to stop taking lessons. You just keep coming, and don't worry about the money." Tears streamed down my face, and I thanked him. When Mom came home, I told her about Mr. Gaska's gift, and she was astounded at his kindness. He continued to teach me for the rest of that school year and into my ninth-grade year.

* * *

The Youth Orchestra rehearsed at IUSB, and one Saturday, my mom was going to be late picking me up. I went up to the front of the music building to wait for her. I was alone because there were no classes on Saturday, and all the Youth Orchestra students had already gone home. As I was waiting, I could hear a student taking a violin lesson in Sarah Peterson's studio. She had been a teacher for many years, and her studio was right next to where I was standing. The student that she was teaching sounded good, but obviously not to Mrs. Peterson because she started yelling at the student. Because the school was closed and the front lobby was empty, the sound of her screaming voice bounced off the tiled floor and echoed up and down the hallway. I felt so bad for whoever was in there. After about fifteen or twenty more minutes of her yelling at the student, I could hear the creaking sound of Mrs. Peterson's studio door opening. Out came Mari, and she was crying. I was in total shock. Mari looked at me, turned to the right, and exited out the side door. I sat down on a bench, facing the front door and waited for my mom.

A few minutes later, Mrs. Peterson came out of her studio and locked her door. She saw me sitting on the bench and came over and spoke to me, saying, "I would love for you to come and study with me."

I immediately thought in my head, *Heck no! You ain't gonna get me in there so you can yell at me like that! Shoooot!* I knew that there was no way that I could work under those conditions, so I smiled at her and said, "Thank you, but I am already studying with Mr. Gaska." Throughout that year, she asked me a couple of other times to study with her, and I always declined and used Mr. Gaska as my excuse.

During my freshman year, Mr. Gaska started to change. He was an older man, so I think he was in the early stages of dementia. He started becoming forgetful and would get agitated very easily. He started harassing me about my weight and things that had nothing to do with music. I started to feel attacked, so I eventually stopped taking lessons from him. That was a very hard decision because I felt guilty for leaving him after all the free lessons and time that he had invested in me. However, I was becoming emotionally damaged by his comments. I stayed with him as long as I could, but I just couldn't take it anymore. So, for my sanity, I felt that it would be better to stop studying with him and be on my own rather than keep studying and endure that emotional pain every week. At the end of that last lesson, I kindly said, "I will no longer be able to come, so this will be my last lesson." He did not ask for a reason; he just wished me well. I knew that he wasn't trying to intentionally hurt me. In his own way, he was trying to help me, but he was losing control of his rational thinking. Mrs. Peterson was probably the best teacher in the area, but I definitely was not going to study with her, so I just stopped taking lessons altogether.

It was Mr. Gaska's kindness that helped me while I was in the eighth and ninth grade. He prepared me to play in the Youth Orchestra and the Philharmonic. I never would have made it into those two orchestras without him. He set me up for success, and for that, I will always be grateful to him and honor him for his service. His kindness set an example for me, and I have paid that forward several times by helping some of my private students that were in financial need, just like he did for me. He taught me about the importance of giving and serving others.

NICHOLAS DANIELSON

In my sophomore year of high school, I auditioned for and got into the IUSB Philharmonic, getting to play with the college students. I really liked this orchestra a lot. The music was very challenging, but I loved the challenge, and I definitely grew from it. Playing in the Philharmonic prepared me for playing in the Ball State and Muncie Symphony Orchestras later when I was in college. At the beginning of the season, they made an announcement that a new violin teacher was joining the faculty at the college. His name was Nicholas Danielson, but he went by Nicky; not Mr. Danielson, just Nicky. When he walked in the door, all the girls looked at him and started swooning over him. He was young and very cute with fairly long, wavy brown hair that fell just above his shoulders. His bangs were long and would fall into his face, so he would always use his fingers to rake his hair backward out of his face. When he did that, the girls would swoon a little more.

The string faculty members played with the Philharmonic and ran our sectionals. We would break up into our sections and work with them to perfect the music. They judged the auditions and conducted juries at the end of each term for the students that studied at the university. Juries were a type of final exam for the students taking private lessons at the school. Each student would have to go and perform prepared pieces and scales for the entire string faculty, receiving a grade afterward. Lessons were considered college courses, so the students received college credit for the course; even the high school students that studied there received credit.

I was still without a teacher at that moment. I certainly didn't tell anyone because I did not want Mrs. Peterson to find out that I was no longer studying with Mr. Gaska. I just didn't want to deal with that drama at all, so I kept that information to myself. Mom's finances got a little better, so she told me that I could start taking lessons again. Now, the challenge was to find a new teacher. I didn't want to go back to Mr. Gaska, and I certainly did not want to study with Mrs. Peterson, so Nicky showed up right on time. The second time I met Nicky, I went up to him and asked, "Do you have any space in your music studio?"

"Yes, I do," he said.

I smiled at him and said, "I would love to study with you if you will have me."

"Great. I will get back with you with some more information about it." I was so excited and was looking forward to studying with him because outside of his good looks, he was a great violinist, and he had a very kind personality.

The next week, we were having seating auditions, and each one of the string students had to go and play for their related faculty member. Mrs. Peterson and Nicky were judging all the violinists, and the auditions were in Mrs. Peterson's studio. When it was my turn to go in and play for them, I was nervous because Nicky had never heard me play before. I practiced hard so I was prepared, but I had butterflies in my stomach. I was so nervous. I walked in and said hello to both, and I played my audition material. They thanked me, and as I was walking toward the door to leave, Mrs. Peterson stopped me and said, "Nicky told me that you want to take lessons here at the school."

"Yes, I do," I responded.

She then said something that completely knocked the wind out of my sails.

"The two of us will talk about it today, and one of us will call you tonight and let you know who you will be studying with."

Dun, dun, dun ... Plot twist! My heart sank. Mrs. Peterson was powerful, and by far the most outspoken person on the string faculty. I just knew, in my heart of hearts, that she would overpower him and force me to study with her. I just smiled, said thank you through my clenched teeth, and walked out. When I got out in the hallway, I almost lost it because the violin life that I knew was soon to be over. I was still very emotionally fragile, so I knew that enduring her yelling would probably break me. There was not much I could do except to pray that Nicky would be the one to call me. So, that is exactly what I did.

When I got home, I paced all evening. It was taking forever for the phone to ring. When it finally did, I paused and looked at it. I was so afraid to answer the phone, but I slowly walked over to it. I took a deep breath, lifted the receiver, and nervously said, "Hello?"

The caller on the other end said, "Hello. Is Kyeni there?"

"Yes. This is she."

"Hello there. This is Nicky."

My heart leapt for joy! My prayers were answered, and I could finally relax. I would have loved to have been a fly on the wall in that studio when they were deciding who I was going to study with. I always wondered if Nicky had to fight for me, or if Mrs. Peterson just accepted that I had asked him and just allowed it to happen. I never asked Nicky about it; I was just grateful that he called, and I moved forward. I studied with Nicky throughout the rest of my high school years.

A period of time during my eleventh-grade year, I stopped practicing and was going to my lessons unprepared. This went on week after week, but Nicky never said anything about it until one day. I showed up for lessons and started playing as usual. When I finished playing what we were working on, he sat there quietly for an uncomfortable amount of time. I am sure it was only a few seconds, but it was silent in the room, and it seemed like an eternity. I was looking at him, and he finally looked up at me and said, "Kyeni, you are one of the best damn players in this town, but you won't even practice!" He said some other choice words after that and lectured me, but I was still processing the first thing that he said, so I didn't hear anything after that. He let me have it (and rightly so)! I was just being lazy. He never said anything, so I got away with it, but he had finally just had enough. (Maybe that was why Mrs. Peterson was yelling at Mari.)

From that moment forward, I didn't want to let him down. He took me on as his student, so I needed to do better. Because of that lecture, Nicky changed the direction of my music career. He helped prepare me to play the Bach Double Violin Concerto with Marc. (Mr. Fisher always chose a senior to play a concerto with our high school orchestra at the end of the school year. Marc and I were chosen. Marc played the first violin part, and I played the second violin part.) I grew so much as a violinist under Nicky's tutelage, and because of his support and direction, I was accepted into Ball State University as a violin performance major. I have always been grateful for him and grateful for the moment that he chastised me. He didn't do it out of meanness but out of care, and because of that one single moment, I am musically where I am today.

Chapter 14

NEIL WEINTROB

Neil Weintrob was my college violin professor. When I went to the Ball State audition, I had a major problem: I had developed pain in my hands, and the doctors were calling it tendinitis. My hands started hurting at the end of my junior year of high school and continued into my senior year. I was living with my grandmother at the time, so she took me to see several doctors, and they could not figure out what the problem was. One of the doctors mentioned that there were musician doctors and suggested that I research them and try to find one. I did what he told me to do and found a few. The closest one to me was a woman in Chicago, so my uncle Joe requested that I come and live with them for the summer and babysit my cousin Chalice, and when my appointment slot came toward the middle of the summer, either he or my aunt Vel would take me to the appointment. Mom agreed and sent me to Chicago on a commuter train called The South Shore. My uncle picked me up at the train station, and I stayed with them the summer before my freshman year of college.

When it was time for my appointment, my aunt Vel took me. I went in and talked to the doctor. I brought my violin as requested, and I played for her. She looked at my technique to see if I was doing something strange that was causing the problem. After she finished her observation, her diagnosis was that I needed to lose weight, so she lectured me about that and then told me that I was not allowed to play my violin for the rest of the summer. "This should be enough time for the swelling to go down. You need to take this seriously because it could be a career-ending injury," she said.

I took her counsel and didn't play my violin for the rest of the summer; I didn't even open my violin case. I didn't play my violin again until it was time for me to go to college. When I finally started to play my violin at the end of the summer, I took it slow and tried to be very careful. I was nervous to play because of what the doctor said, but I knew that there was something other than "my weight" that was causing the problem. I just couldn't figure it out, and my mom did not have the money to send me anywhere else for help, so I just dealt with it. I think this is what contributed to me not applying to any colleges; I didn't know what to do because of the state of my hands.

When I had my audition at Ball State, I auditioned on both the violin and the bass. The whole string faculty was in the room when I auditioned. I wanted to be honest with them, so I told them that I was having pain in my hands, and that the doctors thought I had tendinitis. They sent me out of the room and had a brief conversation amongst themselves. Mr. Weintrob brought me back into the room and told me that if I chose to come to Ball State, he could fix my hands. Dr. Albright then addressed me; he was my state Solo/Ensemble judge on the bass my junior and senior years of high school. He asked me to come to Ball State and play the bass for him after I had finished playing my solo for him during my senior year. That is why I auditioned with both instruments. I was going to go in as a violin and bass double performance major. He looked at me and told me that I was a much stronger violinist, and that I needed to give up the bass so Mr. Weintrob could fix my hands, which, in turn, would allow me to continue playing the violin.

I really wanted to study with Dr. Albright, and I know he wanted me to study with him. However, he saw the wisdom in what Mr. Weintrob said, so he was the one that told me that I needed to sacrifice the bass so I could continue to play music. That really made me sad, but I knew he was right. He was such a kind, gentle spirit, so I took his counsel and immediately made the decision to sacrifice the bass. That decision ended my bass career, but I still play it from time to time in order to demonstrate things for my students.

The injury that I had then, and currently still have, is a tension injury in both of my hands. I used to hold my violin and bow with a lot of tension when I played, so playing that way over an extended period of time is what caused the injury. It is a lifelong injury but working with Mr. Weintrob helped me to learn to manage it. As long as I am playing without tension, I have no pain. I currently teach this concept to all my students to help them prevent injury.

* * *

At my first lesson with Mr. Weintrob, he started working on my hands immediately. This was the most difficult time in my music career, as I had to re-learn, from scratch, how to play my instrument. I had to start over and change everything. I was a freshman in college at the time and had already been playing for nine years, so I had to start all over. I had to learn a tension-free way of holding my violin and bow, and I had to learn both things at the same time. In addition to that, he took the shoulder rest off of my instrument, which is a device that is attached to the underside of a violin or viola and used to support the instrument on the performer's shoulder. I had been using it for years, so I was completely hooked on it. Without it made it very difficult to learn to play because the balance of the instrument was completely different, and my violin kept sliding off my shoulder.

I started complaining and arguing with Mr. Weintrob about the technique because it felt so uncomfortable and foreign to me, and I was just lost. This was the most frustrating and difficult time for me, so I cried regularly. I couldn't figure out how to hold my instrument, nor could I hold my instrument like him. Everything was just uncomfortable, and then Mr. Weintrob told me that I would not be playing any solos for my whole first year during private lessons. All I would be working on was scales and etudes (technical exercises) for the entire year in order to help me change my technique. The day that he told me that news, I was devastated. *How could I go a whole year without playing real music?* I didn't realize that this journey would be so difficult.

When I got back to my dorm room, I just sat down on my bed and started to cry again. I kept telling myself over and over, *I can't do this! This is just too much!* And then something popped into my head. He said that I could only play scales and exercises until I learned the technique. "Ding!" Lightbulb moment! *Stop fighting him. Learn the technique as quickly as you can, and then you can start playing.* From that very moment, I changed my mindset because I was emotionally flying low and had developed a bad attitude toward him. I realized that fighting Mr. Weintrob wasn't working, and, as a matter of fact, the more I fought, the longer it would take me to start playing real music. So, when he saw me trying to make the corrections, he stepped in to help me. He gave me a little, thin pink sponge that was porous, which I attached to the back of my violin. Because of the pores, it gripped onto my clothes, and the violin stopped slipping off my shoulder. That was all I needed, and from there, the rest was easy.

I didn't take his hand position completely, but I compromised, and what I did do was enough to suffice. I worked so hard that first semester and made the necessary corrections, and when I came back from winter break, I started working on my first solo piece at the start of the second semester. He told me that none of his students had ever accomplished that feat. I worked hard, so I was very proud of myself.

* * *

One day during the second semester, I went in for my weekly lesson with Mr. Weintrob. I was working on a piece of music, and Mr. Weintrob had been standing next to me, watching and listening. After I finished playing, he sat down and was quiet for a moment, and then he looked at me and said, "I want to ask you a question."

(This scenario brought back memories of the day Nicky chastised me.) I thought he was going to yell at me for not playing well, but I was completely wrong. What he asked me shook me to the core! He asked, "Were you sexually abused?"

I looked at him and remembered feeling my eyes open wide like a deer in headlights, and then my countenance immediately fell. Before I could say anything, he continued, "I have noticed that every time I come close to you, you move away from me. It appears that you have an issue with me because you seem to be uncomfortable around me."

I was shocked. *How could he have noticed that? If he noticed, how many men had I done this to?* I looked at him and said, "If I am doing that, it is completely unconscious. I do not feel afraid of you or nervous around you."

I then briefly, and humbly, told him what had happened to me as a child. He was the first adult that I had ever revealed this to and, to be honest, it was a relief to get that off my chest. I had been holding onto that secret for so long, so talking about it brought about a huge release for me. When we finished talking, he asked me to go to the library and check out the book, *I Know Why The Caged Bird Sings* by Maya Angelou. He had read it and told me that it would help me, and it did. Our relationship changed after that because I understood that he had my best interest in mind, and he wanted me to start the healing process for my abuse.

I am very grateful to Mr. Weintrob for having the courage to talk to me about the abuse. It did help, and it changed our relationship to where we actually became friends. I didn't fully start to deal with that trauma of the abuse until the Cassie incident, but it did start me on the road to partial recovery.

Mr. Weintrob showed me kindness when I needed it. Not only did he show this in his violin studio, but he also showed me kindness outside of music. One year, I was not able to go home for the holidays because I did not have the money to rent a car, and no one could come and pick me up, so he invited me over to his home to spend the holidays with his family. I didn't have a car to get there, so he came and picked me up from my apartment. I will always be grateful to him and his wife Susan for looking out for me when I was alone. They fed me and took care of me, making me feel like family. When I think about the phrase, "Are we our brother's keeper?" I can honestly say, "Yes, we are!" I know that to be true because of the selfless example of Neil and Susan Weintrob.

Chapter 15

JOHN MEADOWS AND MY NEW TALENT

Oh no! I am short one credit! I only had eleven credits, and I needed at least twelve to be considered a full-time student. If I didn't find a class to take, I would lose my music scholarship and my job as a resident assistant in my dorm, Baker Hall. These two things, plus my other financial aid, took care of all my school costs, so if I didn't find another class, I would lose everything. I was running out of time, so I decided to go to the music building and see what classes were available for one credit hour. As I was looking through the list of courses, I saw a beginning vocal class, and it was one credit. So, I went up to the secretary and asked her if I could sign up for the beginning vocal class. She said, "You have to audition for that class."

"When are the auditions?" I asked.

"Today at 2 p.m. Can you prepare an audition that quickly?"

It was about noon, but I said, "Yes, I can do it!"

She put my name on the audition list, and I ran back to my dorm and flipped through all my vocal music to try and find something to sing quickly, and "Evergreen" by Barbara Streisand popped up. It was one of my favorite songs, so I knew it very well. I ran through it singing a couple of times, and then I ran back to the School of Music to audition. When I arrived at the audition room, one of the vocal professors came out in the hallway and yelled to the auditioners, "If you don't have an appropriate audition piece, here is a hymnal. Pick a song out of here." I wasn't sure if my piece was appropriate or not, and I didn't really go to church, so I didn't know any hymns. He seemed aggravated, so I guess someone had already sung something inappropriate. But I got the courage to go up to him and asked him if my song was okay to sing. He looked at the cover and said, "Yes, that is okay." I was relieved.

They had an accompanist on site to go through our songs with us before we went into the room to audition. I ran through it with him once, and then it was my time to audition. My heart was pounding in my chest because I had never done anything with my voice before. I sang in a church choir for a little while, and I also sang in the shower and in my room all the time, but that was the extent of my singing experience. I would now be competing with other people for a spot in this class, so I wasn't sure how I would measure up to them. We were not allowed to sing in the hallway because the auditions were going on, so I didn't get to hear anyone else singing. To be truthfully honest, I was so focused on going over the lyrics to my song, I probably wouldn't have heard them anyway.

My turn arrived, and I walked into the room. The entire vocal faculty was sitting there, and they were all looking at me. That was very intimidating, as half of them were men and half of them were women. The man that came outside started talking to me first. His name was John Meadows and asked me to tell them a little bit about myself. He also wanted to know why I wanted to take the vocal class. I said, "Hello, my name is Kyeni Bryant. I am a violin performance major, and I study with Mr. Weintrob. I decided to audition because I was short one credit hour, and I thought singing would be a good choice because it could help me develop my ear."

"Have you had any singing experience?" he asked.

"No. I have only done a little singing in a church choir that I sang in for a short time."

"I believe you are going to sing 'Evergreen'?" he asked.

"Yes. That is correct."

"You may begin," he said.

My accompanist began playing the introduction to the song, and I took a deep breath and began singing. I focused on making the song as beautiful and musical as I could. My song was a slow ballad, so if I didn't sing my words clearly, they would not understand what I was singing about. Thus, I made sure that I focused on my diction. Because I had been playing the violin for so long, I rarely got super nervous anymore. However, this was a completely different experience, and my heart pounded the whole time I was singing. During all rests and breaks in the music, I took big breaths to calm myself until I started singing again. I didn't look at their faces at all while I was singing because I didn't want their facial expressions to mess with my focus, so I just found a few spots just above their heads to look at, making it appear that I was looking at them.

When I finished singing the last note, I exhaled with a sigh of relief. The professors smiled at me and thanked me for coming in. For that being my very first vocal audition, I felt like I did a good job, and I was proud of myself. So, come what may, if I didn't get in, I knew I did my best. As I was preparing to leave, they told me that they would hang a roster outside the music office the following day with the names of all the students that made it into the class. I thanked them for their time and exited the room. My fate was now in their hands.

The next afternoon, I walked over to the music building to go and check the bulletin board. There were a lot of lists hanging up on the board because just about all the music faculty taught private lessons, so their rosters were also hanging on the board for students. I was scanning the board from right to left until I finally came across the vocal class roster. I scanned down the list, and my name was not on it. *Oh well, at least I tried,* I thought to myself. I had signed up for double hours with Mr. Weintrob, so I decided to find his roster and make sure that they had the correct number of hours listed. As I was scanning across the board, I saw the name Bryant, (Bryant was my maiden name) so I thought to myself, *Who else in the School of Music has the last name of Bryant?* I went back to check and see who it was, and it was me. I was confused because I didn't sign up for any other classes.

I looked up to the top of the roster to see who the professor was, and it was Mr. Meadows. He was the vocal instructor from the day before that yelled about having the appropriate song choices. They didn't put me in the beginning vocal class because Mr. Meadows must have seen something within me that he wanted to work with. That was a huge blessing because instead of having to sit in a class with other non-vocal majors, I was placed in the private studio of one of the best vocal instructors in the School of Music, receiving one-on-one instruction from him. In addition to that, I received my twelfth credit hour, and my status at the university was saved.

When I arrived at Mr. Meadows's studio for my first lesson, one of the very first things that he said to me was, "You got that voice from the Man Upstairs, girl!" He told me that he wished I had come into the university as a freshman vocal major, which he surprised me by that statement. I knew I could carry a tune, but I didn't know that I had the potential to be a vocal major. I started working with Mr. Meadows, and he let me sing whatever songs I wanted, applying the vocal technique to whatever song I was singing. Of course, the songs had to be appropriate, but I got to choose. He was an amazing teacher, and I learned so much from him. Surprisingly, the most important things that I learned from Mr. Meadows were of a spiritual nature. He taught me that the Lord knew me and was aware of me. He also informed me that the Lord had given me the talents that I had, so I needed to use them to bless others. The small conversations that we had were a foreshadow of what was to come in my life with music.

This opportunity to study with Mr. Meadows opened a new form of musical expression for me. Not only did I have my violin to use as a form of expression, but now I had my voice. I worked diligently on it, and it became an important way for me to communicate my feelings. One of the cool things that I learned about singing was that singing uses different muscles than our speech muscles, so I never had to worry about stuttering at all. I could just focus on the music and the message behind the lyrics. This was the start of my singing career, and I have slowly but surely incorporated it into my life. And just like my violin, I have tried my best to use my musical gifts to spiritually uplift and bless others.

Chapter 16

GOLDSMITH

When my mom was still living in Indianapolis, I went home and stayed with her during one of my Ball State winter breaks. The day that I was leaving to go back to school, Mom's friend Cynthia came to visit from out of town. We spent some time with her, and then she left. Later that evening, Mom drove me back to school for the winter semester. The next day, Mom called me at school and asked, "What is your blood type?"

I said, "B positive."

Mom then said, "Uh-oh!"

She then asked me, "Are you sitting down?" to which I replied, "Yes. What is wrong?"

Mom then relayed this story to me.

"Cynthia called me and told me that you looked like her cousin's sister, but before she called me, she called her cousin and told him. After I hung up with Cynthia, her cousin Terrace called me and asked, 'Is she my daughter?'

"I told him I don't know," she said.

After she told me all of this, Mom said, "There is a good possibility that James may not be your biological dad."

She explained more to me.

"Your dad and I were having some problems when we were dating, and we broke up. While we were apart, I moved to Detroit for a little while. When I was there, I met a man named Terrace, and there is a possibility that he could be your biological father. I don't know for sure, but there is a chance."

She continued, "Before we hung up, Terrace told me that his blood type was B positive."

I thought in my head, *Wow! I'm twenty-four years old, and I am just now finding out that another man could possibly be my dad.*

She then told me, "I'm going to hang up now because Terrace is getting ready to call you."

I hung the phone up, being baffled momentarily, but in my heart of hearts, I think I have always known this newfound information to be true. My grandmother, Florine Woods, on my dad's side had very strong genes. All her children look like her. My dad's genes are extremely strong as well. When I was a teenager, Dad sat Tommy, Trunae, and me down and told us that he had two other sons, Darryl and James. I met James first. He looked exactly like Dad, so there was no question about his paternity. Dad and James were both born on the same date. Both of their first names were James, and James the younger looked like a clone of my dad. I always noticed that I didn't get any of those genes. I didn't look like my dad at all, and I also didn't really favor my mother either.

When I was a young girl, I remember sitting at the kitchen table at my grandmother's house (my mom's mother). I was upset with both of my parents and said to my grandmother, "I think I must have been adopted."

I'm sure many kids think this when they are mad at their parents, so I guess I was no different. I didn't catch this then because I was young, but my grandmother deceptively said,

"I know for a fact that Jean is your mother." (Jean is my mom's middle name.)

She didn't mention my dad at all. Now that I know what I know, I am sure she knew that Daddy was not my biological father; she just chose not to say anything. My grandmother also told me about the Thomas birthmark. My grandmother, my mom, and I all have a birthmark in the same location on our bodies. I knew that I had a birthmark, but I did not know that the two of them also had the same mark until I had that conversation with my grandmother. She showed me hers, and that helped me to know, with assurance, that my mother gave birth to me, and that I was not adopted. I assumed that my grandmother was referring to both of my parents being my biological parents, so I never brought the topic up again.

Back to finding out about Terrace, the phone finally rang. I was so very nervous, but I took a deep breath and answered the call. It was him, the man that was possibly my biological father. I wasn't sure what to say to him, so thankfully he did most of the talking. He told me that he met my mom in Detroit and also told me that he contacted her after she gave birth to me. He said that he asked my mom if I was his child and my mom said, "Did I say she was your child?"

He said it in my mom's voice, inflection, and personality, and I said, "Yea, that sounds like something my mom would say."

He then asked, "What is your blood type?"

"B positive," I said.

"So is mine," he said. We carried on with some small chit-chat. He told me that he had three other children who are all older than me, so I am the baby of the group. He told me that my brother Anthony was nine years older, my sister Tracy was seven years older, and my second brother Terrace (Terry) was five years older than I. He gave me his phone number to keep, and then we hung up. I didn't really know what to say. The whole thing seemed awkward, and I felt a little sad because no one had ever mentioned the possibility of this altered parentage until that time; and if Cynthia had never said anything, I would still probably not know. What I did know at that moment is that I needed to find out if the dad that raised me was or was not my biological father.

I came up with a plan. I would ask my parents what their blood types were (as I didn't know my mom's) and see if mine matched either of them. I would then call the blood bank and ask for clarification as to how blood type between parents and children work. So, I put my plan into motion, calling both of my parents to ask them for their blood types. Mom was first and she said, "O positive."

She didn't even question me at all as to why I was asking. (Obviously!) When I called Dad and asked him, he said, "Why do you want to know?"

I wasn't ready to tell him what I found out. I figured that I should get some more information first and then have a conversation later with him, so I told him that I was working on a project about blood-typing. He said, "A positive."

I thought to myself, *Hmmm … mine does not match either. Let me call the blood bank.*

I called the blood bank, and a woman answered the phone. I then asked her this question.

"Can parents with O+ and A+ blood have a child with B+ blood?" She then asked me, just as my dad did, "Why do you want to know?"

I gave her the same answer that I gave my dad.

"I am a Ball State student, and I am doing a project on blood-typing." She then said, "No. The child would have to have either O+ or A+ blood."

At the moment those words came out of her mouth, reality set in. I now knew for certainty that James T. Bryant was not my biological father. I felt a sense of sadness come over me, but this was now my new reality, so I needed to figure out what to do with this information.

I called my mom and told her what I found out, and in a remorseful tone, she said, "Oh shoot! I'm sorry, baby."

We talked for a little bit, and then I told her I was going to call Daddy and talk to him about this news, to which she said, "Uh oh!"

We both laughed because we knew it was going to be an uncomfortable conversation for me and then hung up. I dialed Daddy's number, and he picked up the phone right away. We chatted for a little bit until the time came that I needed to tell him. I did a big exhale and said, "Dad, do you remember when I called you and asked you about your blood type?"

He said, "Yes."

I proceeded to tell him that I found out he might not be my biological father, and I needed to know for sure if it was true or not. He asked, "What did you find out?" so I told him.

"You have A+ blood. Mom has O+ blood. I called the blood bank, and they told me that the child of parents with those two blood types would either have to have A+ or O+ blood. I have B+." He was quiet for a moment, and then he said, "I'm glad that it is finally out in the open."

His response was completely shocking to me. He continued, "I have always known, but I didn't feel that it was my place to say anything. I am just glad that everything is out in the open now."

I couldn't be mad at my dad for this news because I learned something really important about his integrity that day. Both of my parents had some issues with infidelity, which had something to do with why they married twice and divorced twice. However, Dad knew from the very beginning that I was not his child, but he chose to raise me as his own anyway. His name is on my birth certificate, and he always treated me like I was his biological child. Dad did not use whatever happened between him and my mom as an excuse to get away from being my dad. He treated me like his daughter, and, in his own way, he loved me. I will always love and respect him for that.

The other thing that I respected him for was his encouragement of me seeking out Terrace, my biological dad, and getting to know him. He asked me about Terrace on a regular basis. Even right before my dad got sick and passed away in May of 2021, he asked me how my dad was, and I said to him, "You are the man that raised me, and you are the only dad that I have ever known. Terrace may be my biological father, but you are my dad."

It seems that Dad must have thought in some way that I would abandon him as my dad and go running after Terrace. I definitely had a need to see who Terrace was, and I wanted a relationship with him, but it wasn't to do a dad swap. I already had a dad, and his name was James T. Bryant. I think this conversation cleared up any and all doubt that Daddy may have had about my love and respect for him, as well as his role in my life as my dad. He was my dad and would always have that role in my life.

* * *

From the moment that I found out Terrace was probably my father, I wanted to meet him. We talked on the phone periodically, but it wasn't until several years later that I finally got to meet him in person. One summer, I was going to be up in Indiana, so I arranged to drive up to Detroit to meet him in person. Terrace found a hotel that was close to him and in a safe area for us to meet, and I got everything organized and made the plans. I set out on my adventure and drove all the way from Florida to Indiana and then on to Detroit. The hotel that he selected was nice, and it had a big pool, which I was going to utilize. I called him when I got to the hotel, and he came to meet me.

Terrance knocked on the door, and I opened it. Of course, the first thing that I looked at was his facial features. I wanted to know if I looked like him, and I was a little letdown because I didn't think I looked like him at all. I guess I set myself up for that letdown because in my mind's eye, I had supposed that since I didn't have any major likenesses to anyone on my mom's side of the family, I had to look like him. Nope! It was not what I expected. We talked a little bit, and then he apologized to me because he felt bad that he could not take me to his house. He wanted me to stay there, but his wife wanted no part of it, which I guess I could understand her feelings. All three of Terrace's children were from his previous wife, and his second wife had just found out that he had a child with another woman before they got married, and she probably did not want to deal with "baby mama drama"!

She may have even thought that I was after his money, but what she didn't know is that I am not that kind of person. I am very independent and can take care of myself. I didn't want anything from him but just wanted to know who my father was and what he looked like. When he expressed his sadness for not being able to bring me to his house, I told him that I was not upset at all. I reassured him by saying, "I am not here to see her. I am here to see you. I am not offended at all."

"Thank you," he said with some relief.

I would have loved to meet his wife, but she had no interest in meeting me, and I was not going to force myself on anyone. I didn't want to be the cause of a rift between the two of them, so I just focused on the real reason why I was there, and that was to meet my father. On a side note, we didn't really know each other, so he didn't know that I loved my independence and would have stayed in a hotel regardless of the situation.

After we talked a bit, he took me over to meet some of his family members. I met my aunt Sam and my grandmother and some other cousins. They all treated me with kindness, like I was a member of the family. Terrace took me back to the hotel, and later that evening, my brother Anthony came to visit me while Terrace was there. He was tall and funny with a great personality, and he called me "sis" when he came over. After he left, my other brother Terry came to visit me, along with his two kids. We went to the pool and swam; I had a great time with them. Terry had no problem accepting me as his sister, and even though we had no concrete proof that Terrace was my dad, he just accepted me right away. Because of that, I loved him from the first moment we met.

I stayed in Detroit for two nights, and on check-out day at the hotel, Terrace came to the room, and we talked a little more. Then he walked me up to the reception desk. When we got up there, he told me that he was going to pay for my room. I assured him that I had money, and I could pay for my own room, but he insisted on paying for it. So, I agreed to allow him to pay, but I was able to get him a discount because there was a problem with the beds in the room. The hotel had put the wrong size frames on the beds, so the mattresses were about three inches shorter than the metal frames. When Terry was visiting me with his kids, he did not notice the overhang of the frames and ran his shinbone smack into one of the bed frames, which put a big gouge in his leg. The sound of his leg hitting that metal was so disturbing. I could see the distress on his face, but he took it like a champ.

When they were leaving that day, we went up to the front desk to complain. He showed them his leg, and they gave me a 50% discount on the room. So, Terrace reaped the benefits of that discount when he paid for my room. It was at the expense of his son's leg, but it was a sizable discount, nonetheless.

Terrace told me to follow him across the street to the gas station, and he filled my car up with gas. I resisted allowing him to pay for my gas as well because I didn't want him to think that I was out for his money. I wanted him to know that I could take care of myself, but when I thought about it, I realized that this was not about my pride. He was never able to provide for me as a child, so this was his opportunity to do what he could to take care of me now. It appeared that he was trying to step into the fatherly role that he was not allowed to do earlier in my life, so I relinquished my independence and allowed him to do so for this time.

* * *

I found out about Terrace in 1992 when I was twenty-four years old. For many years, we had assumed that he was probably my father, but we never had any DNA testing done. When ancestry DNA by Ancestry.com came out, my sister Alberta asked me to take the test. She and my mom had done it, and she wanted me to do it too. I agreed to take the test, so Alberta had a test mailed to me. I took it in 2019 and several months later, I got my results back. On my chart, my mom, Alberta, my aunt Hester, and two of her kids showed up. There was another link with the information for a first cousin on my paternal side. I sent her an email to find out about her, but she never replied. Over time, I started looking at some of the links that were popping on my page, and I was seeing a lot of people on my paternal side, but they were second, third, and fourth cousins. None of them had Terrace's last name of Goldsmith, and I didn't know any of them.

In November of 2022, a new first cousin on my paternal side popped up for my profile. She must have just received her results back from Ancestry because she was not on my page before. Her DNA strand had more markers than my cousins on my maternal side. She reached out to me before I even received a message from Ancestry, introducing herself and wanting to know if I was on the McConnell side of the family or the Goldsmith side. My jaw dropped. The answer that I wanted to know all these years had probably just been answered by her. I wrote her back and said:

Hello. Thanks for reaching out. My mom and dad were never married. We have assumed that Terrace Goldsmith is my biological father. We have never had DNA testing done, but we have been in contact for many years now. We have both assumed that he is my father. Do you know Terrace Goldsmith?

She responded immediately and said,

He is my uncle. My mother's brother.

She also said, *You met my mom and our grandmother when you came here to visit. I met you then too. I thought you looked familiar.*

Reading that message gave me a sense of relief and closed the chapter of uncertainty in my life. Finding out who my biological father was allowed me to breathe a sigh of relief. I didn't have to wonder anymore, and that knowledge provided me with peace.

However, learning that James T. Bryant was not my biological dad gave me mixed emotions. I felt gratitude toward him for raising me as his own because he certainly did not have to do that. He could have walked away, but because of that aspect of his integrity, he stayed, provided for me, and gave me his name. I will forever honor him for that. I will always be his, and he will always be mine. But this whole situation made me feel sad because Daddy was relieved to finally get that secret off his chest, and I was glad for him. However, I was saddened because I didn't know this big secret until I was in my twenties. My mom was not sure if Terrace was my father because there were some other potential candidates. I was an adult when I found out, so I was able to deal with the news calmly and rationally, but I didn't realize how hurtful it was to not know the true identity of my biological father until I started unpacking my past with my counselor.

We talked about my feelings a lot during my sessions, because I had a bad habit of holding my feelings in and suffering in silence. That silence led to self-destructive patterns in my life, so opening up and talking about things was an important tool that I had to learn, and my counselor gave me a platform to vent my feelings. Since I was twenty-four years old when I found out, I secretly felt like I didn't have an identity, and I allowed that thought to attach itself to my sense of self-worth for years. Finding out who my biological father was had helped me to feel a sense of belonging. I finally found out that I was a Goldsmith, but surprisingly, I still was in search of who the real Kyeni was.

Chapter 17

BAD CHOICES

My early years of college were typical and uneventful. I was clean as a cucumber and had always been an even-keeled girl. I didn't rock the boat or anything like that with others. In high school, I kept to myself and was an introvert. When I went to college, I found some amazing friends, who gave me an opportunity to explore my personality. I really didn't know who I was before that time because my identity was wrapped around trauma and depression. Besides my roommate Debra, who was my old friend from orchestra class, no one at Ball State knew me or my past. I could now just be free and put some of that craziness behind me.

When I went to Ball State as a freshman, I lived in Baker Hall. Next door to my room was a crazy girl named Susan, but she and I hit it off almost immediately. I used to go to her room and ask for chips, and she would always provide. She was from a little Southeast Indiana town called Brookville that was about forty minutes west of Cincinnati, Ohio. Because of her locale, she had, and still has, a little Southern Indiana drawl. Despite her cute drawl, to me, she was not a country girl. She could have lived in the city with no problem, as she was just cool like that.

I don't know what it was about Susan, but we latched onto each other pretty quickly. I could unashamedly be my awkward, weird self with her, and she never judged me. She just let me be me, and it was Susan who helped me come out of my shell in college. I am the unapologetically weird, quirky person that I am today partly because of her. We eventually became best of friends. I could tell her anything, as she was like a security blanket for me. She had my back, and I knew that I could always depend on her.

Some of my middle years in college brought about some weirdness, where I started trippin' big time. I turned twenty-one and started doing some drinking. I partied a little bit, but that was really not my thing. Guys typically were not interested in me except for the ones that were the worst possible candidates that I always seemed to attract: heavy drinkers, potheads, or junior pimps that would try to immediately get me into bed with them. So, for that reason, I didn't go out too much unless I went with Susan, or with my sorority sisters from Delta Sigma Theta Sorority, Inc.

During that period of time in college, I lived in a condo that had three bedrooms and two bathrooms. There were four of us living there, so I shared the master bedroom with a girl named Minna. We became good friends right away. She was a smoker, and I started asking myself, *What is the big turn-on with smoking for people?* So, I decided that I was going to try it out. I sparked a conversation with Minna about smoking and finally asked her for a cigarette; she gave me one and showed me how to smoke. I tried it out, and it didn't seem like a big deal to me. After that first try, I decided to buy my own cigarettes. I didn't know anything about cigarettes at the time, but I remembered seeing commercials about a specific brand of cigarette, so I decided to get some of those.

Our condo was right behind a liquor store, so I walked out the back of the condo and went to the liquor store. When I got inside, I went up to the counter and looked at the plethora of cigarettes. I never noticed how many different brand names and types of cigarettes there were because I never had any interest in them before. I was standing there looking at them and feeling a bit overwhelmed, so I told the guy at the cash register the brand name that I saw on TV. He then asked me questions like, "Do you want 100's, light, or menthol?"

What did all of that mean? I was totally clueless. He picked up two of the varieties, and I picked the one that looked like the one I saw in the commercial. I bought it and bought a lighter. I went back up to my condo, which was on the third floor of the building and went to my room. I opened the pack, took a cigarette out, put it in my mouth, and lit it. That was the start of my short-time smoking habit. Fast forward about two months, and I went to a voice lesson. I got through about two-thirds of my lesson before Mr. Meadows stopped me. With his kind and concerned way, he said, "I'm not sure what is happening, but there is something going on with you and your voice. Something has changed, and I can hear it in your voice. Whatever it is, you need to think about it and change it." He didn't say it, but I was sure that he knew I was smoking. He probably smelled the smoke on my clothes because I never tried to hide the smell.

He ended my lesson early and, in deep contemplation, I walked home. The next day was a Saturday. I was walking to the music building to go practice. I lit up a cigarette and continued walking. The campus was empty, so I was by myself there. When I approached my old dorm, where I used to be a resident assistant, I started crossing the street. A car approached me, slowed down, and stopped. My sorority sister Janel jumped out of the car and came up to me to say hello. She had graduated the year before and had come back to the school to visit some friends. She looked at my hand and asked, in shock, "Is that a cigarette in your hand?"

"Yes," I said.

Janel knew this was completely out of character for me, as I wasn't smoking when she was at school. You must know I respected Janel a lot. She was a very religious person and had a high level of morals and standards. For me, even though I didn't go to a specific church, I knew that there was a God, and I kept my standards fairly high to live by. Janel knew me very well, and she saw this loss of light in me, which made her sad. She made eye contact with me and said, "I don't know what has happened to you, but it must be something terrible. I cannot believe that you are smoking. I can't talk to you now because I have to go, but when I get back home to Fort Wayne, I am going to call you."

She said goodbye and left. I watched the car drive away and felt completely ashamed. She eventually called me and lovingly expressed her concern over my decision to start smoking and about my standards. I listened to her and allowed her to express her feelings, where she told me that she loved me, and we hung up. I didn't know why I started smoking, as it was a very stupid decision. What I did know was that two important people in my life had just lovingly, but firmly, chastised me over the whole smoking thing. It was fascinating to me because whenever I started to get too far off the mark, it seemed like the Lord would send someone to me, like a guardian angel, to get me back on track. Mr. Meadows and Janel were my two guardian angels at that time, and they helped me to make a course correction. When I went back to my condo, I took one last smoke and never smoked again, and never thought about it again either.

Smoking wasn't the only problem I encountered while I lived in that condo. I was over twenty-one and was in a phase of my life where temptations were placed in front of me, and I just decided to experiment with them. Because the liquor store was right behind us, Minna and I went over there frequently to get liquor, cigarettes, and snacks. I usually just got beer, but sometimes I would get hard liquor like Mad Dog 20/20. One day, I decided to go to the store and get some liquor and drink it while I was watching *The Cosby Show* and *A Different World*. I got a 40 oz. of beer and a bottle of grape Mad Dog 20/20. *The Cosby Show* started first. I drank the whole bottle of beer and started drinking the Mad Dog bottle. No one ever mentioned to me that you should never mix beer and hard liquor; that goes to show how naïve and inexperienced I was. I was just flying by the seat of my pants.

I finished the whole bottle of Mad Dog toward the beginning of *A Different World*. The next thing I know, I woke up after *A Different World* had ended and midway into the next show. I had completely passed out. All of a sudden, my stomach started to feel squishy. I jumped up and staggered down the hallway, trying to get to the bathroom that was in my bedroom. I just barely made it into the bathroom as the heaving began. Just as I reached the toilet, vomit flew out of my mouth and went all over the toilet and onto the floor. The toilet cover was down, so I couldn't quite get it all the way up before the vomit came out. I was so drunk and dizzy that I could not stand still enough to keep my mouth centered over the toilet, so vomit was falling on both sides of the toilet and floor.

I have a problem with vomit; I cannot even deal with my own. I cannot stand the smell of it, the look of it, or the texture of it. Just the sight of it can make me throw up. So, when I was done throwing up, I saw that I had thrown up all on the floor and didn't want to leave a mess for Minna. I grabbed some toilet paper and tried to wipe up as much as I could. I quickly looked at where it was on the floor, and then I turned my head away from it because I knew if I looked at it too long, I would throw up again. So, I took a quick glimpse and then reached down with the toilet paper and tried to get it up without looking at it, but it was slimy, and the feel of it set me off. I thought my stomach was empty, but it sure wasn't. The grossness of trying to get it up made me throw up again. I heaved and heaved and heaved until there was nothing else in the stomach, and then my body heaved some more. The dry heaves were the worse because they made my ribs start to hurt. It was terrible! The whole ordeal made me sweat profusely as well. I was still hung over, so I laid down on the floor and passed out again.

Minna came home and saw me laid out on the bathroom floor because I did not close the door. She did not know what happened, so she knocked on the door and said, "Hey! Are you okay?"

I sat up and looked up at her. I was still very hung over, but in a slurred speech, I was able to say, "Yes. I'm okay."

I got up and grabbed some paper towels. They were thicker than toilet paper, so I figured they would help me clean up the mess easier. I cleaned the top of the toilet seat, the underside of the toilet seat, and the top of the toilet bowl so that my roommate could use the bathroom if she wanted to. I then went into the room, jumped in the bed, and went back to sleep. The next morning, Minna woke me up and said, "Can you clean up the bathroom? There's puke everywhere."

She was leaving, so I said, "Yes. I will take care of it."

She was really nice about the whole thing, so I wanted to make sure that I cleaned it up for her. I got up and did a thorough cleaning. It was so gross, but the vomit had dried up a bit, so it was not too slimy anymore, which made it easier for me to get it up without getting sick. After that experience, I could not drink or eat anything grape-flavored for years because of Mad Dog. The grape-tasting vomit was the most nasty and disgusting thing that I could ever imagine. The thought of drinking alcohol was off-putting as well, so that slowed down my drinking. Lesson learned!

Just a few weeks after that incident, my mom called me from New York and asked me if I could go up to South Bend and check on my grandmother (Mama). Mom had just gotten off the phone with Mama, and Mama told my mom that she felt like she was fading away. This freaked my mom out, so she called me and wanted me to rent a car and go up there and check on her. It was a Saturday, so I was having difficulty securing a car, as I called almost all the car rental companies, but no one had a single car available. There was one company left, so I called them and spoke to the saleswoman, who said they were sold out, but to call back in about an hour because there was one car that someone was supposed to be returning that day. When I hung up the phone, I was silently praying that they would return the car because that was my only option left. I went ahead and started packing my things and tidying up the condo, and in the midst of all that commotion, there was a knock at the door.

Chapter 18

THE START OF A NEW LIFE

I went to the door and opened it, and on the other side of the door stood two nicely dressed young men. They had coats on, but underneath those coats, I could see, from their collars, that they had on white shirts and ties. I said hello to them, and they told me that they were missionaries from the Church of Jesus Christ of Latter-day Saints. The moment I opened that door, I knew immediately I was supposed to talk to these men. I didn't know why, but I felt strongly about it. As we stood at the door, one of the missionaries told me that they had a message they would like to share with me, but because of all the issues going on with Mama, I really couldn't talk to them at that time. So, I said, "I'm not trying to be funny, but I cannot do it today. I really would like to talk to you, but I am trying to get out of town to go and check on my grandmother. I would like to hear your message. Can we reschedule?" They kindly agreed.

We scheduled the meeting for the upcoming Tuesday, and they left. I called the car rental place, and the car came in. I rented it and went home and stayed the rest of the weekend with my grandmother. She was fine, just alone and feeling sad. Me going home gave her some company. She cooked for me, and we spent the weekend talking and catching up. When I left to go back to school, she was in much better spirits.

I didn't realize this until many, many years later, but from the moment that I left those missionaries until they returned on Tuesday, I was constantly thinking about them and was looking forward to their return. I didn't know what I was supposed to learn from them, but one thing I knew for certain was that these were two more angels that God had sent to me. I had been wandering around aimlessly for the past couple of months, making bad choices and doing things that I always said I would never do, like smoking and drinking. Both of my parents did both of those things when I was younger, and I told myself that I would never do those habits. Low and behold, I did the very things that I said I wouldn't do.

The missionaries came over on the requested Tuesday after I returned home from class, and I invited them in. Their names were Elder Johnson and Elder Andersen. Elder Andersen had just recently gotten there, a new missionary from Idaho. Elder Johnson was a spiritual powerhouse and had been on his mission longer, so he was the senior companion of the two missionaries, and he was amazing. When he opened his mouth to speak, I could feel the spiritual power behind his words, and I knew that what he was saying was true. His words spoke to my spirit.

When we got to the end of their message, we scheduled another meeting for the following week and said goodbye. I was totally locked on to what they were saying, and I was sure that they knew it too.

About forty-five minutes after they left, there was a knock at the door. It was the missionaries again, but this time, they were with a woman. I invited them in, and they introduced the woman, whose name was Mary Kaye Lyon. I invited them to sit down, and we had another lesson. We talked about the plan of salvation, why we were here on this earth, and where we had the potential to go. These were topics that I had not heard spoken in that way before, and they spoke peace to my soul. Mary Kaye was wonderful, and I could tell that she was very spiritually in tune as well. They invited me to come to Church with them on Sunday, but I told them that I did not have transportation to get there, so Mary Kaye said that she would pick me up, and I agreed to go.

Sunday came, and just as promised, Mary Kaye picked me up, but she was not alone. Her husband and four children were in the van with her. When I got in the van, they were very friendly, and the kids asked me questions, like, "Where are you from?" and "What are you studying at Ball

State?" on the way to Church. When we arrived at the Church, I followed them as we walked into the chapel. I stepped in and looked around. It was a nice, big chapel, but it was not overly ornate. It was bright and comfortable. I did notice that I was the only African American in the room.

Being the only African American wasn't entirely surprising to me. At that time, the percentage of African American students, and other people of color, on the Ball State campus was fairly low. So, more often than not, I would be the only person of color in my classes at school. This was especially true in the music building, and even more so in my particular major in the string department. I was the only Black violinist my first year. There was one African American male named Monroe who played the viola, and there was one harpist named Elena; that was it in the string department. So, when I walked into the chapel of the Church of Jesus Christ of Latter-day Saints, it was business as usual for me. However, my presence did not go unnoticed. When I walked in, people immediately came over to me and welcomed me to the Church. They were so nice and made me feel completely welcome. I loved my time there; I learned a lot, and everyone was wonderful.

Missionaries are transferred to different areas in the mission ever so often. Elder Johnson was transferred to the mission home, but Elder Andersen stayed and continued teaching in our area. Elder Lewis came and joined Elder Andersen as a companionship. I went to Mary Kaye's home for every missionary lesson after that. The Muncie Ward took me in and treated me like family. I was invited to dinner after Church on a regular basis. The Lyon family picked me up, and oftentimes, another family invited me home for dinner after Church and would take me home afterward. They always gave me leftovers to take home with me; for a poor college student, that was awesome.

I loved my new Church. I loved my new Church family, and I loved learning about the Lord and His role in my life. Learning that I was literally a daughter of God, born of royal lineage, changed the trajectory of my entire life. I learned about the Word of Wisdom, in which I needed to commit to not smoke, drink alcohol, and take drugs. The trials that I had just gone through with drinking and smoking prepared me to make a commitment to not partake of these things ever again in my lifetime, in tribute to my faith in God. That was not a hard commitment at all because the memory of how sick I got on that crazy night was front and center in my mind. I still could not drink or eat anything grape-flavored at that time, so there was no concern about missing Mad Dog.

One of the next lessons that the missionaries taught me about was baptism. I had never been baptized. Because we did not go to any church regularly when I was young, I never had the opportunity to be baptized. On top of that, I struggled with finding the right church that I wanted to join and be baptized. We went to several different churches when I was young. Whenever my mom's friends would invite her to church, we would go and visit their churches. Going to these different churches, I got the opportunity to see people being baptized. The most memorable time was when I went to Calvary Temple for Sunday school when I was about seven years old. One Sunday, our Sunday school teacher invited the entire class to go to her house for an activity right after Sunday school. There were about eight of us in the class. We carpooled with a couple of the parents, and they dropped us off at her house.

She lived on a farm and had several beautiful horses. Everyone rubbed and petted the horses, except for me; I just admired them from a distance. Other than dogs and cats, I have never been a big fan of touching animals because I have a fear of some of them. When I became a musician, I avoided touching animals around the mouth area because they could bite my fingers and ruin my music career, which would affect my livelihood.

We all changed clothes because we were playing outside and exploring the farm. When we went inside to have lunch, we all took off our shoes. I brought my sneakers with me, but they were sweaty and stinky because I often wore them without wearing socks. I didn't realize that we would have to take them off when we came inside her house, so I immediately felt a little uncomfortable. I could smell my stinky feet myself, so I knew that they would be able to smell them too. We all washed our hands and sat around the table to eat lunch. As I have learned as a teacher, kids are very candid in their speech. They do not understand what it means to be tactful, or to just keep their thoughts to themselves. If they think it, they say it. As we ate, one of the kids yelled out, "Somebody's feet stink!" and some of the other kids chimed in and said, "Yeah ... I smell it too."

I was so embarrassed because I knew the smell was coming from my feet, but I didn't say anything. Right after the comments were made, my teacher chimed in and said, "You know what we could do? We could have a ritual foot washing just like in the Bible when Jesus washed the disciples' feet."

My feet smelled so bad that my teacher wanted to have a foot washing with us. That was so humiliating, but luckily for me, the subject abruptly changed, and I was very grateful to my teacher.

One of my classmates was being baptized that day after our activity. So, we started talking about baptism. I guess the water from the foot washing segued easily into the more important washing of baptism. Our teacher told us a little bit about baptism and then asked our classmate to tell us what she felt about her upcoming baptism. She told us how excited she was to be getting baptized, but she was concerned. She had recently broken her finger and had a silver, metal splint on her finger, of which she was not supposed to get wet. She had been toiling over it for days and was really worried about it, so our teacher asked us to all bow our heads so we could say a prayer for her that everything would be okay. After the prayer, they played one game of *Twister*, but I chose not to play because of my stinky feet. I sat back away from everyone and watched the game.

After the game was over, we changed back into our Sunday clothes. The parents came and drove everyone back to church for the baptism. We all sat together as a class to support her. The pastor and everyone that was being baptized walked down the aisle from the back of the chapel to the front. They were all wearing white robes that looked like choir robes. When our classmate passed us, she waved, and we all waved back to her. When it was her turn to be baptized, she stepped down into the font. The chapel was big, so it was hard to see her from where we were sitting. However, there was a big video screen above the font so we could watch it on the screen.

The pastor said a prayer over her, and he then lowered her backward into the water. As she was going down in the water, she raised that broken finger high into the air as she was going down into the water, and all we could see was the silver splint sticking up in the air. Everyone in the chapel roared with laughter.

* * *

If I would have gotten baptized, it would have been at St. John's Missionary Baptist Church; that was the church my grandmother had been a long-time member of. However, I didn't feel that St. John's or any of the other churches that we attended were the right church for me. Now, I was attending a church that I felt completely comfortable with, and I knew that this was finally where I should be baptized. The one holdback was a fear that I needed to overcome, and it could potentially stop me from being baptized. I was embarrassed to talk about it with the missionaries and Sister Lyon, but I knew I had to tell them eventually.

My fear was completely centered around my weight. My baptism needed to be done by immersion, so that meant that whoever was going to baptize me would have to lower me into the water but also have the strength to lift me back up. I was heavy, weighing about 275 pounds at that time. All the baptisms that I had ever seen in my life had been done by immersion, so I have always been aware of the procedure. I had told myself that I had never been baptized because I could not find the right church, but that was only partly true. I was afraid that when I went down in the water, the person that was going to baptize me would not have the strength to lift me back up out of the water, and they would drop me. I would be totally humiliated and embarrassed, and I didn't want to put myself through that, so I never got baptized.

When I tried to explain the problem to the missionaries and Mary Kaye, they thought that I could not swim and was afraid of the water; that was definitely not the case. My cousin Jenny Briggins taught Tommy and I when we were kids how to swim many years earlier when we were at a family reunion. I wasn't the best swimmer in the world, but I could swim, and I knew that I would not drown. It was too weird to try and correct their understanding, so I just let them believe that story.

The day before my baptism, I really started to feel anxious about the whole thing, so I knew that I had to call on my reinforcements to help me get through this one. I called my mom, as she, as my mom and an overweight person, would understand my dilemma. I explained the problem to her, and she gave me the exact counsel that I needed. She said, "Don't you know that your body is buoyant in water? When you go down in that water, your body will just bounce right back up. Besides that, you are doing something for the Lord. He is aware of you and will not let you fall."

That was one of the most important things my mother has ever told me in my entire life. I felt that her words were inspired by the Spirit, and they helped me to relax and feel more comfortable. When I got off the phone with her, I said a prayer and asked the Lord to help me get through the baptism, and I prayed that the missionary would have the strength to lift me.

When I had the final pre-baptism meeting with the missionaries, they asked me who I wanted to baptize me, and I said, "Elder Andersen."

Elder Andersen was a farmer from Idaho. He told me that he stacked bales of hay on his farm. He looked buff and very strong; the muscles in his arms were poppin'! Elder Lewis was small, so that was a no-brainer. I picked the muscular farm boy, and he was happy to oblige. I felt comfortable with my choice and knew it would be okay.

It was May 30, 1992, the day of my baptism. I was all set to go. Sister Lyon borrowed a beautiful white dress from Sister Brown, a good friend from Church that was about my size. I used her dress for the baptism. After I was all dressed in white, I went out in the hallway and talked to Elder Andersen. He was giving me instructions on what I needed to do when I was in the font. He showed me how to hold my hands, and he told me to squat down in a sitting position and then lean back when it was time for me to go under the water. He looked at me, with all the sincerity that he could muster, and said, "I will not drop you." I knew then that he understood my concern, and he was reassuring me and letting me know that I would be fine. It was an answer to my prayer.

I invited some of my closest friends to my baptism, but the only one that showed up was my best friend, Susan. When I told her about my baptism and asked her if she would come, she immediately said, "Absolutely!" Some of my other friends tried to stop me from getting baptized. For some reason, they did not like my Church. They didn't know much about it, but it wasn't the typical African American church, so they mocked it and chose not to come. Despite their comments, I knew that I was doing the right thing for me, so I paid them no mind. Contrary to their behavior was the behavior of Susan. "Poo-Poo" is what we call each other. Neither of us remembers how that nickname got started, but to this very day, that is the name that we continue to call each other when we talk. She was Catholic and attended a completely different church than I did, but that did not matter to her one bit. She came to my baptism because she loved me and wanted to support me. I was content and happy that she showed up.

My mother was all the way in New York when I got baptized, and my other family members were anywhere from one to two hours away from me. Susan was like family to me, and she showed me that I was family to her by standing by my side on one of the most important days, at that point, in my life. I will forever be grateful to her for that act of love and kindness.

The time had finally come for my baptism, so I followed Sister Lyon around to the back entrance of the font. She was prepared for everything. She laid out towels on the floor for me to step on when I came out of the font. She opened the door and led me to the stairs that went down into the font. Elder Andersen was there waiting for me to come. When I got to the stairs, he grabbed my hand and helped me down the steps. When I got down into the font, he turned me around and positioned me, so I was facing left. He said the baptismal prayer and when he was finished, I plugged my nose with my right hand, squatted into the sitting position that he showed me, and leaned back just like he told me, and he lowered me into the water. Of course, it wouldn't be right if I didn't have a little drama. Somebody up there had a sense of humor, but I didn't think it was funny.

My right foot slipped out from under me, and I instinctively released my left arm and did a swimming stroke under the water. When I was completely submerged, Elder Andersen used his farmer boy muscles, and with the buoyancy that my mom talked about, I flew right up out of that water with no struggle at all. Just as he promised, he did not let me fall. The Lord heard my prayers and gave Elder Andersen the strength and knowledge that he needed to protect and support His daughter. My baptism was the start of a new life for me. I left all the crazy things that I was doing behind and focused on changing my life and being the best daughter of God that I could be.

Chapter 19

FEAR NOT

About a year after my baptism, I had to drop out of school again because of finances; it was 1993. I started my schooling in 1986, and this was the fourth time I dropped out. So, this time, I ended up moving to New York City with my mom, catching the evening Amtrak train out of South Bend. It would be an overnight train ride, and I would arrive in New York City around midday the following day. Traveling that distance by train was a first for me. It was comfortable and much more spacious than taking the bus. I could move around and go to a dining car, which was really nice. We made a major stop in Schenectady, New York the following morning because they needed to add some cars onto the train, since we were going into the city. Schenectady was about three hours from New York City. We had a twenty-minute layover there, so we were informed that we could get off the train and go into the station to get food, go to the restroom, and stretch our legs.

Quite a few of us chose to get off the train. I made a beeline right for the bathroom, so I could get in there before some of the other women on the train. The bathrooms on the train were nice and they were a decent size, unlike the bathrooms that you have to squish into on buses and airplanes. I was looking forward to going to a bathroom that was on firm foundation, though, not shaking me from side to side while I was trying to go.

I was one of the first ones into the restroom, and then I found some food to take back on the train with me. I noticed that it was quiet in the train station, so I started to head back to the train, even though I still had about five minutes left, and boy am I glad I did. I got down to the platform, and the train was moving. I thought they were still adding cars, but no! They were actually leaving the station, and we still had about five minutes to go before the train was supposed to leave. They didn't make any announcements or anything; they just started leaving. One of the conductors was leaning out the door, and he saw me. He yelled down to me and asked, "Are you supposed to be on this train?"

"Yes!" I said.

He called up to the driver and told him to stop the train. When it finally stopped, I had to quickly walk down toward the end of the platform. When I got there, the conductor lowered the stairs and let me back on the train. I couldn't believe it. I was almost left in Schenectady, New York, and all my stuff, including my violin, was on the train. That was an important lesson learned. I made that same trip a couple of years later, but I chose not to get off the train that time. That was some scary business because I was all alone, and if I had been left there, I would have been completely lost as to what to do. We did not have cell phones back then like we do now, and I did not have a lot of money on me to stay anywhere or pay for another ticket to New York City, that was for sure. On top of that, I would have had to wait until the next day because that was when the next Amtrak train heading into New York City was scheduled.

Mom, Alberta, and Corey picked me up at Penn Station in Manhattan. It was huge and looked like there were a gazillion people in there. Seeing my family standing there waiting for me was heartwarming. I was so excited to see them. We embraced each other, and they helped me grab my things. I didn't have a lot of stuff because I shipped everything that I couldn't carry to them already. We started heading out of the train station and made our way to the subway system that would get us to the "A" train. The movies that I loved to watch came alive for me on these trains. I had seen many movies that had scenes from the NYC subway, and I was now living in my own scene. However, the one thing that the movies didn't express was the extreme smell of urine in the station. The urine smell was so strong and foul, and I had never smelled anything like it. The smell in Chicago was bad too, but

NYC was twice as bad as Chicago. This was a bit of a culture shock.

We finally caught our train, and Mom taught me my first lesson about New York life. Before we sat down, she said, "Always check the seat before you sit down to make sure that it is not wet." Duly noted!

We arrived home in the late afternoon, and I unpacked. They had set me up to share a room with Alberta. We were back together again, just like old times at our home on Johnson Street. After I was all settled in, I grabbed a phonebook and looked for the closest Church of Jesus Christ of Latter-day Saints, as I wanted to go to Church the next morning. Mom said that she would not allow me to go on my own because I was new to New York, so she said that she would go with me. I was glad that she came with me, but little did she know I was planning on taking my first outing alone on Monday while she was at work. It was part of my plan of not being afraid of the city. My first trip was to an African American museum in Harlem. I got myself there, and I got myself back. Mom about had a heart attack, but I did it and was okay.

I quickly learned how to get around the city by train or bus, and I got a job working in a nursing home doing recreational therapy. Everything was going great in my life. My spiritual life was great, and my family life was great. I was happier than I had been in a long time, but it always seems like when the adversary sees you happy and things are going well for you, he tries to put a monkey wrench in your whole program. I was on a spiritual high and was firm in my faith, so he sent a low flyer to try and knock me off my horse.

One morning, my mom came to me and told me that Auggy had called. We weren't home, so he left a message on the answering machine. He informed her that he was coming to New York the next day and wanted to stay with us for a couple of days. My mom was now aware of his inappropriate behavior toward me as a child, even though I didn't tell her about it until I was twenty-two years old. I had to write an autobiography in my micro-counseling class at Ball State, and I talked about the situation with Auggy in my paper. I didn't think that the teacher would read all those papers, and I don't know if he did, but he read mine. At the end of a class, he asked me to stay behind. I knew at that point that he had read my paper. He asked, "Do your parents know what happened to you?"

"No. They don't," I replied.

He was the second adult, after Mr. Weintrob, that I told my secret to. He encouraged me to tell my parents about it. Even at that point, I was still hesitant to tell them because I didn't know how they would respond. So, he said, "If you do not feel comfortable telling them verbally, you can send them a copy of this paper and let them read it on their own."

"Thank you. That is a good idea. I will definitely think about it," I replied.

After some pondering, I took his counsel and sent each parent a copy of the paper. I called them both ahead of time and let them know that I was sending them something in the mail and that I needed them to read it. Daddy was the first one to reach out to me. He wanted to know what happened and how it happened. I was not specific in the paper but just mentioned the incident without very many details. Daddy didn't necessarily want to know the details about what happened. He just wanted to know when it occurred, how long it occurred, and why I didn't tell them. He was more concerned about my mental state than anything else. Mom contacted me a few days after that, and her response was totally different. She completely went into "woe is me" and guilt mode. She kept saying that she was a terrible mother, which made me feel like I needed to flip the switch and comfort her. Because of her response, I couldn't really discuss any major details with her at that time. Over time, she would periodically ask me questions, and I would respond to her questions.

When Auggy left the message, Mom immediately came to me and wanted to know how I felt about him coming to visit. I was in a different place emotionally than I was as a little girl, so I told her that I was fine and was okay with him visiting. I told her that when I got baptized, I forgave him and symbolically washed my feelings of anger toward him away. However, she had not quite forgiven him and was still angry with him for what he did.

She had not seen him for quite a while, so she was never able to confront him about what happened. Mom wanted to confront him when he came, but I asked her not to because I just didn't see the point in it. He had some emotional and mental issues going on with him now, so I didn't think that confrontation would solve anything.

Mom, Alberta, and Corey were going to be leaving to go to our family reunion in another state. I could not go because I had to work, so that was also another reason why Mom wanted to know how I felt and if I wanted her to turn him away. He was going to come for a couple of days, leave for a few days, and then come back and stay for another night after Mom and my siblings had already gone. This was a concern to her because I would be home alone with him for at least one night. I was an adult, so I was not concerned about him inappropriately touching me at this stage of my life. I told her not to worry and that I would be fine, so she contacted him and told him that he could come.

Auggy arrived the next day as promised. He was traveling with some friends, and they dropped him off at our house. He was not aware that Mom knew about his transgression, and just as I asked, she did not bring it up. We all greeted him and spent some time chatting and catching up. He was pleasant and told us that he was going to the mountains in a couple of days to go and see a guru that he was following. It was a woman leader who he was seeking to gain knowledge from. He and his friends were all going to see her, but they decided to stay a couple of days in the city before they went up to the mountains. They all had people that they knew in the city, so they split up and stayed with their friends and families.

As Auggy and I were catching up, Auggy was sitting on the loveseat directly across the room from me. As we were talking, he stopped, mid-sentence, closed his eyes, and said, "I hear you ... yes, I hear you."

My eyebrows immediately went up, and my eyes got big because that, right there, was pretty spooky. I didn't say anything because I didn't want to be disrespectful, but this was confusing. When he opened his eyes, he looked at me and told me that he was communicating telepathically with his guru. My immediate thought was, *Okay???* It was strange to say the least, and I felt a little awkward. He had been a little different for many years and appeared to have some kind of psychological problem, but I did not know what the situation was. So, seeing this "telepathic" conversation happen in front of me was weird to say the least, but not really surprising with Auggy's past behavior.

We ate dinner and when it was finished, he went back to the living room. He pulled out some books, which were sitting on the coffee table. I came in and sat down to talk to him. I noticed the books, and I asked him about them. I liked to read at that time, so I grabbed the book that was on the top of the pile. I opened the book, and on the first page, there was a depiction of a bunch of circles and lines connected in a diamond-like shape. There was a distinct circle in the middle and one at the very top of the image. He started to explain to me that the center circle represented Jesus Christ, and the circle at the top represented God the Father. He then began to tell me something a little shocking, saying the circle at the top represented God, but there was a way to gain more power and knowledge than God; and that was what he was seeking after. My thought was, *Oh my! That's deep!* Just shortly after he said that, Alberta came into the room and sat down next to me. Her evil detection and deception radar must have lit up. She asked me what I was reading, and I started to explain what he was telling me. I then heard her say, in a very quiet, rapid pace that only I could hear, "Put that book down!"

I tried to continue telling her what he said, and she grabbed onto my lower arm, leaned over, turned her head in front of my face, and made direct eye contact with me to say forcefully, but in a hushed tone, "Kyeni! Put ... That ... Book ... Down!!"

When she said that, I immediately felt the urgency to get that book out of my hand. She had not heard what Auggy told me about the chart, but she felt the loss of the Spirit in the room. After that interchange, she got up and left the room, but I stayed and talked to him a little bit longer. He told me that the next day, he wanted to go into Brooklyn and go to a couple of occult bookstores. He asked me if I would help him get there, but I told him I didn't want to go to an occult bookstore. He got a little aggravated with me and said, "Fine! I'll find it myself!"

I should have let him go alone because all he needed to do was call the transit authority, and they would tell him the most efficient way to get there either by train, bus, or walking. However, I started to feel guilty. Yep, that is my typical response. I always did things for others, even if it was not good for me. I thought about it for a minute, and I knew that he might have trouble finding it, since he didn't know anything about the city, so I rationalized and told myself that I didn't have to go into the stores. I could just show him where they were and wait for him outside. With that in mind, I agreed to help him find the two bookstores. I didn't realize at that moment that it was a really bad decision to go. I should have taken Alberta's signal and walked away from him and his suggestion. I think in my mind I was trying to show him that I had forgiven him, but what I didn't understand was that forgiveness did not mean that I should put myself in harm's way again. The "I hear you" conversation should have been enough witness for me to stay clear of him.

The next morning, I got the addresses to the stores. I called the transportation authority to help me figure out the general directions, and which form of transportation would be best to get us as close as possible to the stores. We left and walked down to the train station and took the connecting trains to get to the two bookstores. They were both in Brooklyn, and one was right around the corner from the other. We got to the first store, and he went in. I was supposed to stay outside, but for some reason, I followed him into the store. There were gifts and trinkets in the front third of the store, while books were the rest of the way back. It looked typical of a bookstore. However, I decided to stay at the front of the store and not go into the body of the store. I watched where he went and waited patiently. He was taking a long time, so I finally walked back to where he was. Once I found him, Auggy said that he was debating about buying a particular book.

While I was waiting for him to decide, I looked at the title of the section of books that he was looking in and noticed we were standing in the alchemy and witchcraft section. *Yikes!* When I saw that, I immediately turned around and walked back to the front of the store. At that point, I started to look around at what was in the front of the store and saw symbols and trinkets that made me feel spiritually uncomfortable. I was ready to go, so I went outside and waited for him. I should have taken my own advice and did that from the very beginning. He finally came outside and decided not to buy the book, but he was ready to go to the next store.

We started walking toward the end of the block. He had a Walkman (a portable CD player) in his right hand. He put the headphones on, and we began to walk. We were not talking while we were walking. He was listening to music, and I was leading him to where he needed to go. There aren't very many trees on the streets of New York City, but this particular street had one tree planted about every quarter of the block. As we were walking, he was swinging his right arm, the arm carrying the Walkman. The next thing you know, his arm swung and hit the tree. I'm not sure how he did that because it didn't seem like his arm was close enough to the tree's trunk to hit it, but somehow, he did. The impact knocked the Walkman out of his hand, and it fell to the ground. I stopped and looked back at him, and the eeriest thing started to happen.

He was standing perfectly still, with the exception of his head. His head looked down at the Walkman, and then up at the tree, and back down at the Walkman and back up at the tree. He kept doing that all the while his Walkman was lying on the ground, with the batteries strewn across the sidewalk. I was standing slightly ahead of him and was watching this whole thing transpire. It was some spooky business, so I finally said, "What is wrong?"

He said, "I think I was supposed to buy that book."

I didn't say anything further. I just waited for him to decide what he was going to do. People were passing him on the sidewalk, and I am sure they were probably thinking the same thing that I was. "This guy is crazy!"

He finally picked up the Walkman and put the batteries back in, and we walked around the corner to the next bookstore. I waited outside this time, but he did not stay in there long. Auggy came back out and said that we needed to go back to the other bookstore so he could buy that book. I never got a clear look at the book he was referring to, but I didn't want to know. I just know what section the book was in, and that was off-limits for me, so I had no desire to know anything more about it.

The next morning, Mom, Alberta, and Corey left to go to our annual family reunion. They left first, and Auggy's friends picked him up a couple of hours later. He was gone for a couple of days, and he came back and stayed overnight before he would leave to go home. He slept in my mom's room this time instead of sleeping on the couch. Auggy told me that he had a good experience up in the mountains, but looking at his facial expressions, it appeared to me that he didn't learn as much from his guru as he expected. I think he was slightly disappointed. He left the next day and headed back to the Midwest. It was kind of a relief because of the occultic things he was into; his whole presence made me feel very uncomfortable.

As I was getting ready for bed, I made sure the door was locked and turned off all the lights. I went into my room and got into bed. As I was laying there, the scariest feeling that I have ever had in my entire life came over me. It was like the hair all over my body stood up. I started to get really scared, and then I became terrified. I felt the presence of something evil in my room, and it absolutely paralyzed me with fear. I knew the Bible mentioned that the third of the hosts of heaven had fallen to the earth when they rebelled against God. I believed that to be true, but I did not understand its real truthfulness until that very moment. I didn't know how many were there, but I just knew that there was a presence in the room that had no light in it. I also knew that Auggy brought that presence with him, and it lingered after he left.

I didn't know what to do because I couldn't see it, but I could feel it, and it was close to my bed. I covered my head with my blanket and started breathing heavily and fast. The air felt thick like pea soup, and my diaphragm expanded and contracted at a rapid pace as the air traveled in and out of my lungs. I was so scared, and I didn't know what to do. Suddenly, a moment of clarity came over me, and the thought of prayer came into my mind.

In Joseph Smith's history, he talked about being overcome by a presence when he went into the woods to pray to Heavenly Father for the first time. So, I decided to pray and ask the Lord for help and protection. I was still a fairly new member of the Church, but I had faith that if I prayed to the Lord, He would help me. I uncovered myself, slid off the side of my bed, and onto the floor. I kneeled and turned my back to the room, then lowered my head and began to pray the most fervent prayer that I had ever given in my entire life. I told the Lord how afraid I was, and I asked Him to protect me and to dispel the evil presence that was in my room and in our house. I stayed down on my knees and prayed for quite a while, and I continued to pray until I had poured my whole heart out.

When I was finished, I got back up into the bed, and I turned my back to the room. I reminded myself that, "faith without works is dead" (Jas. 2:26, KJV). I kept repeating this verse in my mind because it meant I needed to trust that the Lord would take care of me and protect me throughout the night. I laid my head down, but I did not cover it with the blanket this time. I just closed my eyes and kept saying a prayer in my heart, and I went to sleep peacefully.

When I woke up the next morning, my room and the house were clear of whatever presence was there. I felt calm and at peace, and I learned a lot that night. The first thing I learned was that fear is not of God. Fear can weaken us emotionally, physically, and spiritually. I experienced all three of those feelings the previous night, but when I called upon the name of the Lord, it gave me the strength to overcome that fear. I gained a testimony that we are not the only beings on this earth. This earth is occupied by a bunch of unseen others that are attracted to darkness and do not have our best interests in mind.

I learned firsthand that light and darkness cannot occupy the same space at the same time. So, I needed to invite the light into my room in order to dispel the darkness, and when I did that, the darkness had to flee. It is just like going into a dark room and flipping the light switch on. When the light illuminates, the darkness disappears. Most of all, I learned, once again, how much the Lord loved me. He was there for me and protected me in my time of need. He knew what I needed, and He provided for me when I utilized my faith to call upon His name.

* * *

I knew what kind of person Auggy was before he came to the house; I didn't want there to be any conflict between he and my mom. However, I wasn't looking out for my best interest at all, and that has always been a problem for me. I always looked after everyone else before I looked out for myself. This is one of the traits that the counselor was pulling out of me, as an adult, during our sessions. She kept reminding me that I was putting all my energy into making things okay for other people, but then she kept asking me:

"When are you going to start looking out for Kyeni?" and

"Why is Kyeni the last person on your to-do list?"

Those were very good questions that I didn't have an answer to at that time, but I knew that in order for me to move forward in my life, I would need to address them.

Chapter 20

HELLO NEIGHBOR

One day, while still in New York, I was walking back from the train station with Mom and Alberta. When we got close to the house, there was a nice-looking man outside standing next door to our house. As we approached him, he said, "Hello neighbors."

He had a cute, little accent, so I smiled at him and said, "Hello."

When we got into the house and closed the door, Alberta told me that she did not particularly like him. Everybody has their opinions about people, but this was Alberta that we are talking about. I should have listened to what she was saying, as she told me several times that she did not trust him. Alberta has a radar for things like this, and I certainly did not, being naïve and very gullible. Michael was this man's name, and he would speak to me with his cute Trinidadian accent every time I saw him outside.

One day, I was sitting by the front window of our house, looking outside and watching people. Michael pulled up in his car and got out. He looked up and saw me sitting at the window and waved at me. This had been our interaction for the past couple of weeks. He would come home, look up, and wave. I knew what time he generally got home, so I made sure I was at the window. Eventually, I started going downstairs and sitting on the stoop, and he would come up and talk to me. We started to become good friends, though Alberta continued to tell me that she did not trust him. She told me that before I came to New York, he tried to hit on her, and I guess he tried to hit on Mom too. I completely disregarded what she was telling me because I finally had a decent-looking man that seemed to be interested in me. All the other guys that tried to hit on me in college were overtly scummy guys.

I could see their wandering eyes coming from a mile away. They had one thing in mind, and one thing only, and they didn't care who they got it from. I always stayed clear of them, but I finally wanted to be in a relationship with someone. I wanted to be loved, and I wanted someone to care about me.

Michael was so nice to me during this time, so I thought that maybe he was the one. Because of my lack of self-worth and self-esteem, I threw caution to the wind and dove into his deceptive cesspool headfirst. When it came to Michael, I chose to use my own wisdom and not wait on the Lord to guide me. Of all the lessons that I have learned or needed to learn in my life, this was one of the most important ones. I needed to learn not to put my complete trust and faith in man because they do not always have your best interest in mind. I needed to trust in and wait on the Lord, because He will never lead me astray.

The niceties continued between us, and then we exchanged phone numbers. We pretty much talked every day after that. Around the same time, I then decided to go back to school and try to finish my degree, so I made the move and went back to Ball State. When I got to Ball State, there was a problem with my financial aid, and the amount that I was going to receive was not enough to cover my costs, which meant I could not take classes. So, I decided to stay in Muncie and get a job. I was able to get two jobs, working four ten-hour days on and then the next four days off at a big-box store, and on the four days that I had off at the big-box store, I worked at an ice cream shop. I worked between sixty to seventy hours per week.

I didn't have a car, so I had to take the bus when I needed to go to the big-box store. I worked from 11 p.m. to 9:30 a.m., four days in a row at the store. Muncie was a small town, so the bus lines stopped running at 10 p.m. The last bus to the store got me there around 9:30 p.m., so I had to wait an hour and a half before my shift started. However, the time wasn't wasted because that was the time when I talked to Michael. I called him from the payphone in the front of the store, and we talked until it was time for me to go to work. He was so sweet, and I loved talking to him.

At the end of the school year, I decided that it didn't make sense to continue staying in Muncie and working so hard to cover my rent and other expenses, and still not be able to go to school, so I decided to move back to New York with Mom until I could raise enough money for tuition. When I finally got back home, Michael and I picked up our relationship right where we left off. He finally asked me if I wanted to go out on a date with him. Other than Marc, I had not been out on a serious date before, and I had never been on a date with an adult man before, so this was an exciting step for me. I was so blinded by the thought that someone liked me that I could not see what was really going on with Michael.

The day of the date came, and Michael took me to a steakhouse for dinner, and then we went to a movie afterward. We had a good time, and when we got back to the house, he asked, "Would you like to come up to my apartment and hang out for a bit?"

"Sure," I said.

However, I knew better. I was a member of the Church, so I knew that I should avoid things that could be temptations, but I completely threw caution to the wind. He was not a religious person. He was raised in a major religion and went to church when he was young, but when he got older, he quit going. Our standards were completely different, but I was falling in love with him. He had been a complete gentleman all this time we were talking, so I was not concerned about him at all.

We went into his apartment and watched TV. He sat right next to me on the couch, and it got cozy. Actually, it was a little too cozy. It got to a point where it was not good, and it started to become inappropriate. I didn't feel comfortable, so I told him to stop. He didn't, and the next thing I know, he had taken from me that which was precious and sacred. It happened so fast that I was caught completely off guard. He knew exactly what to do, and it appeared that he had probably done that to someone else before. I couldn't believe it. My heart ached, and my countenance fell.

When I joined the Church, I made a promise to save myself for my husband,

and that promise had now been taken from me. I immediately blamed myself for what had happened because if I had not made the decision to go up there, that would not have happened. I was relaying this story to my counselor, and immediately when I blamed myself, my counselor said,

"Uh, uh, uh … You do not get to do that! Did you tell him no?"

"Yes, I did, but…" She stopped me again in mid-sentence and said, "No means no! He should have stopped when you told him to."

With the EAP, they provide ten counseling appointments. I was on appointment #9 out of ten sessions when this memory surfaced, and it set me back emotionally. This was a painful memory I had buried very deep inside of me. I had no recollection of it at all until I started to re-visit my memories. There was so much guilt and shame surrounding this particular incident that I was not able to function properly at all. I ended up having to contact the EAP to request some more sessions with my counselor. Because this issue was different than the original Cassie incident, they granted me another ten sessions to deal with this new revelation. This may have been the big one that really needed to be dealt with, because it brought me to a complete standstill in my healing. Some of the other things that I went through could have caused PTSD, but this one right here was definitely a source of great mental anguish for me. It took me a little while to deal with the guilt and shame of this memory with Michael.

The counselor asked me what happened after the incident. I am sure that she was probably hoping I had called the police and all of that, but of course I didn't. I left his apartment and went home. When I got into my room, Alberta was in bed but was still awake. I showered and got into my bed, and we started talking in the dark. She asked me about the date, and I proceeded to tell her everything that happened. Then I started crying, as I revealed to her the tragedy of what had just happened and what Michael did to me. She could have easily said, "I told you so," but that is not her way.

Instead, she said, "I am so sorry, Kyeni."

I told her it was my fault and took complete blame for the incident.

Because I felt like it was my fault, I never reported it. I just let it go and tried to go on with my life. However, I didn't realize how emotionally injured I was by this incident and how my sense of self-worth was completely depleted by it.

A couple of days later, Michael called. I went back to his apartment, and we talked about what happened. He apologized for what he did and said that he realized that it went too far, and that it probably was not what I wanted. Crazy me accepted his apology and just tried to let it go, and we continued on with our relationship. Shortly thereafter, he told me that he needed to get married so he could stay in the United States, as he was from another country. He asked me to marry him so we could stay together, but if I decided not to marry him, we would have to split up so he could focus on marrying someone else. He told me that he had a great relationship with me, so he wanted to marry me. So, I thought about it for a few days and decided that since he had already taken a part of me, I might as well go ahead and marry him.

In my eyes, I saw myself as worthless. He said that he wanted to be with me, so what else do I have to lose? I did not know it then, but the answer to that question was *A lot!*

We started making plans. I wanted to get married in my Church, but he didn't want to because he didn't want to wait for all the pomp and circumstance. He said that he wanted to get it done faster, so we should go down to the courthouse and get married there, and then later, I could have the wedding that I wanted, and he would start going to Church with me. That made me happy, so I agreed to his suggestions, and we made all the plans.

The night before the ceremony, we were sitting on the stairway in my house, talking about what we were going to be doing the next day. Our plan was to go to the courthouse first thing in the morning. After that, we would go home and change clothes, and then we would take the train into Manhattan and go to the immigration office and file the paperwork to show our legal marriage. After we went through the plan, something told me, in my mind, that this was not a good idea. I am sure that it was the Spirit, but I wasn't listening. I could have stopped it right there before it went any further, but because I was in love with Michael, I figured he was the best that I could get of a husband. One moment of clarity came into my mind, and I paused and asked him this simple question.

"Why do you want to marry me?"

"Because I love you," he said.

He was good ... really good. It was a complete lie, but because I was so blinded by the fact that he said the "L" word, I told myself that he must have been telling the truth. That meant that he wanted to be with me. So, with all the proof that I needed of his love, I went down to the courthouse with him the next morning. Dad and Tommy were in Indiana, and Corey was at school, so with my mom, Alberta, his mom, and his sister with us for support, I married Michael.

As I recalled this memory, the counselor stopped me right there, chimed in, and asked the following question.

"So...because you felt worthless, you married the man that assaulted you?"

Woah...that was deep, I thought to myself.

I paused for a second because I was taken aback, as I had never thought about it from that perspective before. I then started to realize how my lack of self-worth drove the poor decisions that I was making during that period of my life. I truly think the Lord sent this counselor to me because she truly gave me some tough love, which was exactly what I needed. I was living in my own, little, weird headspace, but she kicked me out of that and forced me to look at my decisions from a different set of eyeglasses. That was what ultimately helped me to start healing. I responded to her question and said, "Well, I guess if you put it like that, yes."

She then said, "Well, isn't that what you did?"

I took a deep breath, paused again, and responded, "Yes, I did."

"Okay. Go on," she said.

I continued relaying my story. "We went down to Immigration and got the paperwork going. About a year from that date, we moved to Florida to get out of the city. Michael and his brother had built a house together in

Florida, so when we first got there, we moved in with Michael's brother to give us time to find jobs, get situated, and then get a place of our own. The first night that we arrived there, Michael was sitting in the kitchen and was on the phone. I was in the bedroom, and then I went to the bathroom that was right next to our bedroom door and right in front of the kitchen. As I was going into the bathroom, he looked a little suspect, so it seemed to me like he was doing something sketchy. I went to the bathroom, but I could hear him talking on the phone. Then, I realized what was happening: there was a woman on the other end of that phone. I could tell that he was talking to a woman because of the tone of his voice. Men do not talk to their buddies like that. I went up to the sink and turned the water on, and then I started banging things around so he wouldn't realize that I was listening to him."

"After a couple of minutes, I heard him say, 'I love you too,' and then he hung up and went into the bedroom. When I went back into the bedroom, I asked him who he was talking to, and he said, 'Jessica.' (Jessica was his sister.)

"He said it with no hesitation at all. I knew he was lying because he never talked to her before in that tone of voice. They always talked raucously and loudly, so I had no doubt that he was lying. I didn't know what to do about it, and I didn't want to rock the boat. We had just moved to Florida, so I just let it go."

The counselor chimed back in again and asked another question.

"So ... the first day that you got to Florida, you found out about his deception, and possible infidelity, and you chose to ignore it?"

A period of silence came from me again, and I finally said, "Yes. I guess you are right."

She started writing some things down on her paper and said, "Ok, continue."

She didn't need to say anything because she knew that I knew where she was going with that. As she asked me these types of questions, it made me see how naïve I was. Her questioning made me look at the fact that I contributed to my own pain in that relationship because I wasn't willing to look out for myself. That situation reminded me of the ice at Ball State that was shined up by those snow brushes. The ice was beautiful, but it was deceptive. Even though many of the students knew the ice was dangerous, they chose to walk on the ice anyway and risked their safety because they thought it was the shortest and fastest way to get to class. They threw caution to the wind and slipped, slid, and fell their way to class. Their choice of walking on the ice made their journey longer, harder, and much more dangerous than avoiding the ice altogether and walking on the snow-covered grass.

I was one of those ice-walkers in my relationship with Michael. I did all I could to keep the peace in that relationship and make him happy, all the while injuring myself trying to stay in a relationship with a man that did not love me, respect me, and was unequally yoked to me.

We eventually rented a house a few minutes away from Michael's brother, finally settled down, and started our new life together. Everything seemed to be going ok. We were both working at the time. I got a job as a recreational therapist in a large nursing home in Orlando and was able to get Michael a job in the maintenance department of that same nursing home. It was nice seeing him at work. He would talk to me and smile at me when he saw me. He was nice to everyone, and everyone loved him. Michael was so charming, and everyone at work told me how amazing my husband was, and how nice he was to the residents. For the most part, he was exactly like that at home too.

As we finally settled into life, I wanted him to make good on the promises that he made to me when we got married. I would ask him regularly if he would go to Church with me, but his response was always, "No." One Sunday morning, I asked him again if he would come with me, and he gave his usual reply of "No."

I then said, "You told me that you would go to Church with me after we got married." Shockingly, he said, "I lied!"

He said it in such a cold and callous tone of voice, not even caring how I felt about it one bit. I couldn't even provide a rebuttal to that at all because it just seemed so out of character for him during that time. So, I grabbed my things, walked out the door, and went to Church. That brief conversation was the start of the decline of my marriage. As time went by, he started going out and not coming home until late, or he would go to the payphone and make phone calls. In other words, he was creeping. One day, he said he was going to the payphone to make a call. It got really late, and I had not heard from him. I rang his beeper multiple times, but he didn't respond. Michael finally came home the next afternoon and came in like nothing had happened. I asked him where he had been all night and he said, "I went to hang out with my boys and I drank too much, so I decided to stay there and not drive home."

"Why didn't you return my phone calls?" I asked.

"I fell asleep," he responded. After that comment, I finally got the courage to question him, so I asked, "Are you having an affair?"

He said, "How could you ask me a question like that?"

Of course, he responded that way. He never really answered the question but just deflected it and turned the tables on me. He tried to make me feel like I was wrong for asking him such a question, and he tried to make me feel like I was being paranoid.

A few weeks later, he started sleeping on the floor. He had a slipped disk in his back, so he would sleep on the floor periodically when it was inflamed. He would usually go on a crash diet, drop a few pounds, and sleep on the hard floor for about two weeks. After that, he would come back up and sleep in the bed. However, this time, he had been on the floor for about a month. He was eating normal food and was not crash-dieting anymore. One evening, he was laying on the floor, and I rolled over to his side of the bed, looked down at him on the floor, and said, "It seems like your back is better. Why are you still sleeping on the floor?"

He looked at me dead in my face and said, "I don't love you like I loved my first wife."

My jaw hit the floor, and I thought to myself, *What do I do with that information?* I did the only thing I could do. I rolled back over to my side of the bed, turned my back to him, and quietly started crying. He heard my sniffles and jumped up onto the bed. He knew he had hurt my feelings badly, so he apologized and snuggled up with me.

A few days later, I came home from work, and he had completely moved out of our bedroom and put all his things in the guest bedroom. I asked him what was going on, and he said, "I need some time to work through some things, so I need some time on my own." I was completely blindsided by this change and couldn't say anything to him at all because my feelings were so hurt. I just went into my bedroom and cried.

After that, he just became brazen with his activities. He would sit on the couch and talk to woman openly on the phone while I was in the same room with him. He would come and go as he felt, not telling me anything about where he had been. So, one evening, I came home from work and saw him sitting in the living room, and I said, "When are you moving back into our bedroom?"

He looked at me and said, "I want to keep things the way they are. I don't love you, and I never did. I know I have hurt you, and it makes me feel bad. I feel guilty, so it is hard for me to stay in the same room with you."

When all of this went down, I was trying hard to be a better wife, in hopes that he would change his mind, but he said, "The more you try to be a better wife, the more you are pushing me away from you."

So, with little to no hope that things would change, and hearing his response, I finally took my needs into account. I stood up for myself and spoke my peace. I told him, "I didn't get married to have a roommate. I got married to have a husband, so if you cannot function as a husband to me, I want a divorce!"

Per usual, he responded in the same kind of nonchalant way that he was used to talking to me. He said, "Okay!"

His indifference was so sad to me; that hurt more than anything else. He was trying to protect his feelings and his needs because he couldn't stand seeing the pain that he had caused me, so it was just easier for him to go ahead and get divorced. Our marriage meant nothing to him, as he married me simply to get his immigration papers … Period! It hurt knowing that I was in love with him, but he was not in love with me and never was. What a hard lesson to learn.

I shed so many tears during this period in my life, as I was just completely heartbroken. I had never been treated with such disregard for my feelings before, and I was living in it every day. It got to a point where I just needed to get away for a few days. So, I booked a flight to Louisville, Kentucky to spend a few days with my good friends, Marsha and John Jones. I met them at Ball State many years earlier, and we immediately became best friends. My friend/sister, Jacqueline Barattiero, took me to Orlando Airport, comforting me all the way there, and Marsha and John picked me up from the airport in Louisville and took care of me for those couple of days I stayed with them. While I was there, I had no cares in the world. They encouraged me to be strong as they loved on me and tried their best to help strengthen me. I was able to let my guard down, laugh, and have fun with them; it was probably the first time I had had a good laugh in months.

When it was time to go back to Florida, I wept bitterly. My little heart was just so hurt, and the idea of going back to that environment was just too much to bear, but I knew I had to go back.

When I landed at the airport in Florida, Jaqueline's husband Paul, who I call "Papa Bear," picked me up. Paul is a straight-shooter, and he just came right out and said, "You are unequally yoked to him, and he is not worthy of you." He continued to talk to me and let me know that I was doing the right thing by dissolving my marriage. Paul could see that this relationship was slowly destroying me and told me that the way Michael was treating me was completely unacceptable. I knew he was right, but I couldn't help but blame myself for everything that I was experiencing, because I should have listened, first, to Alberta. She tried to warn me about him back in New York. Second, I should have listened to the Spirit when I was sitting on the stairs with Michael the night before the wedding. I had the chance to change the course of my life and not marry him, but because I made the decision to marry him, I tried everything I could to avoid breaking the marriage, even if it wasn't in my best interest to stay.

I took Paul's counsel, and I followed through with the divorce. As I said earlier in the book, we didn't have any children and no assets, so it was a simple and quick divorce. We had a court date scheduled about four weeks later. The day before the divorce, I asked Michael if we were making a mistake by getting the divorce. I said, "Maybe we should postpone this."

He looked at me and said, "No. I want to keep things the way they are."

I felt just awful. The idea of being single again was scary for me, but it was now my reality.

We went to the courthouse the next day and sat before the judge. She asked us, "What is the reason for this divorce?"

I did not open my mouth, so there was a moment of silence. Michael then said, "There is no love, Your Honor."

That cut like a knife into my heart, but I didn't say anything. The judge then looked at me and asked, "Is that true?"

Trying to hold back tears, I realized that I could not answer in the affirmative from my point of view because despite his cruelty, I was still in love with him. So, I turned it around in my head and looked at it from his perspective. He did not love me, so I said, "Yes, Your Honor. That is true." A tear slowly left my eye and rolled down my cheek. She finalized the divorce, and after two and a half years of marriage, we left the courtroom as single individuals. We then did the unbelievable: we went to Disney World and spent the rest of the day in the theme parks and enjoyed each other's company.

I don't even think it is necessary to mention the details of the conversation that I had with my counselor about me going to Disney with him immediately after the divorce. One would only need to use their imagination to figure that out. *Yikes!*

Chapter 21

ENOUGH IS ENOUGH

So, what possessed me to go to Disney World with him? Brain damage is my first thought. I really think I had temporarily lost my mind, but I guess that was the state of mind I was in at that time. The one thing that I wanted to make sure didn't happen between the two of us was a battle. We had never gotten into a single argument while we were married, so I didn't want to start then. Looking at divorcing couples on the news, television, or in the movies, many of those relationships turned into outright battles between the two people, and that was something I refused to let happen to us. Spiritually speaking, I didn't want that negative energy in my life. I wanted to leave the relationship with some semblance of dignity.

I'm not going to lie; it was very hard for me to deal with some of the challenges that would soon come from our marriage, but I honestly felt that I was doing what was best for both of us. I really cared about Michael, so I didn't want to do anything to jeopardize the relationship that I thought we had. Yes, as usual, I was putting my own needs aside to try and keep the peace, but I would soon learn that the two of us needed to have similar feelings if our plan was going to work for the good of us.

The next reason that I wanted to have a cordial relationship with Michael was because neither of us could afford to move out of the house, so we decided to continue living together temporarily. Did I mention brain damage? I decided to stay in Florida and save my money until December, and then I would move to Muncie, go back to Ball State, and finish my degree. That was the plan Michael and I came up with. I just needed to make it to December, but little did I know that plan was doomed from the start.

The next couple of months went by without any major occurrences. He started his new life and was openly dating. It was painful watching him prepare to go out with his women, but I tried to stay focused and endure the pain for six months until I could leave in December. The major issue that was going on was the fact that we did not set any boundaries or procedures for our new relationship, but just kept going on like normal. We shared food. We hung out and watched TV together when he was home. It was essentially the same relationship that we had right before we got divorced. Unfortunately, our set-up gave me a false sense of hope that maybe, just maybe, he would change his mind, and we would get back together again.

One day after he came home from work, he asked, "Do you want to go shopping and go out to dinner?"

"Sure," I said.

We left and went to a big-box store and did a little shopping. When we picked up everything that we needed, he led us down the check-out lane. He went down the lane first and said hello to the cashier, and then he started helping me unload the cart. I guess my female radar was on because out of the corner of my eye, I could see him look at the female cashier again, and she looked at him. My head was down so they didn't notice that I was checking them out with my peripheral vision, which was enhanced because of my music reading skills. They underestimated my abilities because I saw their whole interaction. I emptied the cart, and he paid for the groceries. The events were kind of interesting to me because his new girlfriend was bagging the groceries of his ex-wife, whom he was still living with and still buying groceries for. I always wondered how she felt about that later when they started dating.

When she finished bagging our groceries, we started walking away. I went first this time, but I turned my head slightly to the left so I could use my peripherals to see what they were doing behind my back. Sure enough, they took a nice, long look at each other. Watching them look at each other like that made me think about that whole interaction, and I wondered, *Why did he take me to that specific store, and why did he take me down that lane? There were other lanes open.* It was disrespectful to me, but even more so, it was disrespectful to her. There were multiple store options in that area. There was one that we used regularly that was close to our house, but he chose to go to that store that was thirty to forty minutes away from our house.

After we left the store, we went to a buffet down the street to have dinner. He liked to go there because he could fill his stomach up and make good use of the money that he spent. I generally only got one plate of food, and some dessert, but he ate enough for both of us, and then some. He was muscular and weighed about 230 pounds, so he had a hearty appetite. He would eat, go to the restroom and empty his bowels, and then come back and eat some more: that was his ritual every time we went there. I would just sit there and watch him get about two more plates full of food after he emptied out. I think he had a pocket hidden somewhere in his stomach.

When he finally finished, we walked outside and started heading back to the car. He took out his cell phone and called a girl and started talking all lovey-dovey to her. That just ruined the good time that we just had. *Why couldn't he have just waited until I wasn't with him?* He talked to her the whole way home, and I was fuming. He was so insensitive, and out of respect for him, I would never have done that. This was just another sign that he had no respect for me at all anymore.

* * *

I was a sales representative that sold attraction tickets at a company called "Ticket and Tours." I went to work the next day, but I was still sad about what happened the night before. I helped a few customers, and then I started to feel strange. I started feeling dizzy and short of breath. I didn't know what was going on, but I did not feel good. I belonged to an HMO for my doctor's office, so I called to see if they could work me into the schedule, but they had no availability. They gave me the phone number for the main office in Orlando, and I called them. Thank goodness they were able to squeeze me in.

When I got in the room, I started telling the doctor how I was feeling, and he decided to do an EKG to check my heart. So, I changed into the gown and waited for the nurse to come back into the exam room. I was in a sitting position on the exam table, so when the nurse returned, she lowered the table down so I would be in a flat position on my back.

When I was finally laying down, she began to attach the electrodes of the EKG to my chest and abdomen. All of a sudden, my body went crazy! I started breathing rapidly because I felt like I couldn't get any air into my lungs. I totally started to freak out. The nurse ran out of the room to get the doctor. Soon after, the doctor ran into the room and asked me what happened and what was wrong. I couldn't answer him, so they ran and called 911. The doctor put some oxygen on me, but the breathing continued to get faster and faster. I could not control it and was so scared that tears started running down my face. (Thinking about this memory reminded me of the pig-in-a-blanket debacle in school. When you can't get air in, it is terrifying.)

The paramedics finally got there, and they tried to get me to talk. I tried to, but the words wouldn't come out correctly because I couldn't breathe. They switched oxygen tanks, loaded me up on the gurney, and took me out to the ambulance. When I was in the back of the ambulance, the paramedic said, "You need to try and control your breathing. If you don't, you are going to start hyperventilating, and you don't want that. It will make everything worse."

He put an IV into my arm and started talking to me, trying to get me to talk and tell him what happened, but when I did, I started crying and choking.

"Ok come on. Stop crying now." Then I thought to myself, *Stop talking to me then!* I just turned my head away from him and ignored him.

They took me to the emergency room, and the doctors asked the paramedic what happened. He gave them my vitals and told them that they tried to get an EKG on me but were unable to get a good reading because the rapid breathing messed up the results. He then told the doctor that my problem seemed psychological, and that he thought I was having an anxiety attack. They transferred me onto the hospital bed and left. The doctor walked over to me and jokingly said, "Are you trying to set a world record for the most breaths per minute?"

I didn't think that was funny at all because I was scared to death. I was breathing so fast that it was like an uncontrollable pant. I didn't laugh at the doctor's joke and just turned my head away from him, and he left the room. A few minutes later, a nurse came into the room and put some sort of shot into a port in my IV, and then she walked up toward the door and stood there and watched me. Suddenly, my breathing started to slow down. Each breath was slower than the previous breath. Pant. pant. pant … pant …… pant ……..… pant ………..……. pant …………..………….. Out!

As my breathing slowed, I could feel my body slowly shutting down. Right as I did my last pant, my eyes started to close. I looked at the door and saw the nurse turn to exit my room, and I was knocked out. I don't know what cocktail mixture was in that shot, but it was some powerful stuff. It shut me DOWN!

However, the shot did its job, and it completely knocked me out so my brain could reset itself. The doctor ordered some tests to check my heart, lungs, and blood, and everything went back to normal. The doctor came back in and talked to me for a few minutes, finally asking,

"Do you have some major stress going on in your personal life right now?" I thought to myself, *That is an understatement.* I looked over at him and said, "Yes." However, I didn't go into any details.

He then said, "You need to get whatever is stressing you out under control because the rate at which you were breathing was very dangerous. You had an anxiety attack, and the stress is probably what sparked it."

After our conversation, he signed my release papers and allowed me to go home. However, there was one major problem. I arrived by ambulance, so my car was still at the doctor's office, and I didn't have any money to call a taxi to take me over there to get it. I was still very drugged up from the medication, so I couldn't even think straight to figure out what to do to get myself to my car. So, I sat in the waiting room lobby and slept for a couple of hours. Even then, I was still drugged up, but I came up with a plan. Michael had already left work, so I would wait until he got home, and then I would call him and ask him to come and pick me up, which he did. When I got in the car, he asked me what happened and showed concern. He dropped me off at the doctor's office to get my car, and then we drove back home in our cars.

I really should not have been driving because that medicine was very powerful. I was so sleepy and was having a hard time staying awake and staying focused on the road while driving. I wasn't on any medication, and since I joined the Church, I didn't partake of alcohol, caffeine, or anything like that. So, my body was in shock and did not know what to do with the drug that was now inside of it. When I arrived home, I went right to bed, and I think my body shut down before my head could even hit the pillow. Michael checked in on me to make sure I was okay, and I appreciated that. I stayed home from work the next day to plan my next move. I called my grandmother and told her what had happened, asking her if I could come home early and stay with her for the five months until I went back to Ball State in January 1999. She told me to get out of there as soon as possible and come home.

I contacted my friends Paul and Jacqueline and asked them if I could stay with them after I graduated in order to give me time to find a job, and without hesitation, they said, "Yes." I was truly grateful for them because my plan would not have worked if I didn't have the time that I needed to acquire a new job. It was such a blessing to have them in my life. They knew what I had gone through in my marriage, and they helped me get out of it. I am a firm believer that the Lord places certain people in our lives to help us as we work our way through our earthly sojourn.

I know that Paul and Jacqueline were placed in my life because they have been the best of friends for me, just like Alberta, Susan, and Marsha and John Jones. All six of these people have played vital roles in my life and have been a safety net for me when I was falling. And all six of them were part of my inner circle, despite their distance from me, when I was navigating this new direction in my life as well.

I was going back to familiar territory where I would be loved. So, the stress of the unknown was now removed. Preparing myself to put my two-week notice in for my job was a little more challenging because I really liked everyone that I worked with. The owners were an older British couple named Mike and Pat. Despite having lived in Florida for well over twenty years, they managed to keep their rich British accents. I loved listening to them talk because they were very cheeky and extremely candid. They took a liking to me from my very first day of my employment, and they trusted me. I made them a lot of money through selling attraction tickets and booking weddings and vacation rentals. So, when I informed them that I was leaving in two weeks, they were sad to hear that I was leaving, but they were also proud of me for going back to finish my degree. They threw me a little going-away party and even gave me a little pocket change for my trip.

Michael worked on my car for the few days leading up to my trip. He put new tires on because I would be driving in snow, and he wanted to make sure that I had good treads on the tires. He also changed the oil and replaced the thermostat because it was faulty. So, the car was ready to go. I loaded the car the night before, so all I had to do the next morning was jump in and go. I slept well, and when I woke up the next morning, I felt content. I got up and got dressed and did one final sweep of the house. I loaded my overnight bag into the car and finally my violin. Meechy was always the first thing out of the car, and the last thing in the car, when I was traveling. I then popped my magnetic CB antenna on the roof of the car, and I was ready to go.

I took one last look at the house, and then I turned and looked at Michael, as he was standing in the driveway. I thanked him for fixing my car and making sure that it was road-worthy. We said our last goodbye, gave each other a hug, and I got into my car. I sat in the car for a moment, closed my eyes, and did the first thing that I always did before I pulled away from my house when I was traveling. I folded my arms and said a prayer of thanksgiving, and asked the Lord for guidance and protection for everyone that was traveling on the road and for me on the journey that I was about to take. When I finished, I put my car into gear and drove to the end of the driveway. I took one last look in my rearview mirror and slowly pulled away. As I drove away, tears of sadness and relief streamed down my face.

I cried bitterly for the first ten minutes of my drive, but it was a cleansing cry. I didn't realize how stressed I was living in that house with Michael. It was so dark and heavy there, but now a huge weight had just been lifted off my shoulders. I could now relax and focus on the road ahead of me. The further away I drove, the more optimistic I became. The tears eventually dried up, and peace filled my heart. I couldn't wait to see my family in Indiana and was now excited about the future.

I didn't need to rush to get to Indiana, so I decided to make the drive in three days instead of one day, like I had done in the past. I found a hotel north of Chattanooga, Tennessee, where I watched TV and rested up that night. The next day, I drove to Louisville, Kentucky, and stayed overnight with Marsha and John Jones. We, of course, stayed up, talked, and laughed until late in the evening. I got up the next morning, gassed my car up, and drove the final four-and-a-half hours to home. I was so happy to see Mama, and she was happy to see me. I unloaded my car and placed everything back in my old bedroom from my senior year in high school. The familiarity of my room brought me a tremendous amount of joy and peace. Although I missed Michael, I was very happy to be away from him. Now I could fully heal and start to move on with my life.

I was home now, and because I quit my job early, I needed to quickly find a new job. A new big-box store had recently come to town a couple of years earlier, and they were hiring. I went down and applied, and they interviewed me while I was there. I had previous experience working at another big-box store as a cashier, so they hired me as a cashier right on the spot, which I was very grateful for. I needed to work hard and save a couple of thousand dollars to cover my tuition for the upcoming semester. Because I was living with my grandmother, I didn't have to pay rent, so that helped me save more.

When September came along, I applied to be a substitute teacher with the South Bend Community School Corporation. I wanted to see if I was really cut out to be a teacher, as a professor at Ball State advised me, so subbing was the perfect job to give me some teaching experience.

When I started subbing, I was able to sub for some of my old teachers. I subbed for Mr. Fisher, Mr. Keys, and my sixth-grade teacher, Mrs. Mitchum. Her class was terrible with a capital "T." The other sixth-grade teachers told me that she had some issues with the administration, so they loaded her class down with every possible problem child they could find in the sixth grade. They also had difficulty finding subs to take her class because her class had a reputation. I was new to subbing, so I didn't know about her class and signed up to take her class when she was out for three days. Those kids gave me a run for my money on the first day, but I hung in there with them and blessed them with kindness. After the first day, the kids started to be nice to me. They settled down and allowed me to work with them on their assignments.

That subbing job put the teaching itch in my heart, and I knew that I was choosing the right direction for my life. I continued to work both jobs until it was time for me to go down to Muncie and attend school. Muncie had the same big-box store there. It was also new, so my boss helped me transfer my job down there so I could continue working. My dad saw that I was working hard to save the money that I needed to finish my last semester, so he stepped in to help me. With Dad's help, a scholarship from the School of Music, and the money that I saved, I was able to finance my last semester of school. With the financial support that I received, I was able to quit my job at the big-box store in Muncie and just focus on school! That was a huge blessing because trying to balance all the classes and working until late at night was a huge source of stress for me.

After thirteen years, I finally received my Bachelor of Music degree and proudly walked across that stage in front of my family and friends. I took the long road, but I was so proud of myself for finally getting it done. I went back to Florida in June of 1999, applied for a teaching job, just like Dr. Mueller told me to earlier in the book, and was hired at Denn John Middle School in Kissimmee, Florida. I was finally able to start my life over.

* * *

That four-year period of time with Michael was probably the most difficult time of my life. Michael, as charming as he appeared to be, was another low flyer, and he almost completely destroyed me. Re-living this part of my life and walking through it with my counselor was very difficult, but it was the big thing right beneath the surface that needed to be addressed. My mind buried that one experience deep because part of the pain that I endured was because of some of the decisions I personally made. I had to walk through that topic with my counselor because it hurt so much. Allowing that memory to come forth really cut me deep, but it also enabled me to see I had lost all sense of who I was, and that I had viewed myself as nothing for a long time. That is what the adversary wanted me to believe. He didn't want me to regain the knowledge of my true identity in God because that would give me power over him.

These two chapters about Michael appeared to be focused on his transgressions, but in actuality, he was who he was, and he was that way before I chose to marry him. He showed me who he was on the night of our first date. That was his true self, but I somehow chose not to see him for who he was. I was hoping that I would be able to change him into the man I wanted him to be for me. Unfortunately, we cannot change people; they must change themselves.

Prior to meeting Michael, I was already in pain because of my past traumas and relationships, but despite that, I needed to trust God and wait on Him to lead me to the right companion. Because I was being impatient, I didn't want to wait for the Lord's time, so I used my own warped sense of judgement in choosing Michael, and that forced me to walk down a slippery slope. All the signs were there for Michael's deception. The Lord was trying to show me and tell me what I needed to do, but my eyes were shut, and my ears were closed. I made the choice to start that trial, so I had to walk through it in order to learn my lesson.

Even though it was very hard, the Lord did not abandon me during this time and placed many angels in my life in the form of my good friends. I had to lean on some of them more than others during that time, and I don't think I would have gotten through it without them. Paul and Jacqueline were probably the most actively supportive in this time, with Paul supplying me with tough love, and Jacqueline being a soft cushion for me to land on.

I made some bad decisions pertaining to my relationship with Michael, but that gave Michael no right to treat me the way he did, nor the right to take from me that which he had no right to take. When I was talking about this period of life with my counselor, I thought that I had forgiven Michael, but I realized that I hadn't. I buried the trauma and put it behind me, or so I thought. It took me a couple of years to work through that period of my life, but despite the pain, I knew that I had to forgive him. I had to release all that hurt, guilt, and pain so that I could finally move on with my life and be free.

That period of time brought me so much sadness, but it forced me to learn and grow. I have forgiven Michael, and I did that as a vehicle to allow me to forgive myself as well. I have chosen to lay the injuries of that relationship at the feet of the Savior because He has already atoned for them. Michael crossed over in October of 2013 in a tragic car accident. His brother Milton called me to notify me that Michael was critically injured and was in the hospital; he passed away a couple of days later. I felt a tremendous amount of sadness for him because it appeared that he had straightened his life out. He re-married, had a child, started going to church, and was working with his wife in a family business. His wife knew about our history. She invited me to the funeral, and I went and paid my respects to him, to her, and to their daughter. He is on the other side now, and I pray for him and the family that he left behind.

Chapter 22

THREE BEAUTIFUL ANGELS

After I had been teaching for two years after graduation, I decided that I wanted to go back to school and obtain my master's degree in music performance. I was not sure what prompted me to do that, but the idea took up shop in my mind so I started doing some research on schools that I could attend that did not require me to take an entrance exam. I hated taking those types of tests. I didn't want to go back to Ball State; I was completely done with Muncie, Indiana, and I wanted a change of pace. As I was doing my research, the University of Las Vegas (UNLV) popped up. Some friends of mine moved out there a few years earlier, and they loved it. So, I decided to investigate the program and apply.

I contacted the violin professor and introduced myself. He was very pleasant and kind. I felt like I could definitely work with him if I got in. Auditions were coming up, and this time, I was on top of things, not procrastinating like I did with Ball State. The cool thing about UNLV was that I didn't need to take a graduate entrance exam; it was not a requirement for that school. I just needed to audition on my violin. I filled out my application to audition, but it felt very strange to do so because I never had the desire to go back to school. After my long stent at Ball State, I thought I was done with school. I wasn't sure where that desire came from, but I decided to act upon that prompting anyway.

A few weeks later, I received an audition date. Now, it was real, so I had to take things seriously and worked really hard on my audition material. I needed to play two contrasting pieces, so I decided to play the first movement of "the Prokofiev Violin Sonata, No. 2 in D Major," and "the Adagio from

Sonata No. 1 for Solo Violin" by J.S. Bach. I had been out of school for a while and wasn't working on any violin literature, so I was out of practice big time. I was only playing simple things to demonstrate technique to my private students, occasional performances at Church, and the periodic wedding gig. So, when I started working on the Bach piece, my hands were like, *What are you doing?* Building up my stamina after going for so long without practicing music at my level was exhausting. My muscles would tighten up, and my triceps became fatigued after about ten minutes of practicing. Each piece was about three minutes of strenuous, nonstop playing, so I needed to really push myself because the audition was only a few weeks away.

When the audition day arrived, I flew out to Las Vegas. I rented a car and drove to David and Heather Lusvardi's house, some friends of mine. They used to live in Florida but moved to Las Vegas a couple of years earlier. They let me stay with them, so that saved me a lot of money on hotel expenses, and it was great catching up with them. They had a baby since they left, so it was fun seeing them as parents. The following day, I drove through Las Vegas and went to the campus for my audition. It was a nice-size campus, and when I arrived at the music building, they had escorts waiting for those that were auditioning. They walked us to a holding area where we could unpack and warm up.

My turn came, and I was escorted to a music studio. There were two professors sitting in the room waiting for me. I told them a little bit about myself, and then I started playing my audition music. Considering the fact that I was out of practice, I played well, and I was pleased with my performance. The violin professor complimented me on my audition, so I felt good about it.

I flew back home because I needed to go back to work on Monday. A couple of weeks later, I received an email congratulating me on my audition, and I was awarded a full graduate assistantship. My tuition would be covered, and I would be getting a stipend. The assistantship required that I play in the orchestra, teach lessons to some of the incoming violin students, and teach some ear training classes. I definitely would be a lot nicer than the teacher that I ran into at Ball State, who was insensitive to my speech impairment as you recall.

I resigned at the end of the school year in Florida; that was very difficult because I loved the staff at Denn John, especially my principal, Linda Caswell. She took a chance on me and hired me as a first-year teacher with no official teaching experience. I was a music major, but she hired me out of field to teach an exceptional student education class with students that had some learning disabilities, because that was the only job available at Denn John when I applied. She was like a mother to me and supported me the whole way through that first year at my school. I was only allowed to teach out of field for one year, so the following year she created a music position for me at Denn John so I could stay at the school. I have always been grateful for her because she believed in me when I didn't believe in myself. Linda was the one person from my job that I was going to miss the most when I left.

I made plans for my new life in Las Vegas. I did my research online and found a studio apartment in Las Vegas. I was able to work with the property management over the phone and online to get most of the paperwork done before arriving. They were very accommodating with this request. I got all my plans in order, and I flew to Las Vegas to finalize everything and get settled.

I only saw my apartment complex on the computer, so when I pulled into the complex, I was very happy with my choice. It was a nice complex, and it had lots of trees and plants all around. I went directly to the rental office, signed the final lease, and picked up my keys. My studio apartment was only about 400 square feet, but it was cute. It was furnished so I didn't have to buy any furniture. I cleaned the apartment and stayed the weekend. I got everything organized, locked up my apartment, and headed back to the airport. I flew back home to Florida, and a few days later, I packed my car, said goodbye to my friends and Alberta (she had moved to Florida after she graduated from college), and started my drive across the country.

I drove up to Indiana first so I could visit my dad and my grandma.

Dad and I went over my route with my atlas and his big, trusty-dusty map. We used maps back then and didn't have GPS. Dad, being a military man, made sure that Tommy and I knew how to use and follow a map. He would be tracking me just like he did for every trip that I went on. He always took down the make, model, and license plate number of my car. I would contact him every two hours and give him the highway that I was on, the closest city or town, and the mile marker, so he would log the time. That way, if I ran into trouble, he could tell the police my details and the time that he last spoke to me. He was always my extra pair of eyes when I traveled. Even though he wasn't physically with me, he was always right there behind the scenes, watching over and looking out for me.

Dad checked my CB and my antenna to make sure that they were connected correctly so I could contact truckers if I ran into trouble. He told me that truckers knew everything that was happening on the road, and they alerted each other while driving. He was right about that because I listened to them as I traveled. My handle was Echo 1. The truckers saw my antenna, so some of them chatted with me as I was driving on the interstates.

Before leaving, Dad took me to a gas station and filled my car up. He gave me a big, strong, daddy hug, kissed me on the cheek, and I hit the road. I didn't know when I would see him again, but I knew that he loved me, and I loved him. I had so much gratitude in my heart for him at that moment. Our relationship had grown so much over the previous few years, and he became very affectionate toward me. When I was a child, he never told me verbally that he loved me; he just wasn't that type of person. I knew he did, but he just wasn't affectionate like that because he didn't grow up receiving that type of affection from his mother. He could not give me what he didn't have at that time.

However, when I became an adult, he changed when he started going to church, and he made sure that there was no question of his love for me. He professed it and showed me through his actions that he did. I knew that he loved me, and I made sure that he knew that I loved him. This trip would be the furthest away from him that I had ever been, so pulling away and watching him in my rearview mirror was bittersweet.

After I got over the initial sadness of saying goodbye to my dad, I started to enjoy the adventure that I was embarking on. My little Toyota Echo was filled to the brim with all my things. Other than the things that I stored at the home of my good friends, Paul and Jacqueline Barattiero, just about everything that I owned in the world was in my little car. I took Interstate 80 all the way across the top of the country. I drove for about an hour and a half until I arrived in Chicago. I had lived there before, and had visited the city many times, so it was very familiar territory, but going out of the west side of Chicago was the real start of my adventure. I had never exited that side of Chicago.

I drove through Illinois for a while and eventually crossed into Iowa. I felt like I was a pioneer. Other than my aunt Hester and her kids who lived in California, I was going to be the farthest west of any of my immediate family members. Not only that, but the route that I was taking was virtually the same route as the early Latter-day Saints that trekked across the country centuries ago. There were sign posts all along the road mentioning the pioneer trek.

The first day of driving was my longest day. I drove about 525 miles across a lot of flat farmlands and got to a hotel in Lincoln, Nebraska. The second day, I drove about 445 miles, and I stayed in Cheyenne, Wyoming. The drive was very peaceful. I listened to music and sang my way across the country. When I crossed into Wyoming, I was headed into mountain territory; it was amazing. I saw some real buffalo or bison for the first time. Outside of a zoo, I had never seen them before in the wild, and it brought tears to my eyes for two reasons. First, they were beautiful, but second, they were not free to roam; they were in captivity in a fenced-in area that was set back from the road. It brought extreme sadness to my heart because these beautiful creatures should have been free to roam and enjoy their lives, not be behind a fence. The Rocky Mountains were great, but they were very different than the Smoky Mountains. The Rockies were exactly that. Rocky! They were beautiful in their own way, and there were some trees, but the Smoky Mountains were lined with deep, lush, green trees everywhere. The Rockies were starker and much more treacherous.

It was extremely windy, and they had to put up wind barricades to try and break up the flow of the crosswinds that whipped across the highway. Even with the barricades, the wind pushed my little car to and fro, so I had to be extremely alert because of that. The wind would come out of nowhere and push my car a couple of feet; that was very scary. My plan was to drive all the way into Salt Lake City, Utah, that night and get to a hotel there, but the wind was so bad that third day, I had to stop outside of Rock Springs, Wyoming, and hunker down for the night. I could hear the wind howling all evening and could only imagine what it was like for those pioneers walking through those mountains and encountering wind like that. It gave me a lot of respect for their journey.

The next morning, the wind had died down, so I got up and ate some breakfast and hit the road. I drove a bit and headed south into Utah. I would be taking Highway 15 all the way down and into Nevada. As I was heading south, I made a planned stop in Salt Lake City and decided to go to the Joseph Smith Memorial Building and watch the movie, *The Testaments*. It was a movie about the events in the Book of Mormon that the Church had released. I heard it was good, so I wanted to see it. Since I was going to pass through the area, that would be the perfect place to stop, watch the movie, and get a bite to eat. When I arrived in Utah, I made my way down to Temple Square in Salt Lake City and found a parking spot. I grabbed my violin and put it on my back. (I have backpack straps on my case.) I never leave my violin in the car because heat can damage it, and it can also be stolen, so when I have my violin with me in the car, I always take it in with me wherever I am going. It doesn't matter if it is a grocery store, a restaurant, or a doctor's office. I try to plan ahead so I don't have to carry it, but sometimes you just can't help it. I was traveling, so on my back was my only option.

I walked through Temple Square, which was beautiful and peaceful. I peeked into the Tabernacle and got to see the place that I had seen on TV so many times. When I beheld those organ pipes with my very own eyes, my heart leapt with joy. As I left there, I went into the visitor's center and saw the Christus statue, whose grandeur was incredible. I stayed and looked at it for a few minutes. It made me think about the sacrifice that the Savior made for me and His love for me. He loved me so much that He was willing to lay down His life for me. I will be forever grateful for His love, and for the love of my heavenly Father. Everything that was happening in my life at that moment and beyond was because of Him. This experience of driving across the country was also a huge blessing, giving me an opportunity to see the beauty of this country while also some alone time to ponder my life and where I was being led.

When I left the visitor's center, I headed toward the Temple. I could feel the Spirit so strong as I walked the Temple grounds. There were multiple couples that had just been sealed, which means that they were married for time and all eternity in the Temple. The Temple is the only place that one can be sealed. Looking at the couples and the joy on their faces was so heartwarming. I didn't wait to be sealed the first time I was married, but standing there looking at those couples reminded me of how important it was to me, and that I needed to have faith and wait on the Lord so I could be sealed in one of His Temples.

I left the Temple and walked across the street to the Joseph Smith Memorial Building. I acquired my ticket to see the movie and waited a few minutes before they led us into the theater. It was a nice theater, with beautiful ruby red curtains that covered the movie screen like the theaters back in the old days. The seats were comfortable, and because the theater was not full, there was plenty of space for me to lay my violin across the seats to my right. A couple of sister missionaries that were serving a mission told us a little bit about the movie, and then the lights dimmed, and the movie started.

The movie was amazing. The last scene of the movie just caught my breath. The lights went dark, and a recording of the Tabernacle Choir started playing. They were singing a song called, "This is the Christ." The text of the song was by James E. Faust and Jan Pinborough, and the music was written by Michael F. Moody. I sang this song several times in the past, but the Tabernacle Choir sang it slowly and with such peace and beauty; it absolutely touched my heart.

As the lights slowly came on, I started wiping my eyes, and as I turned my head and looked around, I could see other people wiping their eyes as well. We all just sat there for a moment and pondered what we had just seen, and then slowly, people started to get up and leave. It was like no one wanted the experience to be over. The spiritual message of God's love for us was so powerful that I just couldn't get up right away. I had to sit and ponder it for a little while longer.

When I finally started to move, I noticed two ladies in front of me. They stood up at almost the same time that I did. One of them turned around and saw me standing there and said, "Wasn't that an amazing movie?"

"Yes, it was!" I replied.

The other lady turned around and said hello to me, and we sparked a conversation. Noticing my case lying on the seat, one of the ladies asked me, "What is in your case?"

"It is my violin."

"Oh wonderful! Are you playing somewhere in Salt Lake?"

"No. I am just passing through. I was accepted at a graduate program at UNLV, and I am headed there now. I just stopped in Salt Lake to see this movie and get some lunch."

"Well, we are going upstairs to the top floor of this building. There is a nice restaurant up there. You should come and join us," she said. Her friend joined in and said, "Yes, you should."

I agreed to join them, and we exited the theater. We took the elevator up to the top floor and went into the restaurant, where we ordered our meals and began to carry on a conversation. They told me that they had been friends for over forty years, and they got together every year and had a friend's weekend together. They decided to stay the weekend in Salt Lake this time. The ladies were very inquisitive and wanted to know all about me. They wanted to know my conversion story and how long I had been playing the violin. They were so friendly and kind, and I loved our conversation. When we got close to the end of our meal, I got up and went to the restroom. When I returned, they looked at each other, and one of the ladies said, "If you will play something for us on your violin, we would like to pay for your meal."

I was taken aback at the request, but then I said, "Thank you, but you don't have to pay for my meal."

"We know, but we want to. You just need to agree to play for us."

They sat and looked at me while I pondered my next response, and as I looked at them, I could see a sincere sense of love in their eyes. They didn't know me, but I felt like they loved me with a Christ-like love I had not seen before. So, I smiled at them, and I agreed to their request and thanked them for their offer. To be honest, I was going to get something cheap to eat at a fast-food restaurant because I was now going back to school and needed to put myself on a student's budget, so I needed to save money. The restaurant that we were eating at was quite costly. I bought the cheapest thing on the menu, but it was still expensive. The ladies somehow must have known, so their gesture was a blessing to me.

They paid for our meals, and we exited the restaurant. There was a little spot down the hallway next to the elevator that had a window facing Temple Square. When we stepped over there, one of the ladies said, "Ok. Let's hear it." It was just the three of us, but I looked around to see who was out in the hallway, and they said, "Don't worry about them." I was thinking to myself, *Wow! They are serious!* I took my case off my back, opened it, and removed my violin. I grabbed my bow and tightened it, peeking over their shoulders to see who was there in the hallway. They were standing in front of me with their backs to the restaurant and smiled at me as I began playing "the Allemande from the d minor Partita" by J.S. Bach. I closed my eyes and just allowed myself to feel the music, and when I did, I was no longer concerned about who was or wasn't watching me. It was all about the music, and I wanted to play my best for those two sweet ladies.

When I finished my last note and pulled my bow away from the strings, the two women clapped and thanked me for the performance. My playing had not disturbed anyone; it was just a private performance between me and those sweet ladies. I thanked them for the applause and the meal. I then packed up my violin, put it back on my back, and we took the elevator back down to the first floor. I thanked the ladies for their company and for the meal, as they each gave me a hug, and then we departed.

Those two women did something to me that day, showing me unconditional love. They were Caucasian and I was African American, but they absolutely did not care. This was true of all the wards (congregations) that I had attended in my Church. From the very moment I joined the Church of Jesus Christ of Latter-day Saints, I always felt loved by the members of my wards. These two ladies had a measure of the light of Christ that I had never experienced before, both living lives that were completely focused on the Savior. His light was radiating out of them, and I could feel it.

That whole experience was a miracle to me because I just happened to be traveling across the country and just happened to stop in Salt Lake City on that day at that time. I should have arrived in Salt Lake City the night before, but the wind stopped me. I walked around Temple Square first and then walked over to that building. All those things happened exactly as they were supposed to because the Lord wanted me to meet these two amazing women, my angels. They have probably crossed over to the other side by now, but I will forever remember their kindness toward me.

* * *

I left Salt Lake City and drove all the way to Las Vegas. It was late in the evening when I arrived, so I took my violin into my apartment and left everything else in the car to be unloaded in the morning. Since my apartment was furnished, I immediately jumped into my queen-size bed and called Daddy to let him know that I made it safely. Then, I quickly fell asleep. When I woke up in the morning, I unloaded the car and put some things away. I was tired, so I sat on the couch and relaxed. The independence felt good. I was alone, but I didn't feel alone because I knew the Lord was with me.

The first thing I did, after unpacking, was go to the grocery store. I went and purchased food and stocked my refrigerator and pantry. After I did that, I went to find the Temple, which I could see up on a hill down the road from me. I didn't have the address, but it looked close so I just decided to drive toward it. So, I started driving toward the hill that I saw it sitting on, and I then realized that the hill was a lot farther away from me than it appeared. Because of the size of hills and mountains there, they always appear closer than they actually are. It was on my side of town, so I just kept driving. I followed the roads around and turned where I thought I was supposed to, and there the Temple was. When I saw it down the road, I immediately felt the Spirit; that has been the case for every Temple I have seen with my eyes. The Spirit always testifies to me that it is a house of the Lord.

I drove into the parking lot and parked. I wasn't dressed to go into the Temple, as that was not my plan for the day. I just wanted to go and sit on the grounds and pray. So, that is what I did. I got out of the car and walked over to the side of the Temple, and I sat in the beautiful green grass there. I said a prayer of thanksgiving to the Lord for helping me to arrive in Las Vegas safely, and when I finished, I sat there, meditated, and breathed in the peace of the Temple grounds. I stayed there for about an hour, and then I headed back to my apartment.

Later that evening, I went down to the famous Las Vegas Strip. I parked at the Bellagio hotel and walked through the casino; it was very fascinating. There was a stark difference in mood walking through that casino than what

I felt earlier at the Temple. The building itself was massive, and it had a beautiful garden area in the front. I walked through the garden and out the front door because I was headed to the fountains that were outside in the front of the building. I could have stayed out there all night. They have water fountains that move to music and lights; it was so good. I stayed there through several performances of the water fountains show and then walked down the Strip for a little bit. It was dark outside, and there were some very interesting characters out there. Some of the people that I ran into were very drunk, cursing, and acting crazy, so I walked back to the Bellagio, went to my car, and drove home.

My next task was to find the ward that I was zoned for. I decided to go to a singles' ward, so I looked it up and found it in the phonebook. The meeting was in the late afternoon, so I decided that I would go to a different family ward in the morning every Sunday, and then go to the singles' ward for single members that were between eighteen and thirty years of age in the afternoon. I wanted to make sure that I stayed focused on spiritual things while I was there. There were a lot of wards in the Las Vegas area; as a matter of fact, there were twenty-two stakes in the Las Vegas/Henderson area when I was there. On average, each stake is about eight wards, with each ward generally having somewhere between 250-500 people.

I was shocked to find out how many Latter-day Saints there were in the Las Vegas area. With there being so many wards to pick from, I just opened the phonebook, closed my eyes, and pointed to a spot on the page, and wherever my finger landed, that was the family ward I went to that Sunday. It was awesome. I even visited the ward in Henderson that Gladys Knight attended. She wasn't there the Sunday I was there, but when I spoke to the members, they told me that they always knew when she was home because her voice was so distinctive and powerful in the ward. The time that I was spending in Las Vegas was so spiritual. Outside of going to the occasional movie, pretty much everything I did was spiritual in nature.

After I had been in Vegas for several weeks, my graduate advisor set up a meeting with me, so I went to the campus to meet with him. When I got there, the first thing he said was, "The School of Music offered too many graduate assistantships this year. Because of that, we do not have enough money to honor your assistantship." I couldn't believe what I was hearing and thought to myself, *They couldn't have figured that out before I quit my job and moved all the way across the country?* I looked at him and said, "I just moved across the country with the understanding that my school cost would be covered. What am I supposed to do now?"

He said, "We will give you a few private students to teach so you can get in-state tuition; that is all we can do. I will walk you over to the financial aid office, and you can apply for some financial aid and see what they might have available for you."

I was really mad, but I kept my composure to see the options available. He walked me over to the financial aid office, which was close to the music building. They had me fill out a financial aid application and told me to come back in about an hour, and they would know if I qualified for any aid. I returned and when I sat down with the financial aid advisor, she had a smile on her face and said, "Congratulations! You qualify for $28,000 in loans; that will cover your master's program." I guess I looked at her in a strange way because she said in question, "Isn't that great?"

"No. Not really. It's loans. I will have to pay those back. Aren't there any scholarships available that I don't have to pay back?"

"No, I'm sorry. There aren't," she said.

"I'm already paying back my undergraduate loans, so taking out more loans is very concerning to me," I said.

"While you are going to school, it will defer the payments of your undergraduate loans until you are finished with your master's." I sat quietly for a moment.

"I need a little time to think about it before I agree to anything," I concluded, to which she said, "Here is my card. Give me a call when you have made a decision."

I went back home feeling completely defeated. I just kept thinking to myself, *I drove all the way across the country to get here because I had received the promise of an assistantship, and now I have nothing. No income! No job! No nothing! How am I going to support myself and pay my bills? How am I going to pay my rent and my car note?* The assistantship was enough to cover all my expenses. Now, I would have to go and find a job again.

However, I got right on it to find a job, getting a newspaper and looking in the "Help Wanted" section. The first thing I did was contact the Las Vegas school district to see if I could teach. When I spoke to them on the phone, they told me that I was not qualified to teach in the state of Nevada because the requirements were different than they were in Florida. On top of that, they would not honor my temporary license, so teaching was out. Now what? I decided to look for a job anywhere. I had worked in a pizza shop and an ice cream store before, and I worked at three different big-box stores on their stocking crew that stocked the shelves and as a cashier, so I could do any of those things. I got busy and started putting in applications.

Many of the places that I applied to did not contact me back. When I was called by the other places, they told me that I was overqualified because I had been a teacher. I explained to them the situation with the certification requirements and that I was willing to work in any job, but they just said that I was overqualified and would not hire me. My most recent job was my teaching job, and I had put that down on all the applications, and three of the jobs, which actually replied, told me that I was overqualified. I thought that these places would want someone that was intelligent and responsible, but that was not what they were looking for. Maybe it's because I was living in Vegas, but whatever the case, it was shocking to me. I put in applications for several weeks, and nothing panned out.

I finally found a potential job at a private day school. I would need to work during the day, and then I would go to my evening graduate classes. The problem was that orchestra class met in the middle of the day at noon, so that would interfere with my work schedule. So, I met with my graduate advisor and explained the scheduling conflict. I told him that since they denied me the graduate assistantship, I needed to find a job to support myself. I asked him if he could exempt me from orchestra so I could work, and he rudely said, "No! I will not exempt you! Your program requires that you play in the orchestra."

His response was very frustrating, so I said, reminding him again, "I drove all the way across the country and moved here with a letter that said your school was giving me a full graduate assistantship. When I arrived, you told me that you ran out of money and could no longer give me the promised assistantship. I have signed a lease, and I have bills to pay that would have been covered by the assistantship. I now must get a job to support myself. If the orchestra meets at noon, and my classes start at 5 p.m., what kind of job can I get? How can I work to support myself with that schedule?"

He replied, "You are going to have to quit your job if you want to be a graduate student. We will give you a couple of students to help you get in-state tuition, but that is all that we can do for you. You will have to take out loans to cover your tuition."

I didn't know what I was going to do. I did not feel comfortable taking out loans for that large amount of money because the pay for a teacher with a master's degree was only a $2,000 difference in the state of Florida. I felt strongly that it would be a bad financial decision to take out $28,000 in additional student loans as a teacher and continue paying the $15,000 in loans that I already had from Ball State. I would be in debt for the rest of my life.

I sat in my apartment and cried because the circumstances surrounding me going to school took a 180-degree turn. Nothing was working out as planned, and I didn't know what to do, so I decided to get down on my knees and pray until I had an answer. And that was exactly what I did. I poured out my heart to the Lord and pleaded with Him to show me what direction I should take.

I stayed on my knees until about 3 a.m. I got so tired that I started to doze off. I woke myself up, and the thought popped into my mind. *Call your old principal in Florida and ask if your old job is still available.* The moment that thought popped into my mind, I felt at peace. I thought about it for a moment, and I knew that was exactly what I needed to do. I got up, got in my bed, set my clock for 8 a.m., and went to sleep. At 8 a.m., I got up, said a prayer, and called Mrs. Caswell, my previous principal. They patched me right into her, and she was happy to hear from me. I told her what was going on and that I wanted to come back to Florida. I asked her if my job was still available, and she told me that she had moved the class schedule from music to a foreign language and had already offered the job to someone else. However, the teacher that she offered the job to was considering leaving Denn John to work somewhere else, so Mrs. Caswell told me that she would contact that teacher and find out what her plans were. If the teacher was going to leave, she would change the allotment back to music. She told me that she would call me back after she spoke to the other teacher.

When I got off the phone with Mrs. Caswell, I still felt at peace, even though I had no promise of a job. I was tired, so I turned over and went back to sleep. Just a few minutes later, my phone rang. I thought it was Mrs. Caswell calling me back, but it wasn't. It was Delores McMillan, the principal of Parkway Middle School in Florida. She told me that she got my phone number from Mrs. Caswell and explained that she had just called Mrs. Caswell because her chorus teacher had retired, and she was having a difficult time finding a replacement. She wanted to know if Mrs. Caswell knew of anyone or had interviewed anyone recently that was qualified for the job. Mrs. Caswell said, "I have the perfect person for you!"

She then said, "She gave me your number, and I called you immediately. She told me that you were in Las Vegas. Are you interested in coming back and working in Kissimmee again?"

"Yes, I am!" I said.

She interviewed me over the phone, and when she finished, she offered me the job, which I gladly accepted it. She asked me how long it would take for me to get back to Florida, and I told her that it would take about two weeks to get everything situated in Vegas and in Florida. She told me to contact her when I got back to town. I was completely shocked; in a matter of a few hours, the Lord told me to contact my principal. I called her right when the school opened. If I had procrastinated, or waited even just a few minutes longer, the plan could very well have been foiled. Mrs. McMillan called Mrs. Caswell a few minutes after I got off the phone with her initially. Mrs. Caswell would not have known that I needed a job and wanted to come back home and could not have recommended me to Mrs. McMillan had I not called when I did. The outcome could have been completely different.

I have always felt that Linda Caswell was an earthly guardian angel for me. When I returned to Florida in 1999, after I finished my degree at Ball State, I needed to get a job as a teacher, and there were no music jobs open at the time. The assistant principal at Denn John Middle School, Michael Vondracek, was a fellow musician. A friend of mine that worked at a local music store knew that I was looking for a teaching job and told me that he was playing a gig with Mr. Vondracek that evening, and that he would put in a good word for me. The next day, Mr. Vondracek called me and asked if I could come in to interview for a job. Of course, I said, "Absolutely!"

The next day, I went in, we talked, and he liked me. They did not have a music job available, but they had a self-contained exceptional student education (ESE) position available. He told me that I would be teaching language arts, math, science, and social studies to a classroom of students that had special learning needs. He told me that he felt confident I could do this job and asked me how I felt about it. I knew that this was my opportunity to get my foot in the door of the school district, so I said, "I can do it." He told me that he could not make the decision himself; the principal had to do that, and she wasn't there at that moment, but she would be there at the school in a few minutes. He asked if I was willing to wait for her, and I told him, "Yes."

As promised, she arrived quickly, and when she went into the office, he went in and talked to her about me. She called me into her office, and I immediately felt a connection with her. She spoke to me with such kindness and respect, saying, "Mr. Vondracek really likes you, and I respect his judgment. I think you will fit in well here at Denn John." She hired me on the spot, and from that very moment, she was like a mother to me and looked after me.

Mrs. Caswell could not offer me my previous teaching position back when I wanted to return from Las Vegas, but she did the next best thing for me that she could. She gave her friend my name and provided a reference to help me acquire another job. Because of her, I was able to come right back to Florida and resume my teaching job at a different school within the school district the very next school year. Since I started the very next school year on time, there was no break in my employment, so I did not have to re-apply. I only had to take the state-required tuberculosis test, and when that came back clear, I went right back to work. Along with the two ladies in Salt Lake, Mrs. Caswell was my third angel that summer, and I have no doubt that the Lord used her for my good.

Several people told me that I wasted my time and money moving to Las Vegas and coming back without my master's degree. It might appear that way, but that is an uninspired perception. That whole trip was an act of faith for me, a two-month period of complete spiritual growth. I spent my time in the Temple and doing spiritual activities. Because most of my time was spent doing spiritual things, my testimony of the Lord grew substantially. I leaned on the Lord the whole time that I was away, fortifying myself and putting on the armor of Christ. I was not supposed to go to UNLV; I was sent there to grow and to learn to depend on the Lord, and that was exactly what I did.

I went through the Hoover Dam, and I took US 40 on the way back home; it was a more southern route. As I was driving, I saw some signs about the Grand Canyon. When I saw the sign that said exit here for the Grand Canyon, I could not pass up the opportunity to see it with my own eyes. I saw it from the air when I flew to Vegas, and I was amazed then, but driving there, getting out of my car, walking to the rim, and beholding the Grand Canyon with my very own eyes was the most incredible sight I had ever seen. It was a reminder that there was someone bigger than myself, and that He who created this canyon knew me and loved me. He knew what I needed, and He would always be there for me.

Chapter 23

SINGLE AGAIN

After returning to Florida, and starting my new job as a choral teacher, I started going to the young single adult activities at Church. I also started to travel to different young single adult conferences in Florida and Georgia. Eventually, I aged-out of the young single adult program because I was over thirty, so I had to start going to the singles groups, which were for people over thirty. Most of the people in the group were much older than I was, but there were no guys that I was interested in. I received a blessing years earlier from Brother Norman Ellertson when he and his wife were serving their mission in our ward in New York, and the blessing told me to, "Seek diligently for a mate." I thought I had been doing that, but it wasn't working out.

One day, a good friend of mine suggested that I go online and try one of the online dating services that were set up for people of our faith. I didn't even know something like that existed, but if I was going to seek diligently, I needed to try everything available to me. I went online and did a search for a dating site. I found three of them: one was called *Mingle*, one was *Planet*, and the other one was *Singles*. *Mingle* seemed to be the biggest one at that time, so I signed up for that one first, and then I eventually signed up for the other two.

I didn't have any preference on race, as long as he was a good person and would treat me right. So, when the first guy sent me a flirt, which is a notification that someone is interested in you, I had no issue with the fact that he was Caucasian. We talked for a good while. He was nice, but there was something off about him. We got to know each other fairly well, and we talked online almost every day. However, that changed when I found out he was immoral and wanted his women to engage in some very strange acts. He told me that he was searching for that special woman that would agree to his strange desires. I was not the one for him. *Bye, bye now.*

The next guy was from the Ivory Coast. He was nice, but he was madly in love with me in about four weeks. He wanted to come to America and spend the rest of his life with me, but he needed me to send him some money so he could come over here. Because of what I had gone through with Michael, that situation sent up a red flag for me almost immediately. I avoided the conversation about that and just tried to get to know him a little better. After a few more weeks of chatting, he brought it up again and said that we could not be together if he couldn't get over to America. So, I told him that I did not have a lot of money, but I could probably come up with $200. He replied and said, "That isn't enough. You need to send more."

I was totally bothered by his response, so I wrote him a letter back saying, "I told you that I did not have any money to send to you, but I would try to scrape up $200. You then told me that it wasn't enough. It is not my responsibility to supply money for you. You are a man, so you need to come up with a plan for you to get here."

Well, that did not sit well with him. He wrote me back and said, "You should never speak to a man like that … In the future, make sure that you watch how you address a man!"

I read his letter and said to myself, *I am glad I wrote him that letter because his true personality came out, and I would definitely be subservient in that relationship. Gotta go!*

I ended that relationship almost immediately. Being in a relationship where the woman is not allowed to speak her mind is the last thing that I needed.

I was having very little luck with these guys online, but I was determined to keep searching. I got a message from another guy whose name was Jacob, and he lived somewhere in Wisconsin. He was pretty cool, and we hit it off right away, talking for hours on end and starting to get close. We eventually started talking about marriage and what we wanted in a marriage. I told him about the basics, like someone to support me, love me, etc. When he responded, he said, "I want someone who can handle me in bed, and someone that has a good libido." *Red light! Red light!* With all the drama that I just went through with Michael, you would think that I had learned my lesson. Nope! I just let that go right on by and pretended like I didn't hear it. You know the old adage, "The same trial keeps coming around until you master it"? Well, that is exactly what was happening to me. Another low flyer came gliding my way, along with the two other low flyers before him on the same website.

We eventually made plans for Jacob to come and visit me, even with his admission about intimacy. He was going to go to a conference first, and then fly to Florida and meet me. I booked a hotel by the airport and picked him up. We went to the hotel to hang out. Jacob was going to leave the very next day, so the plan was for me to stay at the hotel and hang out with him for the night, and then take him to the airport the next day. Of course, that was a bad decision. For some reason, I just made crazy decisions when it came to men. Jacob was at least a Christian and was very active in his church; however, that was his big deception. He was not following the standards of his church at all. Instead, he was wrapped up in a pretty church costume on the outside, but underneath that costume, he was on the lower levels of the low flyers!

Before Jacob came, we had a conversation about my expectations when he arrived. I told him that we would not be doing anything sexual at all, and if that was what he wanted, then he shouldn't come. Jacob was not exactly happy about that, but he said that he loved me and wanted to meet me in person and spend some time with me. I reserved one room for both of us, and of course, that was a bad idea because when we arrived at the hotel room, the first thing he wanted to do was fool around. I rejected him multiple times, so he was mad at me. Jacob started sulking, so I went down to the pool. He didn't want to go because he was mad, so I left. When I came back, he was nicer to me, which was still his plan. He was going to win me over with kindness now.

We talked for a little bit, until Jacob eventually tried to do a little something. We cuddled and got close, but it got a little too close. I started to get uncomfortable because things were starting to get out of hand. Jacob thought that he had worn down my defenses, and he almost did, but something within me flashed a brief memory of what Michael had done to me so I immediately moved away from him. I pushed him back and turned my back to him. At that point, he realized that he wasn't going to get what he wanted, so he sighed out of frustration and stopped trying. I was grateful for that.

We woke up the next morning and went downstairs to have breakfast. Jacob was very quiet and didn't have much to say to me; it was like he was sulking. I guess the time that we spent together was not worth the price of his plane ticket. After that, I took him to the airport. He gave me a hug and told me that he would call me when he got home. His face and his body language showed that he was not happy, so we just said goodbye, and that was it.

I waited for him to call me when he got home, but he never called. One day, two days, and then three days went by and no word from him. Finally, he called and told me that he was visiting a friend in New York City, which was why he had not gotten back to me. We talked for a little bit, and then he told me that he would call me when he got home, but he never did.

* * *

The encounter that I had with Jacob really made me feel unclean, so I arranged a meeting with the bishop of my ward to talk to him about what had taken place between Jacob and I while he was there. I was feeling guilty because I knew that I should not have let it get that far. Even though I was able to stop us from going any further, I put myself in a dangerous position, and it could have gone really wrong. After our conversation, I knew that my relationship with Jacob could not go on because he did not respect me or my standards. Even worse, he was not living up to his standards at all, pretending like he was spiritual when he was not.

The day after we spoke, I was checking my email and received an email from an unfamiliar woman. I opened the email and read it. The email said, *I am the wife of Jacob, and I would like to know the nature of your relationship.*

I was shocked and totally caught off guard. I thought to myself, *Wow! Why am I so unlucky with men?*

I absolutely did not want to get involved with any foolishness, so I wrote her back and said,

I don't know you, nor do I know what is going on, but I don't want to be involved in it.

The next day, I received an email from a girl named Jessie.

Hello there. My name is Jessie.

She then listed her email address and explained in her email,

I am sure that you have seen my name on some of the emails that Jacob sent out.

She was correct. I did see her name on top of several emails that he had forwarded to multiple people. She continued and wrote,

I have some important information about Jacob. Can you please give me a call?

She supplied her phone number, and at that point, I was curious about what was going on. So, I called her, and she started to tell me her story. The first thing she asked me was, "Did Jacob tell you that he was going to Nevada for a conference?"

"Yes, he did," I said.

She then proceeded to tell me this incredible story.

"He came to Nevada to meet up with me. We were engaged to be married." My jaw hit the floor because he and I were talking about marriage. She continued and said, "The conference had a morning session and an afternoon session. After the morning session was over, we went back to my apartment for lunch, and he wanted to be intimate with me and then go back to the afternoon session. I am a religious girl, so I didn't give in, and he was not very happy about that." That sounded very familiar. She continued talking.

"He stayed the night and told me that he had some business in Florida."

She then asked me if I lived in Florida, to which I said, "Yes."

"So, he left me and went to go see you?"

"Yep! I picked him up at Orlando Airport."

She continued with her story:

"We were engaged to be married, so I told a friend about him. He was an officer in my church, so he wanted to check up on Jacob and see if he was a good guy. He asked me for his name, city, and any other information that I knew. I knew the name of his church, so I gave him that too. He did a little research to make sure that Jacob was who he said he was before we went any farther with our marriage plans. I was so glad that he checked him out for me because he found out that Jacob was married. I was totally crushed because I was going to marry that man. I couldn't believe that he would do that to me."

She told me that she decided to do a little research on her own. I don't know how she did it, but she was able to find the phone number of Jacob's wife, and she called his wife. Jessie told his wife everything, and I do mean EVERYTHING! She told her that he had been to Nevada to see her, and that he was headed to Florida for some business. Jessie sent his wife one of the forwarded emails because she figured that some of the names on there could be women that he was interacting with. That is why his wife sent me that email and was trying to find out the nature of our relationship. It all made sense now, and I felt awful for his wife. I wish that was the end of the story, but it unfortunately was not. Jessie continued with her story:

"She told me that Jacob did not have a job. His wife had a good job and made very good money, so she was supporting the two of them until Jacob found work. All the money that he was spending flying around meeting women was actually his wife's hard-earned money." When Jacob left me in Florida, he stopped in New York before he went home. While he was doing all this traveling, Jessie had contacted his wife, and when he finally got home, his wife was supposed to pick him up at the airport, but it wasn't her that he found waiting for him there; it was his father-in-law. His father-in-law brought a bunch of his things and gave them to him at the airport, telling

Jacob not to go back home. Jacob was able to make his way back to New York, and that is why it took him so long to call me after he left.

I thought the story was over, but sadly, his treachery went a lot deeper than that. His wife contacted his church to let his pastor know what he had done. His pastor contacted him and confronted him about his wife's allegations, to which he did not deny it. From there, the pastor started an investigation because Jessie sent his wife some of the forwarded emails, and the emails had quite a few female names on them. They wanted to find out how bad the situation was, so his church formed a disciplinary committee, and they started contacting the women.

My name was on the email, so they contacted me. They wanted to know about our relationship and if he had injured me in any way. I told them about his visit, but that we were not intimate. I explained to them that he tried, but I ultimately refused him. They then informed me that I was one of the lucky ones. He had deflowered many women all over the country, as far away as Hawaii. Many of these women were devastated, and he had damaged them emotionally. I guess he told all these women that he was going to marry them. His pastor told me that the pain was deep for many of these women, and his heart ached for them. I could not believe that Jacob did such a horrible thing. More than that, I couldn't believe that I almost allowed myself to become a victim again.

Alberta warned me about him, and I realized I was making the exact same choices with these men that I made with Michael. Again, my need to find love outweighed my sense of reasoning. I was on the same path that I took with Michael, but at the eleventh hour, I was able to gather my senses and protect myself. I was very tempted, but I had enough strength to avoid Jacob and his intentions. Luckily for me, he stopped and didn't proceed, or I could have been one of those women.

* * *

Jacob was the third online guy that didn't work out, so I said to myself, *Three strikes and you're out. Forget it! This is just too much!* The men that I was encountering were supposed to be religious guys, but they were all "wolves in sheep's clothing." They were lying in wait to pounce on their prey. I did not want to deal with that anymore, so I canceled my accounts on two of the online dating sites. I had purchased a lifetime membership on the other one because it was a more economical deal. So, for that one, I just logged off and didn't log back on. At that point, I decided that I would just have to accept that I would not find anyone, nor would I marry during this lifetime.

Chapter 24

LAUREL FALLS

After all the drama with online dating, I avoided the whole online thing because I was just fed up with it. A lot of the men on the sites seemed to have no morals whatsoever, and many of them had no desire to get married. They were just wasting time, and some of the men were not religious at all on the sites. Others were religious in the past but were now non-practicing and had gone the way of the world. They were just on the sites to prey on innocent and naïve church girls, trying to lure them over to the "dark side."

After multiple months of being logged off the dating sites, I paid for a one-month membership and logged back onto *Planet*. I started checking for any new profiles that had come onto the site since I left. One popped up; the man's name was Jonah (Chuma). He appeared to be very religious, which was very refreshing to me, especially after the previous guys. I didn't think anything would come of it, but I decided to send him a message, so I wrote, *Nice profile*. He replied, and we started to communicate back and forth. This time, I was determined to be more cautious.

I had been talking with Chuma online for a few weeks, and things were going well. He was very different than the previous three guys that I had encountered online. He was living in Minneapolis, Minnesota. He was a nice man and very mature. We started talking regularly while I planned a vacation for myself. It was summer, and I wanted to get away for a little bit. I love waterfalls, so I decided to go to the Smoky Mountains. I told Chuma that I was going away for a little bit, but I would continue to write to him while I was away.

I was actually talking to two guys: Chuma and Peterson. Peterson lived in

Atlanta, so we decided to meet up on my way to the Smoky Mountains. His friend helped me secure a hotel in the Peachtree area of Atlanta and gave me her corporate discount. I didn't ask for help, but I really appreciated their thoughtfulness in helping me find discounted lodging. It was a nice hotel and saved me quite a bit of money.

I arrived in Atlanta and connected with Peterson. He came to the hotel, and we visited for a little while before he took me to do some touristy things. So, we walked down the street and took the Metropolitan Atlanta Rapid Transit Authority train (MARTA). The first thing that I noticed was the train station was very clean, not smelling like the train stations in Chicago and New York City; this was a pleasant change. We got off a few stations away and walked to a place called Atlanta Underground; it was a neat shopping area underground in downtown Atlanta. We walked around and checked out the area, and then we had lunch in the food court. We had a great conversation and enjoyed each other's company.

Before I left Florida, Peterson asked me if I had ever seen any of the Martin Luther King Jr. historical sites in Atlanta before, and I told him that I had not, so part of our plan was to go there. I am so glad I did, as it was a very reflective visit for me. Walking in the areas that Martin Luther King Jr. walked, and seeing where he was buried, brought a sense of gratitude but also sadness. I will always be grateful for the sacrifice that he made for us.

Peterson and I walked quite a bit that day, and my feet were screaming but I didn't say anything. As we were walking back to the hotel, there was a nice restaurant right down the street from the hotel. We passed it that morning when we left and discussed eating there for dinner. So, we stopped there as planned and had a nice, early dinner. He was a perfect gentleman and paid for my meal. As usual, we had a great conversation, but that was about it. There were no sparks or anything like that, just two people hanging out and enjoying each other's company.

After dinner, he walked me back to the hotel, and we said our goodbyes. I was relieved that Peterson was kind and respectful and was not trying to get me in bed. After my experiences with Michael and Jacob, I think I had finally learned my lesson. If I expected these guys to respect me, I had to respect myself first.

When I first met Peterson, I knew that he was not the one, but my experience with him was great, and he showed me that there were some nice and respectable guys out there. Chuma was very different. He was an active member of my Church, The Church of Jesus Christ of Latter-day Saints. I could tell that he loved the Lord and was serious about his beliefs. This was a pleasant change from the previous men that I had encountered. After Peterson dropped me off at the hotel, I went right in and typed a message to Chuma. He was a much more promising candidate, and I was enjoying our conversations because they were intellectually intriguing. I told him that I would continue to contact him while I was traveling and wanted to make sure that I kept my promise.

I left Atlanta the next day, a Saturday morning, and the journey to the Smokies was so peaceful. When I turned down the road to enter the national park, it was so serene. The trees were majestic. The road was winding and curving through the park, and every so often, there would be an open vista that I could see through the trees and into the beautiful landscapes surrounding me. After I drove for a bit, I saw a sign off to my left that said Laurel Falls. I kept driving because I was headed to the visitor's center that was a little farther down the road. When I arrived at the visitor's center, it was bustling. People were all over the inside and outside of the building. I worked my way in and through the crowd, finding a shelf that had maps, postcards of the mountains, and a book about the waterfalls in the park. I picked up the book and opened it. One of the first waterfalls that I saw in the book was Laurel Falls. In my heart, I immediately knew I was supposed to go there.

I paid for the book and went back to the location where I saw the signage for Laurel Falls, and I pulled in. There were quite a few cars there, so I realized that this was a popular spot. I got out of the car and changed into my sneakers and started to walk toward the trailhead. The trail was cut out along the mountain. As I started to walk up the trail, there was a sign attached to the side of the mountain that said,

Laurel Falls, 1.3 miles from here.

I thought to myself, *That is pretty far, but that's why I came,* so I started to walk.

At that period of time, I weighed 325 pounds, so I immediately got winded. As I looked ahead, I could see people coming down the path. The path up the mountain is a zigzag; it is straight, and then you make a left-hand turn along the mountain, and then you turn the corner of the mountain to the right. It continues this straight, left, right-turn pattern all the way up the mountain. When I started up the first straightaway, I could see a group of people turn the corner and come down the mountain. I immediately noticed that the path they were walking on was a steep downgrade. I was at the bottom of the same path that they were walking on, so that meant I had to walk up that steep incline. Fear immediately set in, but I kept walking. I made the left turn and started walking up that incline. I got to the corner and turned right. I took a few more steps, while telling myself, *You cannot do this! It is too hard! You'll never make it up there!*

I had only been walking for a couple of minutes, but I was already completely exhausted. My heart was beating so fast.

There is no way I can make it, I told myself.

When those thoughts came into my mind, I started to feel defeated. I was angry with myself, so I started to cry. I had driven all the way there from Florida, and I could not even get a fraction of the way up the mountain to see the waterfall. I turned around and took a few steps toward my descent until something in my head told me to stop and pray. I turned back around, stopped dead in the middle of the path, and faced the ascent. I tried to calm myself, so I took a deep breath, slowly exhaled, and started praying. Even though there were a lot of people on the mountain that day, no one came from behind me or in front of me while I was praying. I opened my heart and said, *Please Father, give me the strength and the courage that I need to make it up this mountain.*

I continued to pray and plead for the Lord's help, and when I finished, I started walking upward again. I took a few more steps, stopped again, and started crying because I felt like this was just too hard for me to do. My body was too heavy. Every step felt like my lungs and my heart were going to explode, like the strike of a sledgehammer to my chest. My faith was waning, and my hope was fading, but suddenly the thought came into my mind, "… faith without works is dead" (Jas. 2:26).

I paused for a moment and thought about those words. I then realized that I had just prayed and asked the Lord for help, but I was getting ready to give up before I allowed Him to help me. With that in mind, I started walking, focusing on each step. Step … step … step … breathe … step … step … step … breathe … Every few seconds, I talked to myself.

Faith Without Works is Dead! … Keep Walking… Control Your Breath! … Faith Without Works is Dead … Keep Going … Slow Your Breathing Down … Step … Step.

The tears continued to stream down my face because this walk was so hard, but I chose faith, and I chose to trust in the Lord instead of fear. And I kept walking. My body seemed to know that I wasn't going to stop, so it started to work with me. My breathing got a little easier, and my mind was more focused. I got to about the halfway mark of the trail, and I noticed that a little further ahead was a stone seat cut out of the side of the mountain. My heart leaped for joy! It was like the Lord put it there just for me. So, I started walking with more hope and more vigor toward the seat.

With much excitement, I made it to the stone, and I sat down. It was the most miraculous feeling in the world. Sitting never felt better. I took several deep breaths, and I was able to get my heart rate to slow down. I rested for a little while, which made all the difference in the world for me. When I got up and started walking this time, I was much more comfortable and confident with my trek. After I walked a little bit more, I noticed that the hike seemed easier. When I observed my surroundings, I noticed that the incline had leveled out. The path was not as steep as it was before, so the walk was less taxing on my body.

My stride lengthened, and my heart was beating strong but steady. After a few more minutes of walking, I arrived at Laurel Falls. I couldn't believe it. I made it! The tears again began to flow, but this time, they were tears of gratitude. I knew that the Lord intervened on my behalf, and I was so grateful to Him for that. He took the time to teach His daughter about faith, and He helped me to know just how much He loved me. Laurel Falls was beautiful, but Laurel Falls was not the reason I was there. I was there to learn the much-needed lesson on trusting in the Lord. I also needed to learn that it was not enough to believe *IN* the Lord. I needed to *believe Him.*

I lacked faith when I engaged in my last few relationships. I did not have faith enough to wait for the Lord to help me find the right mate. If I had sincerely prayed about Michael and Jacob, the course that I ended up traveling on would have been very different. Different might have been just fine, but I am realizing now that the whole point of being here on this earth is for us to learn and grow. I have learned the things that I have because I have experienced many trials, temptations, and heartache throughout my life. These trials have made me stronger and more observant of those around me.

I remember a quote that was given by Allan Pratt when he was the Orlando South Stake president in our Church many years ago. He said, "The hottest fire makes the strongest steel" (Allan Pratt, speech, Church of Jesus Christ of Latter-day Saints Orlando South Stake Conference, Orlando, Florida, April 2000). That quote has stuck with me for all these years because it reminds me we are able to grow because we experience trials. It is like trees. Trees grow to become strong when they endure wind and the elements. When the wind blows, the tree learns that it needs to become thicker and wider to endure the force of the winds. We must also endure the forces that come our way. We all will respond to different types of forces that are dependent upon our own life experiences and locations, but as we do our best to endure to the end, we become stronger and wiser.

When I reached the top of Laurel Falls, I spent some time looking at the falls and pondering the miraculous experience I had just gone through. It was life-changing because I could not have gotten up there alone. It took every ounce of faith that I had, but yet, that was still not enough. The Lord came in and intervened on my behalf. It was as if He was walking with me, lightening my load and encouraging me the whole way. On the descent back down the mountain, I was able to look at the beauty of the surrounding scenery. I missed most of that on my way up the hill because I was distracted about the strenuous task at hand. I felt like I needed to focus on my steps and my breathing just to make it. Now that those two things were under control, I could enjoy the beautiful workmanship of the Lord's hands. This beauty was there on my way up, but because of my perceived difficulty, my mind would only allow me to see the struggle; I couldn't see the beauty that was right in front of me. As I thought about that, I started to think about all the amazing things I had probably missed in this world because of distractions. My shortsightedness would have been different if I kept my mind focused on the Savior and not the world.

Chapter 25

CHUMA—HE IS NOT WHAT I EXPECTED

The story of how Chuma and I met is nothing short of divine intervention. The Lord knew that we both needed someone, so I feel that He lovingly intervened on our behalf. I have had so many things happen in my life that showed me the Lord was aware of me, so this experience with Chuma was no exception.

When I signed off the online dating sites, Chuma was not on any of them. When I chose to re-join *Planet*, his profile was there. Chuma lived in Minneapolis, Minnesota. One of his Church leaders told him that he needed to start dating and look for a mate. He told his leader that he did not see anyone of interest in his Stake, so the leader told him to try an online dating site. Chuma complied and went out and bought a computer, later figuring out how to log onto *Planet*. He was not very computer-savvy (and still isn't), so that was a bit of a challenge for him, but he eventually figured it out. When he created his page, it was right after I canceled my memberships to the online dating services.

I decided that I was going to wait for the Lord to help me find the right man this time, and if that meant I would need to be single for the rest of my earthly life, so be it. I was done trying to do things my way; I decided to let the Lord guide me this time. Eventually, I started receiving emails from *Planet* to come back, but I ignored them. A few more months went by, and I got another request to re-join *Planet*. I thought about it and decided to pay for one month. If I didn't find anyone, I was going to cancel that membership for good.

When I finally logged back onto *Planet*, it was May of 2003. I did my usual thing. I put my filters in and started checking for any new profiles that had come onto the site since I left. One popped up: it was Chuma's profile. There was no picture on his profile, and in the past, I didn't open any profiles that didn't have a picture. However, I had just come back, and something told me to check out his profile. I clicked on it and started to quickly scan his page. One of the first things he talked about on his page was the importance of the Lord in his life, which was very refreshing. I didn't think anything would come of it, but I decided to send him a short message. I wrote,

Nice profile.

That was it. I didn't think he would reply, so I just kept it short and sweet. Later that day, I saw that I had a message from him. *Hmm, that is interesting.* I opened the message and read it. It said:

What is nice about it?

I didn't expect him to write me back, so I had not even thought about how I would respond. I thought about it for a minute and wrote,

I liked the fact that the Lord was the most important part of your life.

This started our back-and-forth communication. Chuma was completely different than any of the guys I had talked to before. He asked me questions about my goals and pursuits. He wanted to find out about me and my moral framework. I also asked him similar types of questions. He still did not have a picture on his profile, so I asked him to post one. As I mentioned before, Chuma and technology were not best friends, so he did not know how to post a picture. He had to go find someone to help him with that, but he eventually figured it out.

To be honest, when I saw Chuma's picture, I wasn't really attracted to him. He wasn't unattractive; he just wasn't what I visualized for myself. (That was probably my problem.) I had this vision of what my mate might look like, but none of the men I had been with in the past even fit that image. Since African American men were never really interested in me, I figured that I would probably end up marrying a Caucasian man or a Polynesian man. I was really attracted to Polynesian men, so I thought it would be awesome to be married to one. Unfortunately, none came my way. However, a lot of men that I was running into were from Africa, and that included Chuma. He was from Kenya, but he was now living in the United States.

At this point, we were talking daily, and we started to get close. Chuma then asked if we could start arranging to meet. He wanted us to meet up so we could see if we were compatible, and I agreed. I originally planned to fly out there to Wisconsin, but my plans changed, and I decided to drive. We had a family reunion coming up on the 4th of July weekend, and in 2003, it was going to be held in Milwaukee, Wisconsin. My mom was going to be driving by herself, so I made plans to drive with Mom until we got to Indianapolis, Indiana. From there, I would rent a car and follow the family to Milwaukee on Thursday. I would stay overnight in Milwaukee and then get up and drive to Minneapolis to meet Chuma on Friday morning. Everything went perfectly as planned.

We arrived in Milwaukee Thursday evening on July 3rd. I stayed overnight and visited with some of the family members that had already gathered there. Early Friday morning, July 4th, I got up and started driving to Minneapolis, which was about five hours west of Milwaukee. Everything was great until there was a tornado warning. The highway that I was driving on circled around the downtown area of a small city I was driving through. As the road was circling around, I could see the funnel cloud lowering and getting ready to form into a tornado right in the center of town. I started to get scared because I was too close to it, so I pumped the gas and started going about ninety miles per hour so I could put some distance between me and the tornado that was forming. I have always wanted to see a tornado up close, but I didn't want to see it that close and not today.

When I was able to put some distance between the forming tornado and me, I started to slow down and breathe. The further away from the tornado that I got, the slower my heartbeat became. As scary as it was, I wished I had been able to stop and watch the tornado from a safe location because I have always been fascinated by them. However, I was in unfamiliar territory, so I was definitely not going to turn around to go back and get a look at it. I proceeded toward Minneapolis, and the rest of the drive was easy, with no problems finding Chuma's house.

When I pulled up to his house, he was waiting for me, and he came down the steps to meet me. I got out of the car, and he gave me a hug. He looked true to his picture, so there were no surprises there. He was about 5 foot 7 inches and thin. He was from Kenya, and he enjoyed running. Chuma was not a competitive runner like the famous distance runners from Kenya, but he enjoyed running for exercise. He looked younger than I was, but in actuality, he was eight years older. I had no issues with that because he was about the same age as Michael.

The thing that piqued my interest in Chuma was his personality and his love for the Lord. He was an active member of our Church, and that was something I certainly toiled over when I was married to Michael. I was always at Church alone because he would not come with me. Chuma was very active in his ward in Minneapolis. We talked a lot about it, and how he spent time serving in the Church and serving the members of his ward. His spirituality was what really attracted me to him, not his looks. This was very strange to me, but I just went with it.

He led me into his house and introduced me to his roommate. He then took me into the kitchen where he had made oatmeal with raisins for us to eat for breakfast. We talked for a while, and then he planned for us to go and see some gardens and a waterfall in the area. The gardens were very nice, but the waterfall … loved it! It was beautiful. Getting to the waterfall was challenging for me because we had to walk down about four flights of stairs. Going down was fine, but I was getting worked up in my mind because I knew I would have to climb back up all those flights of stairs in a few minutes, and it was going to be bad.

We were down there at the falls for about fifteen to twenty minutes, and then it was time to go back up. I grabbed onto the railing and slowly started to make my ascent. The first flight was fine, but I had about three more flights to go. The struggle was real, and my body started to slow down. I was embarrassed; it was our first meeting together, and Chuma got to see firsthand my biggest weakness: my weight and how it affected my life. He was kind and gracious and told me to take my time. I had no choice in the matter. My body said, "Stop." So, I paused at the top of each flight to catch my breath.

This experience was like Laurel Falls all over again, but the spiritual experience at Laurel Falls prepared me for this. I struggled, but I accepted the struggle. Despite being embarrassed, I kept pushing. Chuma saw the true me in all my glory; there was no hiding from that. When we finally got to the top, I huffed and puffed because I was completely out of breath, but I didn't really want him to see how compromised I was just walking up those flights of stairs. So, as we started walking in the park that surrounded the waterfall, I started focusing on controlling my breathing. I needed to slow my heart rate down, so I started to take long, deep breaths. We walked for a bit, and then we found a big tree and sat down under it. We talked about my weight and my health. I was honest with him about where I was with it, but I also told him that I truly wanted to lose weight, and I was going to work on it. He was understanding and encouraging, and I really appreciated that from him.

After we left the park, he took me to The Mall of America. I'd always wanted to go there, so I was excited about that. I knew that there was an amusement park inside of the mall. So, I was looking forward to checking that out. Chuma does not like rides, so he was definitely not going to be riding on anything. I love amusement park rides, but I had not been able to fit into the rides for years, so I couldn't have ridden anything even if I wanted to. We walked through the amusement park, and I watched the people riding on the roller coaster. It looked like fun. There was also a water ride. He asked me if I wanted to go on the water ride and I said, "No. That's okay. I don't need to go on anything." I didn't tell him that I couldn't ride anything, but I knew that I couldn't. He didn't push it because he didn't like rides, but he would have been willing to go on the water ride if I wanted him to. I thought that was a sweet gesture.

We walked around that massive mall; I could not believe how big it was, two to three times the size of a typical mall. Despite the size of it, I kept track of where we were, and I remembered the landmarks of the mall so we could get back to the correct door to go to the parking garage where we parked. There were multiple parking areas, so to forget that information would be tragic. My dad taught me about looking for landmarks, and Walt Disney World taught me about the importance of remembering where you parked your car, so I made sure I knew where we were in relation to the car at all times. However, Chuma got lost and forgot where we parked. He must have thought that I was lost too, but he didn't know I rarely get lost.

As I was leading us back to the correct location for the parking garage, he kept asking me, "Are you sure we are going the right way?" I kept insisting I was sure. I knew exactly where I was going because we parked close to the amusement park. I guided us back to the correct parking lot, and we left and went for dinner.

The first major, spiritual thing that we did occurred Saturday morning when we went to the Temple together in St. Paul. After my previous trials with men, doing things that would bring us spiritually closer to the Lord was very important. Knowing that each of us was worthy of going into the Temple was very important to both of us. To me, this knowledge meant that God was in the center of Chuma's life, and he was doing his best to live out his faith. Walking out of the Temple with him next to me was very special. I could start to visualize him as a husband. We were two very different people, and our personalities were at opposite ends of the spectrum, but the major thing that we had in common was our faith. We both loved the Lord, and we wanted to do the right thing with the Lord at the forefront of our decision. Attending the Temple was an important step in our progression toward a relationship.

We continued making more spiritual memories because on Sunday morning, he picked me up at the hotel and took me to Church with him. Everyone was really nice, and they were interested in seeing the girl that Chuma was "dating." I guess he was an eternal bachelor in his ward, so it seemed like they were happy to see him with someone. Later that night, Chuma came back to my hotel room, and we talked. I had absolutely no concerns about him doing anything inappropriate with me while he was in my hotel room because his level of integrity was extremely high. He was a perfect gentleman the whole time we were together. The big question for me was, *Where do we go from here?*

I had always had this dream that I would fall head over heels for someone, and we would have a passionate, whirlwind kind of relationship; that was what I was seeking with my other relationships. However, this relationship with Chuma was different. We were both older, so it was a more laidback and mature relationship. It was completely different from what I dreamed of, but for some reason, it felt more grounded. I thought about my question a little more, and then I got up the courage and asked him, "Where do you want to see this relationship going?"

"I want us to get married," he responded.

I didn't know it at that exact moment, but that was his proposal. What he meant to say was, "Will you marry me?"

However, that was not how he said it. We talked some more, and then he went home and came back the next morning. In our conversation, he confirmed that he wanted to marry me, and I felt that was the right decision, so we started to make some preliminary plans. I had already packed my things, so he grabbed my suitcase and we walked to my car. I got into the car and rolled the window down. We were saying our goodbyes, and I thanked him for the weekend. He bent over, leaned into the window, and gave me a quick kiss goodbye. Our time together was wholesome and clean with no drama.

This whole thing was strange. I went to Minneapolis single, but I was leaving as an engaged woman. I was now engaged to a man I had only been talking to for a couple of months. It was hard to explain, but all I knew is that it just felt right. In my other relationships, I was looking for romance and passion and all of that. There is nothing wrong with that, but for me, that type of emotional focus only brought me sadness. Chuma was different: he was calm and kind, soft-spoken but intelligent. He was a deep thinker, and he loved the Lord. These characteristics just seemed more attractive to me than what I was looking for before. He was eight years older than me, so he was much more mature and grounded. I felt like he would love and take care of me, so I felt safe and comfortable with him. I felt like *I loved him* as a person, but I was not *in love* with him in the typical sense of that word at that time.

All I knew was that it just felt right. I felt like I was being led in his direction, and I knew that I would find safety and peace with him. With my relationship with Michael, I felt like I was controlling the situation, but this time, I surrendered the fate of this relationship over to the Lord. I decided that if it was meant to be, it would happen. I would let the Spirit guide me, and I would follow His lead. The Spirit testifies of the truth, but I wasn't listening when it came to my previous relationships; however, my ears were wide open this time. Even though it was not what I expected, I chose to surrender.

I drove back to Milwaukee and told everyone my news. Of course, some of my family members thought I was being crazy and reckless, but I was okay with that. They were entitled to their opinions, especially since they were not aware of the previous relationships I had been in. I listened to their comments, and I pondered all of them, but in the end, I figured that the Lord knew best. So, Mom and I drove back to Indianapolis. I turned in my rental car, and I drove back to Florida with my mom. When I got home, it was surreal because I was engaged to a man that I had only physically seen once. I told myself I was crazy several times, but I still felt like I was doing the right thing. My heart and mind were content.

I needed to start preparing myself to marry again. It wasn't just a physical preparation that needed to be done. I needed to prepare myself emotionally and spiritually. The psychological aspect would have been important too, but now when I look back at that period, I realize I had already forgotten all the traumatic things that had happened to me. I remembered aspects of my divorce, but I had completely forgotten about what happened between Michael and I the night of our first date. My brain had already locked away the painful incidents with Michael, the stuff that happened with Auggy, and most of the things that happened at Marquette Elementary. That approach was what allowed me to survive and move on.

Chuma wanted me to make plans to move to Minneapolis, but I did not want to because I was a teacher. I had a career, and I had tenure. I didn't want to start all over, and I definitely did not want to move to a state that had a lot of snow, which was definitely the case with Minnesota. Chuma owned a small cleaning business, but he decided that he would shut his business down and move to Florida. I was very grateful for that important decision he made.

Chuma came to visit me at the end of September, so that was the second time I physically saw him, and the first time that he had met any of my family members. I was living with my mom and Alberta at that time, so he got to meet them. They both had positive thoughts about him. We also went to Paul and Jacqueline's house, which allowed Chuma to meet two of my dearest friends. After we visited for a bit, Jacqueline took our engagement photos. This was kind of a marathon weekend because we would not physically see each other again until he came for our Temple sealing in July.

* * *

One evening in May of 2004, I made spaghetti for dinner. I went to bed that night, and something was dragging me out of a deep sleep. I was laying on my stomach, and then I felt something weird happening on the right side of my abdomen. I was still unconscious at that point, but whatever was going on in there, it was pulling me out of my sleep. I remember myself starting to lift my right side up off the bed, and when I became alert, I felt massive pain on the right side of my body. The pain was so intense that it startled me and caused me to jump into a standing position in one movement. Once I was standing, I immediately felt nauseous, so I ran to the adjoining bathroom to go and throw up. I got there just in time and leaned over and started heaving. All the movement from lying to standing to bending happened in a matter of seconds, and unfortunately for me, that was not enough time for my body to equalize the flow of blood up to my brain, so I started to black out.

I knew I was in trouble because I was in the bathroom with a toilet, tub, and sink, which could all kill me if I fell down the wrong way, so I quickly turned and started walking as fast as I could back to my bedroom to try and get back to the bed, but I didn't make it! I did get out of the bathroom and onto the carpet in my room just as my body hit the floor. My brain was out before I reached the floor, so I didn't feel the pain of the fall. A little bit later, I started to slightly come to, and I could smell blood. I could feel that my lips were warm and wet, but my brain would not let me wake up yet, so I blacked out again.

I don't know how long I was out because when I jumped up, I didn't look at the clock. It was still dark, and somewhere in the middle of the night. When I finally came to, I felt awful. My face hurt, but my body ached too. That is probably because I fell face down on the floor, and I was still lying in that position. I rolled over and touched my lip because it felt wet. I was alert now, and I could smell blood. I knew I was hurt, so I started calling out for my mom. We lived together but she was down the hall, sleeping in her room, so she didn't hear me at first. I got up off the floor and got into the bed and called her again, and she finally heard me at that time. I told her that I had blacked out. She didn't get up. We were talking from our rooms. She asked me if I was okay, and I told her that I thought I was. I just wanted her to know what happened just in case I blacked out again. I told her to go back to sleep.

We had state testing at school that day, and I needed to administer the test to my students, so I needed to pull myself together and try to get ready for school. I got up and went into the bathroom to look in the mirror because my face was throbbing really bad in several areas. When I looked in the mirror, I was shocked. All the skin in the center of my upper lip had been removed by a carpet burn. (Why all my major injuries are mouth injuries is a mystery to me.) All the brown pigment was gone, and there was only white tissue showing. There was also an injury to the tip of my nose and in the indentation of my nose that was in between my eyes. I don't know how that could have possibly happened because it seems like the shape of my nose would have protected that area. Somehow, my nose flattened out enough to allow the carpet to burn the middle of that indentation.

My face was a complete mess. I should have stayed home, but of course, I was looking out for the kids and not for myself. I laid back down to nap a little bit longer because I still had a few minutes before I needed to get up. Even after that nap, I felt horrible, but I got up and went on to school.

After the testing was over, I called the doctor's office from work and got an emergency visit to see the doctor. I went up and told my principal that I needed to leave, and I went straight to the doctor. When I arrived at the doctor's office, the nurse asked me why I didn't go to the hospital, and I told her that I was a teacher and we had state testing that morning. She gave me a strange look, and I knew she was right. I should have gone, so all I could do was shrug my shoulders in acknowledgment of her look. When I got in to see the doctor, he immediately sent me to get blood tests. They did a rush order on the tests, and the results came back showing that my liver enzymes were extremely high. He sent me to a specialist, and it was determined that my gallbladder was loaded with stones. The pain that I felt came from a stone that had gotten lodged in my bile duct. It eventually passed, which gave me some relief. The doctor told me that I needed to have surgery to remove my gallbladder.

With all that craziness going on, Chuma and I ended up moving our Temple sealing up one month. I had the surgery on May 27, 2004. The plan was to do the surgery laparoscopically, which would be less traumatic to my body because they would only put three holes in my abdomen. However, if they ran into trouble, they would have to cut my abdomen open. I really didn't want the doctor to cut me open because that would lengthen my recovery time. However, they made me sign a waiver saying that it may be necessary for the bigger surgery if complications arose. I felt weird signing that, but I did it.

Luckily for me, the Lord blessed the hands of the surgeon, and everything went fine. I came out of recovery easily with no problems. My stomach was numbed up very well, so I didn't feel any pain. I only felt the tightness of the stitches in the three incision areas.

I did everything the hospital needed me to do to go home the same night. I basically just had to drink some liquid, go to the bathroom, and not take any pain meds. My nurse was not very nice. Her bedside manner left much to be desired, so I wanted to get the heck out of there. They sent me home, and Mom took me to my apartment. She lived close by, so she was able to help me if I needed it.

Chuma flew to Florida the next day, May 28th. Since I just had surgery, I was in a bit of pain. Chuma was flying into Orlando Airport, and that meant I would have been in the car for about an hour to go pick him up. That would have been brutal on my abdomen, so I gave Mom and Alberta a picture of Chuma just in case they forgot what he looked like, and they went to the airport and picked him up. They came back to my apartment with him. He dropped his things off, and they picked me up as well. We then drove to the courthouse and applied for our marriage license. (In Florida, you must have your license for seventy-two hours before you can get married.) I could hardly move, and I needed help, but since Chuma was there, he jumped right in and started taking care of me.

We secured the license, went back to the apartment, and I got back in bed. It was only one day after the surgery, so considering that, I was doing very well. The seventy-two-hour wait was exactly what I needed to recover before our sealing. I was still sore, but I was able to move around a little better. We went to the Temple on Tuesday, June 1, 2004, and were sealed together for time and all eternity. We were surrounded by my mom, Alberta and her new husband Ikenna, Paul and Jacqueline Barattiero, my good friends Paula and Leilani Ita, and all my other close friends from Church.

We kept the reception on our original wedding date in July, and that was when we celebrated with family, friends, and colleagues. We had a great time. My dad and his wife Diane flew in for the occasion, and I was grateful that he was able to make it. He and Diane, along with Tim and Glorimar Hefner, who are some close friends from Church, jumped right in and helped with the decorations and the setup of the cultural hall in our Church building. They did a great job.

Chuma and I were married pretty much on our fourth date. I wouldn't necessarily recommend that to everyone, but we knew that we were supposed to be married. The Spirit led us to each other and testified to each of us that we were supposed to be together. Because we listened to that still, small voice, we were prepared to be sealed for time and all eternity in the House of the Lord in Orlando, Florida. That sealing is what has kept us together these past nineteen years. We have had our moments just like all married couples do, and yes, we get frustrated with each other frequently. I guess that is to be expected, but because we made a covenant in the Temple, it has given us more of a reason to work through our challenges. We both know that if we stay on the path, and keep our covenants, we will be together forever, and that is our ultimate goal.

Chapter 26

BEECH MOUNTAIN

My music career has been a blessing and saved me when I needed it. It has been there for me my whole life, as it, in and of itself, has been like an alter ego for me. That has been problematic at times because my identity has been centered around music. I would go to work and teach music, come home and teach music in my private music studio, direct my youth orchestra on Saturdays, and then go to Church and perform and teach music on Sundays.

Sometimes, living the life of a musician can be completely draining, and it definitely has its ups and downs. The ups are usually sharing your gifts with others, teaching children to love music, or using it as a spiritual gift to bless others. The downs, for me, usually have to do with being overly busy and performing too many concerts. In my younger years as a music teacher, I took my kids to perform all over the place. Our busiest times of the year were during Christmas and during the months of April and May, when we had a lot of major performances going on at school. One particular year was brutal. Between my school concerts and my personal ones, I had done about twenty performances that school year, as well as all the rehearsals surrounding those performances. When I got to the month of May, I was completely burned out. Reading and playing music became a chore. I would be looking at the music, and I knew what note I was supposed to be playing, but my brain would play a totally different note. I used to always call this my Month of May Syndrome; that phenomenon had been happening for several years.

My brain would just get tired of reading music. Plus, I had all my regular music obligations that I would do weekly. I wouldn't finish my work until 8:30 or 9:00 p.m. every night, and then I would go into my weekend obligations.

The year 2008 was a recipe for disaster for me.

In addition to all that craziness, Chuma and I were aggravating each other. We were still in the early years of our marriage, so we were still trying to figure the whole marriage thing out. We were older when we got married. I was thirty-six and he was forty-four, so we were pretty set in our ways and needed to break some of our single people habits. He had never been married before, and I had, but unsuccessfully. We were having a rough go at it and just could not seem to get along. We were also not communicating at all, and when we did talk to each other, it generally ended up in an argument. I would say right, and he would say left. I would say up, while he would say down. I was miserable.

When it got to the middle of May 2008, I decided that I'd had enough. I needed some time away from everything. I just wanted to go away and be by myself, and I especially did not want to do anything involving music. Don't ask me about it! Don't look at me, and don't talk to me about anything involving music! I just wanted to be left alone!

I loved the mountains, so I decided that I wanted to find a place to retreat up in the mountains. My plan was to stay for five weeks and focus on myself. I looked primarily for health retreats, but they were super expensive, and I definitely could not afford any of them. Next, I started looking at cabins in the mountains. I saw some that were gorgeous, but you had to pay for those pristine views. Living on a teacher's salary would not allow me to do that. So, I started looking for short-term apartments to rent.

After a little searching, I saw some advertisements for rentals at ski resorts. The summer would be off-season, so many of them had some decent deals. My search led me to a resort called Pinnacle Inn in Beech Mountain, North Carolina. It was the highest resort on this side of the Smoky Mountains. This looked promising, so I went to their website and checked it out. It looked amazing to me. I checked out the price, and it was just over $1000 for the entire five weeks. That was a fraction of what I would have paid for the other places that I was looking at, so I went and talked to Chuma about what I wanted to do. He never really questioned why I wanted to go, as he knew I was burned out from work and music. (He didn't know that he was part of the problem why I was burned out, so I just left it at that.) He told me to go ahead and go, so I called the resort to get some more details, and I booked one of their ski suites for the summer. It was such a relief knowing that I would be leaving in a couple of weeks, and those felt like the longest two weeks of my life.

As my trip approached, Chuma decided that he wanted to come with me for the first few days. *Really? Oh boy!* That was my first thought, but then I realized I would be gone for the entire summer, so I could understand why he would want to go. We had never been apart for that long since we had been married, so this would be something new for both of us. The one thing I can say is that we trusted each other. We have never felt insecure about our relationship with one another, so that wasn't the issue. He was going to be alone all that time, so I think he was going to miss me. At that moment for me, I was not going to miss him. (So, I thought.) I needed to breathe. I needed some one-on-one time with the Lord, and I wanted to focus on my health. I wanted to put myself first in my life for once, as I was doing everything for others, but I wasn't making or taking any time for myself. This trip was about me.

I packed my car on Thursday night because Friday was the last day of school for teachers. The plan was to go to work and then immediately hit the road after work. I got all my work done. I cleaned and packed up my classroom and prepared all the instruments for summer storage. After the staff luncheon, I jumped in my car. I contacted Dad because, of course, he would be tracking me. After that, I hit the road. I was so excited to finally be leaving, and I was going on my own on Friday. I would stay overnight in the southern part of North Carolina and then drive the rest of the way on Saturday. Chuma was going to rent a car and join me on Monday. The drive was great, and I took my time since I was going to make the drive in two days. The hardest part was driving through Jacksonville, Florida, during rush hour. Larger cities and rush hour are like oil and water; they just don't mix. After I passed Jacksonville, it was smooth sailing from there. I drove until late in the evening.

When I crossed into North Carolina, I needed to find a decent place to stay, so I kept driving until I found a well-lit area with multiple hotels around. One can never be too safe when you are driving alone.

I found an appropriate hotel after driving around for a bit, where I checked in and hunkered down for the night. I called my dad to let him know that I was safe, and he took down all the hotel information. I then called my mom because she just about had a nervous breakdown every time I traveled. Chuma was the next call. When we finished talking, I ate some dinner, watched a little TV, and went to bed.

Saturday's drive was the best part. I woke up in the morning, got breakfast, and hit the road. I could see everything because it was daylight and was heading into the mountain region, which was just beautiful. The deep green of the trees, the beautiful highs and lows of the landscape, and the mountainous hills were just stunning! I found a few scenic overlooks that had parking places to allow you to stop and admire the beauty of the Lord's hands. I really loved being by myself because I could stop wherever and whenever I wanted to. When I saw something cool or interesting, I pulled over. I had time to kill because I couldn't check in until after 4 p.m., so I just explored the area until check-in time.

Beech Mountain is a ski community in Banner Elk, North Carolina; it is literally on top of a mountain. I drove through the little town of Banner Elk and eventually found the turn for Beech Mountain. I started driving up the road, which was a steep, winding, and curving road all the way up the mountain, and some parts of that road did not have side barricades. It was a little scary in the summertime, so I could only imagine what it would be like in the winter with snow and ice on the ground. It would be dangerous!

When I got to the top of the hill, I started driving through the neatest, little, quaint town. I still had a few minutes before check-in time, so I explored the town while I waited. Beech Mountain had a little pizza/hamburger joint and a cool country store, which was an older, historic home that had been converted into a store. Most of the items in the store were trinkets, souvenirs, snacks, and basic supplies. If you wanted major groceries, or if you wanted some different restaurant choices, you would need to go down the mountain into Banner Elk, which is only a couple of miles. Right down the hill from my resort was a beautiful ski slope, and there were chalets all situated on a winding and curving road up the left side of the slope. It was incredible. I thought the road leading up to Beech Mountain was crazy, but this road was ridiculous. You cannot go up there in the winter if you don't have great driving skills. The road was so steep; I just don't know how it is possible for people to drive up there in the winter without sliding backward down that hill. That is a no-driving zone if your skills are sub-par.

I finally checked into my resort and rested for a few minutes because I was winded. The air was much thinner up there, so I struggled to breathe properly. After I unloaded my car, I rested for a bit more and started preparing to go grocery-shopping so I would have food to eat for the next day. Before I left, I grabbed my phone and searched for the closest church building of The Church of Jesus Christ of Latter-day Saints. I wanted to go to Church in the morning and thankfully found one just a few miles away. It was down the hill in Banner Elk, and a couple of miles down the main road to the right. I got in my car and went down the hill to go shopping. Later, I got what I needed and loaded the car. On my way back, instead of turning to go up the hill to Beech Mountain, I drove down the road and found the Church so I would not have to do that in the morning. I went back to my apartment and ate my first meal. I unpacked some of my things and got my clothes prepared for Church. I called Chuma to let him know that I was safe, watched a little TV, and went to bed early.

The next morning, I woke up, ate breakfast, and got prepared for Church. I drove down the hill and went back to the little chapel that I had found the previous evening. I was among the first ones there. The chapel was tiny, a little bit bigger than the typical size classroom in Florida, so I knew the congregation that met there was fairly small. There were rows of chairs set up, and the rows were divided down the middle to create two sides. There was a podium up front in the middle of the room, and off to the right, there was a piano. I sat down on the right side of the chapel, about two rows back from the piano. No one had come into the chapel yet, so I was alone.

Sitting alone gave me a few minutes to pray. I also pondered my life and why I was in Banner Elk. While I was in deep thought, a woman walked into the chapel and was carrying a CD player. I knew exactly what that meant; it indicated that they did not have a piano player in this little branch. At that moment, just like I used to see in cartoons when I was a child, a little devil popped up on my left shoulder and an angel popped up on my right shoulder. They were talking to me in opposition to one another. The devil started the conversation, saying, "Don't you say nothin'! Your plan was to come here and not do any music at all."

Then the angel said, "The Lord gave you that talent so you could bless His children."

"Don't you listen to that! You are a visitor. They don't even know you, and they don't know that you can play," said the devil.

The angel immediately jumped in and said, "Why would you make them sing to a recording when you can sit down at the piano and use your talent and bless them with live music?"

This conversation between the two of them continued on my shoulder until I finally got up and walked over to the lady, asking, "Do you have a pianist in this branch?"

"No. We don't have anyone that plays the piano here," she said.

"Would you like for me to play?" I inquired.

"Do you mean right now, or do you mean next week after you practice the music?"

"Well, what hymns are you singing today?" I asked.

(All of the hymns that she told me were staple hymns we sing regularly at Church.)

"I know all these hymns. I can play them."

"Really? You can play them right now?"

I gave her a little smile and said, "Yes. I can."

"That would be great!" she said.

After this conversation, I played the piano that day, and every week that I was up in the mountains.

This conversation with the sweet sister changed everything for me. It made me realize that the gift of music I had was given to me by God, and it was my responsibility to use it to bless others. The stress that I was feeling was not because of the church stuff, or even the school stuff. It was because I had overbooked myself and planned too many things. I didn't leave adequate space in my spiritual schedule to use my gift for the Lord's children. I filled it with things that were not important. From that day forward, I stopped overbooking myself, especially around holiday season, and that made all the difference in the world. I have never had a moment where I have felt completely burned out like that again.

The reason for that is the fact that I learned to say, "No," or "I'm sorry, but I am not available." Before that, I never said no unless there was a legitimate conflict in my schedule. People asked, and I would just keep piling things onto my schedule. This was happening not only for me personally, but I piled on the performances for my school kids as well. It was just too much! Learning to advocate for myself was something very new to me, and the time that I spent in the mountains that summer was an amazing opportunity to reflect on what was going on in my life and make course corrections for the future.

The week that Chuma was with me was a great opportunity for us to leave our home environment and connect with each other in a beautiful place. He got me out of the apartment and encouraged me to start walking. We walked up that steep road next to the ski slope, which I didn't think I could do yet. My goal was to do it by the fifth week after I had acclimated to the altitude, and after I had dropped some weight. I had no plans to go up there a couple of days after I arrived, but he insisted that I do it. He walked with me to help me jump start the health portion of my trip, and he cheered me on all the way up that steep road.

To my surprise, I made it to the top. It was so hard, but he was not going to let me fail. We had a good time together, and it reminded me of why we chose to marry one another in the first place. He left at the end of that week, and I left the mountains a few days early because I missed him and wanted to get back home to be with him.

Chapter 27

THE SHOES

Many years had gone by since my Beech Mountain experience. It was an amazing spiritual experience for me. Chuma and I had grown a lot since that summer, and we slowly started to become closer. My feelings about being burned out with music had not returned because my perspective was different; however, that did not mean I didn't get tired from time to time. Concerts were always exhausting because concert days were generally a very long day for me. I tried to combine all my schools into one concert instead of multiple small concerts at each school. It would make for a long day, but I could just do one big concert and be done.

My school orchestra had an activity at Harmony High School one Saturday night, so when I finished, I was totally exhausted. By the time the last parent picked up their child from the school, it was about 8:30 p.m. Chuma and I had moved out to Poinciana, so it was at least a one-hour drive to my house, that is if there was no traffic. I left the house that morning at about 5:45 a.m., and by the time I got home that Saturday night, it was 9:30 p.m. Chuma was working nights as a security guard at a major theme park, so he was just leaving to go to work as I arrived home. I had just started to wind down, taking off my clothes and getting ready to eat some dinner. I was assigned to give a talk in Sacrament meeting at Church the next day, so my plan was to finish writing the talk and then go to bed.

Just as I got settled, my cell phone rang. It was Chuma; he forgot his black shoes and inadvertently put his white sneakers on instead of his black shoes that are required for his work uniform. As he was telling me the problem, I knew in my mind he was getting ready to ask me to make the forty-five-minute drive to his job to take him his shoes. This was a source of contention between the two of us because he used to forget stuff at home all the time when we lived in our other house that was in town. I was constantly taking his stuff to work. Today was not the day for him to ask me to do that because I was completely wiped out.

After he told me the situation, he was quiet for a moment. So, I asked him, "What are you going to do about that?"

"Will you bring my shoes to me?" he then asked.

Well, I lost it! I threw an adult tantrum on the phone! He listened and let me yell at him. In his mind, he had a problem that needed to be solved immediately, so he said, "I can just call an Uber, and you can give them my shoes." I knew that was not going to work because of how far we lived from his job, so it would have cost a fortune for the Uber driver to take his shoes there. So, I angrily said, "I'm coming!"

He thanked me, and I said, "BYE!"

Of course, it was not the nicest goodbye, but that was how I felt at that moment, and that was all I had to give at that point. I hung the phone up and started screaming. I was so mad at him, as well as tired and frustrated. I started crying while I was getting dressed because it was after 10 p.m., so it would be after midnight when I finally got back home. I was so exhausted, and the thought of having to make an almost two-hour trip back and forth was too much for me to handle at that moment, but I got in the car and started driving.

While I was driving, I started coming up with scenarios of how I could show Chuma how mad I was.

Scenario #1–Chuma worked at a border gate behind one of the theme parks, so I would just do a drive-by, slow my car down, roll the window down, and throw his shoes out the window. Then I thought, *That's not going to work because the border gate is set back a distance from the road, and he would not be able to leave his post to go and get them.*

Scenario #2–I would just pull up to his kiosk and throw the shoes at him and then peel off, squealing my tires in the process. This will show him how mad I am, but then I thought, *That is not going to work either because it will ruin the tires on my car, and I would have to pay to have them changed.*

Right in the middle of all this mental drama, my sister Alberta called. I thought to myself, *How did she know that I needed her at this moment?* Alberta is definitely one of my guardian angels. She is always there when something is going on with me; it is as if she senses it. She immediately knew, by the tone of my voice, that I was upset. She asked me what was wrong, and I told her what happened, and that I was tired and still needed to finish my talk. She immediately said, "It was just an accident. Chuma is a good man."

"No, he's not!!" I said in a tearful voice because I had been crying.

"Kyeni, stop it! You know he's a good man." She then instinctively asked me, "What is the topic of your talk?"

"That is not important right now," I said.

She then said, "I want to know. What is the topic?"

"I don't want to talk about it," I repeated again.

I didn't want to talk about it because I wanted to be mad. I didn't want her to talk me down because at that moment, I felt justified in my anger. She asked the third time, "What's the topic?" so I finally said it.

"Obtaining and strengthening a personal testimony despite adversity."

Right after I told her my topic, I knew that I needed to repent. I allowed my emotions to overpower my reasoning. We talked for a little bit longer, and then we hung up.

After that, I calmed down. I started to pray and talk to my heavenly Father. I was still driving at the time, but I knew He would still hear me whether my eyes were opened or closed. I asked Him for forgiveness, and I asked Him to give me the strength that I needed to accomplish this task. I just talked to Him like a dad and told Him how tired I was and how I was feeling. After my prayer, I felt better, and my mind was clearer.

Miraculously, my exhaustion went away, and I got a burst of energy. I could see things more clearly. I realized that Chuma called me to ask for help because I was the only one who could have helped him at that moment. He could have gotten in a lot of trouble for being out of uniform, so it was me that needed to help him. The Savior sacrificed everything for me, even His very life. He did that out of love for me, so who am I to not be willing to sacrifice for my husband?

During the rest of the trip to Chuma's job, I felt at peace. He called me and told me to leave his shoes at the kiosk, and he would pick them up from there. When I got there, I pulled up to the kiosk and told the guard that I was Chuma's wife, and I was dropping the shoes off for him. He took the shoes, and I drove and made the U-turn around the kiosk to go back out the other side and exit. As I was passing the kiosk to go out, another security guard flagged me down and asked me to stop. I stopped and rolled the window down. The guard asked me if I was Chuma's wife, and I said, "Yes." He then proceeded to tell me that Chuma was a great guy. He told me that Chuma had always been nice and kind to him, and he really liked him and appreciated him. I then thanked him and said, "Yes. He is a nice guy." It was another humbling moment to hear a perfect stranger testify to me about the goodness of my husband. The Lord's tender mercies always prevail.

This whole situation was a testimony-strengthening opportunity for me. It showed me some areas that I still needed to grow, but most of all, it showed me how much the Savior loved me and loved my husband.

They say when you don't master something, it keeps coming around until you do. Well, there must be some truth in that because Chuma left his wallet at home with his license and his work documents in it. He has done very well about not forgetting his stuff because of the last incident five years ago. It is now 2023, and we have moved to Polk County, which is even further away from our jobs.

I was talking to him on the phone when he discovered that he had forgotten the wallet. He needed his work documents, but he didn't want to directly ask me to bring the wallet to him. So, instead of doing that, he explained how badly he needed it without telling me that he needed me to bring it to him. Of course, I was aggravated because I wasn't going to get back home until after

1:00 a.m., but I didn't want to repeat what happened last time.

He was working at a new location in the theme parks, so I asked him for directions to get there. I got dressed, got in the car, and took off. I was trying very hard to stay positive, but it was starting to get difficult. I was tired, so I turned on some music to distract my thoughts and to keep my brain active while I was driving. The music was loud and bouncy, and I listened to it for the first few miles, but I noticed that my negative thoughts about the situation started to really creep in. I realized that it was probably the music, so I decided to put on some religious music that was more spiritually uplifting.

I had just recently downloaded a song by Yahosh Bonner. He is an actor, TV show host, and fellow musician. He had released a song titled "What A Dream" (written by Obeeyay, edited by R. Bagley, mixed/mastered by C. Cliff, and photographed by D. Gerald). The video for the song had recently come out. I really liked it, so I decided to turn the song on. I was so glad I did because my countenance changed immediately. I started singing the lyrics to the song, and I started to think about the video, which featured his beautiful wife and children. In other words, his family. One part of the song said, "You can be my number one for life … You know I ain't goin' nowhere … because I will always be there. Our ups and downs whate'er I don't care. I will always be there. I will always be there" (© 2022 Yahosh Bonner). This section of the song really hit me hard because after the Lord, Chuma is my family and "my number one for life." I needed to start thinking about him as my number one.

I played that song on repeat all the way to his job and back home. Music can be so powerful, and I was so grateful for it at that moment. Yahosh's beautiful singing and the message behind this song kept me focused on the covenants that I made with my husband in the Florida Orlando Temple nineteen years ago. The Lord didn't say that this life would be easy, but He did say He would be with us, and He certainly has been throughout my life.

I still haven't quite mastered this part of myself yet because I still had some negative thoughts in my head, but I did much better than the first time, and that is progress.

Chapter 28

MY TRUE IDENTITY

I was on session fifteen of twenty sessions with my counselor when I realized I was okay and didn't need any more sessions. It was bittersweet, but I was ready to move on with my life. The journey back into my past was absolutely brutal at times. I was shocked to see how much of my life was hidden away. Not only did my mind lock away all the painful things, but the good memories were also locked away with them. Walking back through my past set me free in ways I cannot fully describe, but it allowed me to see myself for who I was then, and it gave me the freedom to become who I want to be now.

My perspective on trials has completely changed. My experience with Cassie, as traumatic as it was, ended up being one of the biggest blessings in my life. It was another witness to me that my Father in heaven was aware of me and loved me. I was stuck and didn't know it, so used to the daily ins and outs of my life that the unhealthy, destructive, and impractical behaviors I engaged in had become my comfort and peace. I had told myself I was unworthy and worthless so many times that I actually believed it. The negative self-talk was a constant thing, so engrained into my mind that I didn't notice I was doing it. It was silently eroding away at my sense of identity and was almost as if I didn't like the person that I was, and I was creating a new person to replace her.

There is nothing wrong with growing and becoming a new person because it is all about mindset. However, my growing was a result of self-hatred and not of love; that was at the root of most of my problems. That self-hatred started when I was a little girl standing in the yard, having that conversation with my mother when we were leaving my dad. I was mad at myself for choosing to go with her, because in my mind, that choice resulted in me being injured. That result had nothing to do with my choice, but that is how I interpreted it. Most of the other poor decisions I made in my life were the direct result of a false sense of identity that had developed throughout my life. Even though a lot of positive, spiritual things had happened to me, I was still carrying around all the pain that I went through.

The big things my counselor and I spent a lot of time working on were the following questions:

"Why is everyone else in your life more important than you?"

"Why do you go out of your way to do for others at your own expense?" and

"When are you going to include yourself in your own life?"

These were not the only questions that we addressed, but they were the ones that hit me the hardest. Talking to her about these questions was one thing, but having my close family members bring the topic up was quite another thing. Toward the end of my dad's life, I talked to him about the Cassie incident and my counseling sessions. I also talked to him about some of the traumas that I had experienced and hid away. His main goal for me was to open up and release all the things that were hidden. He wanted me to talk about it so I could be free of all those demons. He was being a dad and was doing all that he could to help his daughter before he crossed over. I didn't know it then but the time he spent talking to me would be one of the most important gifts he would ever give me and leave with me before he passed on.

In one of our conversations, Dad said something that was extremely profound. He said,

"I have always wondered why you were always trying to one up yourself. Why were you always doing things to make yourself look better and better? I couldn't figure it out until now."

I sat quietly for a moment because his comment caught me off guard, and I didn't know what to say. I thought about it for a moment, and I finally said, "I didn't realize that I was doing that. I just thought I was doing stuff because I wanted to, or because it was beneficial to someone else."

Later that evening, I started really thinking about what he said, and I couldn't really see what he was talking about, so I called Alberta and talked to her about it. I told her what Dad said, and to my shock, she said, "He is right."

Alberta never beat around the bush with me, so I knew there had to be some truth in the statement. She said, "You stay busy because you are always busy saving others and not yourself."

Ouch! That is brutally honest, I thought to myself. She continued and said, "You spend all of your time helping others as a tool to somehow make yourself feel good about yourself."

I thought to myself, *She is right. I always stay busy, but I have never looked at it from this perspective before.*

She continued and said, "You always try to find the next big thing to validate yourself. When your life or your decisions are getting out of control, you do big things with the underlying reason of helping others. Somehow, you have convinced yourself that you are not worth the effort alone. You have to include others as a motivator. When you do the big things, you always find an element to help someone else instead of focusing on yourself."

That was a lot to take in. I really didn't know what to say and was quiet for a moment until she said, "This isn't necessarily a bad thing. It is just who you are; it's your personality."

That was a huge epiphany for me, and it opened me up to do some real self-reflection. I am finding out new things about myself every day. This was a huge one.

I have learned so many things that resulted from an unfortunate event in my classroom. These things have given me great cause to pause and reflect on my past life, and my life as it is today. I am starting to see a picture of myself through a different set of eyeglasses. I am finally free to live and accept myself for who I am, and I am finally starting to like who I see.

Over the years, I had forgiven everyone that had ever wronged me in my life. I allowed the waters of baptism to help me forgive everyone that had hurt me up to that point in my life. Years after my baptism, I forgave Michael, as well as all the men that I was involved with during the dating process, and I felt good about that forgiveness. I didn't feel like I was holding back forgiveness toward anyone. The problem was that there was a big, white elephant standing in the middle of my room I was completely oblivious to. I forgave everyone else except myself; that is where I needed to start, and that is what I am working on today.

It was just by happenstance that Cynthia showed up to my mom's house, or was it? So many unexplainable things have happened in my life, so this could very well have been orchestrated by my heavenly Father. He always seems to come in at the very moment I need Him, or at a point in my life when I am mature and strong enough to handle the situation. Without some sort of intervention, I might never have known who my biological father was. It was by talking with my counselor and working through all the trauma from the past that helped me to remember that I had a true identity, and that identity was not tied to my human existence. It was much bigger than that. Over the years, I tied my identity to the trauma because I blamed myself for all the pain I had experienced in my life. I attached my identity to those problems.

When the violin came along, it gave me a false sense of peace. I have had four violins in my life, and all of them became my surrogate comforters and companions. They became the objects that I allowed people to see me through. Not only was it just the violin, but eventually music in general. People saw me as Kyeni the violinist, Kyeni the pianist, and Kyeni the singer. In a way, I even saw myself as those things.

When I began to play the violin, the violin became an extension of my personality. When I held my violin, it was in front of my face, so it became a tool for me to hide behind. The beautiful sound that I was making out of my instruments became attached to my identity. I felt like people would see and hear the beauty of the violin, and that beauty became the person I wanted to be. The violin masked all the pain and trauma that could be seen through the eyes of the person behind it. Those eyes were mine. The violin became my perceived protector, and, in a way, it became a savior. As long as I was engaging in music, I felt safe, like I had a safety net around me.

The Cassie experience interfered with those protective safety nets, and I began to feel vulnerable. I wasn't safe anymore. My counselor tapped into my false identity immediately and helped me to understand that music was something I did, but it was not who I was. The Lord gave me music when I was young to help me get through the things that I was going through, but I somehow attached music to my identity in an unhealthy way. So, going through that event in my classroom forced me to look at my life, changing my identity from something temporal to something spiritual and eternal. Those eyes from behind the violin, my eyes, needed to come out of the shadows and into the light. They needed to see who I truly was. They needed to see that I wasn't just an injured, little, nameless girl. I was much, much bigger than that. I was a spiritual being living a very temporal existence. My true identity was attached to my real parentage.

My real father is the God of all creation. If He is my true Father, then I am His daughter, born of royal lineage. I am much more than the broken person I had identified with my entire life. My earthly experiences taught me much, but the most important thing that I learned was that my heavenly Father has always been here with me. He has been a part of my life this whole time. When I look back at all the experiences I went through, He was there in some shape or form. I was never alone; His Spirit was there, or He showed up as one of my friends, teachers, or as a person in authority to help me through a situation. He used others that were in my life to help lead and guide me. He always stepped in when I needed Him the most, and He stepped back when I needed to learn and grow. He allowed me to experience the things that were necessary for my progression.

I am still a work in progress, and I have a lot of work to do to become who I truly want to be, but I am now on the path to properly travel that journey with new hope and optimism. There is no longer a question mark next to my earthly name. I know now that I am a Goldsmith, but more important than that, I know my true identity.

I AM A DAUGHTER OF GOD!

Reflections

Re-living my life gave me many opportunities to reflect upon the things that I was learning. Below are some thoughts and questions for you to reflect on that might be helpful if you have experienced any trials or struggles in your life. These questions come from the things that I have gone through in my life.

1. I buried all the trials that I was experiencing in my life and only dealt with them when I was forced to as an adult, which caused me to have to painfully re-live my entire life. Are you holding onto any unresolved situations of abuse or any past trials that are keeping you stuck, not allowing you to live your best life in the present?

2. The incident with Cassie, as bad as it was, ended up being a blessing to me because it is what started me on my path to healing. Have you had any pivotal incidents in your life that have caused you to look at your past to find healing and understanding?

3. I was the object of bullying when I was in elementary school, and it proved to be very detrimental to me emotionally and physically. The constant barrage of negative comments became my self-proclaimed identity and contributed to a loss of my sense of self-worth. Were you ever the object of bullying when you were in school, and if so, how did you handle it? Were you able to separate the negative comments from your sense of self-worth?

4. I never felt comfortable or had enough trust in my parents as a young girl to talk to them when I was experiencing all the abuse. I felt like they were so caught up in their own issues that they would not be able to help me. What was your relationship like with your parents?

Were you able to talk to them about your feelings and needs when you were a child?

5. Music is what helped me get through my childhood. It provided me with an outlet of expression that I could shift my attention to. Do you have a hobby or a talent that has been a blessing and a positive influence in your life?

6. Developing an understanding about God and who He is was the catalyst that kickstarted periods of healing throughout my life. Having a relationship with Him through the Cassie incident and what transpired after that really strengthened me and helped me work through the process of healing. Do you have a spiritual practice in your life that you can draw upon for strength, or is there a role model or a thought process that gives you encouragement that you can lean on when needed?

7. Where are you in the process of discovering who you are and learning what your divine potential is?

www.ingramcontent.com/pod-product-compliance
Lightning Source LLC
Chambersburg PA
CBHW060907120626
46553CB00001B/242